CRIME, Justice and Literature

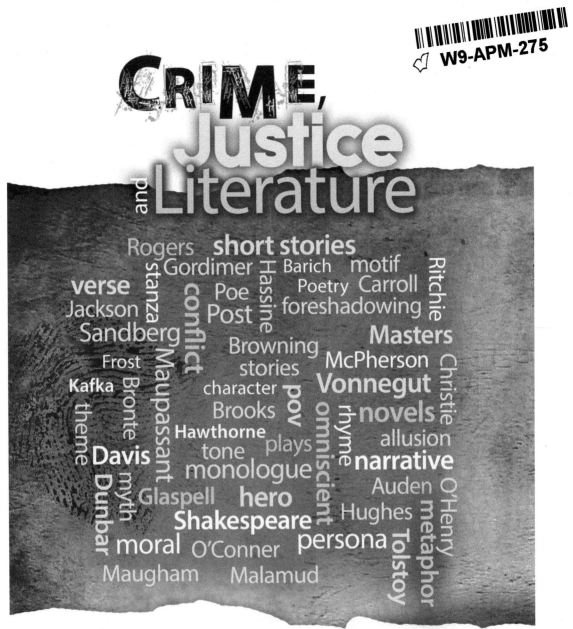

Rogers **short stories**
Gordimer Barich motif
verse stanza Poe Hassine Poetry Carroll Ritchie
Jackson conflict Post foreshadowing
Sandberg Browning **Masters**
Frost Maupassant stories McPherson Christie
Kafka Bronte character **Vonnegut**
theme Brooks pov **novels**
Hawthorne plays rhyme omniscient allusion
Davis tone monologue **narrative** O'Henry
Dunbar myth Glaspell **hero** Auden metaphor
Shakespeare Hughes
moral O'Conner persona Tolstoy
Maugham Malamud

Edited by
Larry Karson ▪ **Claudia Slate** ▪ **Rebecca Saulsbury Bravard**
University of
Houston-Downtown
Florida Southern
College
Florida Southern
College

Kendall Hunt
publishing company

www.kendallhunt.com
Send all inquiries to:
4050 Westmark Drive
Dubuque, IA 52004-1840

Published in the United States of America

Contents

[handwritten: Second Paper]
[handwritten: Anwser 5 questi...]

*****Note:** Those works asterisked are not included in this anthology but may be available on the Internet or at your university or college library.

Introduction

For many of us, literature serves as our introduction to crime, criminals, and the criminal justice system. From the classic novel *Les Misérables* with Javert relentlessly pursing the ex-convict Jean Valjean for a petty crime to Frank Stockton's timeless tale of the arbitrariness of love and justice in "The Lady or the Tiger," stories give us an appreciation of social control and how it works. As the justice system does in publicly prosecuting an offender, so do these tales help define the boundaries of acceptable conduct within our culture, informing all as to the consequences, intentional and unintentional, of one's potential actions.

Storytelling, however, goes beyond simply reinforcing social codes. Our entire justice system employs storytelling with individual and collective voices. The victim. The suspect. The officer. The prosecutor. The defense attorney. All use stories to present their interpretations. Some even recognize that the system is not necessarily about justice, fairness, or even the law but rather entrenched social and cultural codes.

As one form of storytelling, literature has the capacity to bring stories into any classroom. Literature speaks to the human condition while also personalizing—and humanizing—the law. As Steven Engels remarks in his article, "Teaching Literature in the Criminal Justice Curriculum," literature develops students' empathy as well as their critical thinking while also fostering a better appreciation of the effects of the justice system on individual lives, effectively depriving crime statistics of their sterilization and emotional dispassion.

As fewer students take courses in the humanities, literature used in the criminal justice classroom may also be the only opportunity for some students to be exposed to the ideas and views expressed in these works, let alone being offered the opportunity to become more culturally literate. Incorporating literature into the classroom opens an otherwise unnoticed door for students.

Novels such as *To Kill a Mockingbird*, *Crime and Punishment*, *The Stranger*, *Of Mice and Men*, and *Lord of the Flies* have long been recognized for revealing the human condition and society's response to it. Numerous short stories and poems also address these same concerns. Law schools have recognized this, offering classes in Literature and the Law under various titles for years. Jurists such as Richard Poser have written on the subject. The Modern Literature Association published *Teaching Law and Literature* to assist professors with teaching such a class. Collected works of literature formatted from a lawyer's perspective have included Thomas Morawetz's *Literature and the Law,* Fred Shapiro and Jan Garry's *Trial and Error: An Oxford Anthology of Legal Stories,* Thane Rosenbaum's *Law Lit—From Atticus Finch to the Practice: A Collection of Great Writing About the Law*, and Elizabeth Villiers Gemmette's series of works titled *Law in*

Literature. Gemmette's works include *Law in Literature: Legal Themes in Short Stories*, *Legal Themes in Novellas*, and *Legal Themes in Drama*. Our project, therefore, is not without precedent.

These aforementioned books target law school students, but none is devoted to the academic fields of criminal justice and criminology. One such work, Paul Dow's *Criminology in Literature*, focuses on stories illustrating criminological theory but is almost forty years out of print. *Crime, Justice, and Literature* fills that vacuum by bringing together a collection of poetry and short stories addressing a variety of criminal justice concepts. Organized to parallel many introductory criminal justice textbooks, this reader offers undergraduate students in criminal justice a vital tool to assist in their understanding.

The three editors, two English professors with an expertise in literature and a professor of criminal justice with a number of years of service in law enforcement, bring an interdisciplinary focus to the work, making it distinctive within the genre. This intersection of literature, criminal justice, and criminology is the heart of a liberal arts education, a recognition of the interconnections found across cultures and communities.

We emphasize poems and short stories over novels because they are succinct works (one of the most effective possibly being Gwendolyn Brooks' classic "We Real Cool"). Further, they allow close readings to uncover the layers of meaning and their applicability to the American criminal justice system. These readings span the field of criminal justice, including policing, the court system and corrections, encompassing victims and criminals, the defense and the prosecution. All have a story to tell, and some of the greatest writers in Western literature have shared these stories with us. We hope you, the reader, find as much joy in them as we have.

LK, CS, & RSB

Postscript

*Some works believed to be significant in an anthology such as this could not be included due to various copyright concerns, but the original poem or short story is generally available via the Internet or through a university or college library. Those works are identified with an asterisk.

Section 1

Overview of the Criminal Justice System

Chapter 1

Introduction to Criminal Justice

What Is Crime?

"The Hill" and "Hod Putt" from *Spoon River Anthology*
by Edgar Lee Masters

Edgar Lee Masters (1868–1950) was a Chicago labor lawyer who had grown up in western Illinois. In 1915 he published a collection of free verse poetry, written in the form of epitaphs, under the title *Spoon River Anthology*. The poems, inspired by people he knew in his youth, described the reality of small-town America, undercutting, along with Sherwood Anderson's *Winesburg, Ohio* and Sinclair Lewis' *Main Street*, the myth of a Midwestern rural community of tranquility and morality. Known as literary realism, these works challenged the prevailing view of an agrarian life promoting a personal ethic of integrity, self-reliance, and religiosity in counterpoint to the urban world of commercialization, corruption, and crime. Instead, through the epitaphs of the dead who no longer had anything to lose by concealing the truth, Masters exposed the hypocrisy, the sordid secrets, and the delinquencies of the residents of the rural town he called Spoon River.

The first epitaph, titled "Hod Putt," is prefaced by the poem "The Hill," an introduction reminding the reader that "All, all are sleeping on the hill." Whether "killed in a brawl" or "died in a jail" many of the individuals in the cemetery became involved in the criminal justice system prior to their death. In the epitaph "Hod Putt" the concept of committing a crime as well as one's motivation in doing so, is also in the forefront. Hod Putt, having lived in poverty for many a year and seeing how others grew rich by abusing the law and avoided repaying what was owed to others, decided to "innovate" himself by robbing a traveler, unwittingly killing him, and leading to Putt's execution. Yet even though Putt was hanged for his crime, Old Bill Piersol, the businessman, eventually ended up close to Putt's grave, his riches not preventing the two of them from a "Sleep peacefully side by side."

Sharp business practices, though bordering on fraud, by definition are considered legal or are otherwise ignored by law enforcement. One example seen on television is the selling of a product at a low price, such as a set of knives or scissors, with a second set being given for free by just paying "shipping and handling." The concern is that the cost of shipping and handling is not included in the ad and can far exceed the actual cost of shipping the two sets of knives. Another example is a robo-call that is used to obtain donations for law enforcement or veterans groups, yet 80 percent of any donated money goes to the "administrative costs" of the solicitor with only 20 percent being forwarded to the law enforcement organization or veterans.

"The Hill"

by Edgar Lee Masters

WHERE are Elmer, Herman, Bert, Tom and Charley,
The weak of will, the strong of arm, the clown, the boozer, the fighter?
All, all, are sleeping on the hill.

One passed in a fever,
One was burned in a mine,
One was killed in a brawl,
One died in a jail,
One fell from a bridge toiling for children and wife—
All, all are sleeping, sleeping, sleeping on the hill.

Where are Ella, Kate, Mag, Lizzie and Edith,
The tender heart, the simple soul, the loud, the proud, the happy one?—
All, all, are sleeping on the hill.

One died in shameful child-birth,
One of a thwarted love,
One at the hands of a brute in a brothel,
One of a broken pride, in the search for heart's desire,
One after life in far-away London and Paris
Was brought to her little space by Ella and Kate and Mag—
All, all are sleeping, sleeping, sleeping on the hill.

Where are Uncle Isaac and Aunt Emily,
And old Towny Kincaid and Sevigne Houghton,

Edgar Lee Masters, "The Hill," *Spoon River Anthology,* 1916.

And Major Walker who had talked
With venerable men of the revolution?—
All, all, are sleeping on the hill.

They brought them dead sons from the war,
And daughters whom life had crushed,
And their children fatherless, crying—
All, all are sleeping, sleeping, sleeping on the hill.

Where is Old Fiddler Jones
Who played with life all his ninety years,
Braving the sleet with bared breast,
Drinking, rioting, thinking neither of wife nor kin,
Nor gold, nor love, nor heaven?
Lo! he babbles of the fish-frys of long ago,
Of the horse-races of long ago at Clary's Grove,
Of what Abe Lincoln said
One time at Springfield.

———————— ৪৯ ————————

"Hod Putt"

by Edgar Lee Masters

HERE I lie close to the grave
Of Old Bill Piersol,
Who grew rich trading with the Indians, and who
Afterwards took the bankrupt law
And emerged from it richer than ever.
Myself grown tired of toil and poverty
And beholding how Old Bill and others grew in wealth,
Robbed a traveler one night near Proctor's Grove,
Killing him unwittingly while doing so,
For the which I was tried and hanged.
That was my way of going into bankruptcy.
Now we who took the bankrupt law in our respective ways
Sleep peacefully side by side.

———————————

Source: Edgar Lee Masters, "Hod Putt," *Spoon River Anthology,* 1916.

Critical Thinking

Bankruptcy laws are written to offer an individual or business the opportunity to restart their life without the financial consequences affecting them indefinitely, but current bankruptcy laws do not allow a student carrying college loans that are financially crippling her from discharging that debt.

Why is student loan debt not allowed to be included in any bankruptcy proceedings? Should they? If allowed, how might that affect banks from providing future loans to students?

White-collar crime has been defined as "a crime committed by a person of respectability and high social status in the course of his [or her] occupation." Is a businessman who intentionally goes bankrupt to avoid paying his creditors a criminal? If not, should he be?

If a business had workers killed because the company didn't invest in the best safety equipment for them—but did meet a minimum national safety standard—should the company executives be held criminally liable for any deaths? What if the company had previously lobbied the legislator to keep the safety standards minimal to save the company money?

In deciding what a sharp business practice is and what should be considered illegal, what kind of standard should a court use? Should it be what the jury thinks? Only what is specifically and distinctly mentioned in the law? Or is there some other standard that needs to be considered?

History of the Criminal Justice System in America

"Mrs. Hutchinson"
by Nathaniel Hawthorne

Nathaniel Hawthorne (1804–1864) was a significant novelist and short story writer during the American Renaissance, known for his contributions to negative Romanticism, particularly his complex use of symbolism, allegory, and ambiguity; probing the inner, often dark, recesses of the human mind; and exploring the consequences of Puritans' obsession with sin. Although most famous for his novel *The Scarlet Letter* (1850), Hawthorne's short stories are early masterpieces of the themes, characterizations, motives of human behavior, and the role of the artist that would appear in his novels. One such early story is "Mrs. Hutchinson," published in 1830, which explores the psychological and historical landscape of the New England Puritans, especially their obsession with transgressions of biblical law and concomitant gender codes. It highlights this culture's often misogynist view and treatment of women, a theme that Hawthorne would investigate thoroughly via Hester Prynne in *The Scarlet Letter*.

"Mrs. Hutchinson" (1830) is ostensibly a profile of Anne Hutchinson, infamous for her role in the Antinomian Controversy that took place in the Massachusetts Bay Colony from 1636 to 1638. First, she held Bible studies in her home, offering her own interpretations not only of the Bible but also of the sermons by important ministers of the time (including John Cotton). Second, she directly challenged church hierarchy (and state hierarchy, too, since Puritan New England was a theocracy) by offering her own religious views that went against legal and theological doctrines of the Puritan state. Thus, by speaking so openly, Hutchinson challenged patriarchal authority, eventually resulting in her trial, conviction, and expulsion from Massachusetts Bay Colony in 1637 and excommunication from the church in 1638. Ironically, her excommunication only increased her notoriety and confirmed her place in history as an agitator for religious freedom in colonial America.

The story begins with a commentary from the narrator posing as a kind of judge of Anne Hutchinson and her legacy. Referring to her as "Mrs. Hutchinson" could be a polite mode of address, but the narrator's tone suggests that he is just as horrified by Hutchinson's behavior as his Puritan forefathers almost 200 years earlier: "there are portentous indications, changes gradually taking place in the habits and feelings of the gentle sex, which seem to threaten our posterity with many of those public women, whereof one was a burthen too grievous for our fathers." However, the narrator's stance is typical of Hawthorne's narrators, who assume such a position to challenge readers on their supposedly "enlightened" points of view. In this case, Hawthorne, as he does in *The Scarlet Letter*, sets his story in Puritan New England to comment on contemporary (nineteenth-century) views of women as much as seventeenth-century views. Indeed, the narrator remarks, "[w]oman's intellect should never give the tone to that of man, and even her morality is not exactly the material for masculine virtue." As Hawthorne wrote this story, early women's rights agitation was already occurring in England and stirring in the United States. Thus, the narrator's commentary questions the double-standard applied to women when prosecuting them (in the courts of law *and* public opinion) and describes men's often misogynist reactions to female power. Further, the narrator wonders if women are prepared to deal with the tremendous backlash they experience as a result of transgressions such as Hutchinson's. As you read the story, think about how American society currently reacts to women who have or seek power.

After his commentary, the narrator begins his sketch of Mrs. Hutchinson, noting she "was a woman of extraordinary talent and strong imagination" who advocated for religious freedom and reform from strict New England Calvinism. The first half of the sketch details Hutchinson's first interrogation by the current governor of Massachusetts and a group of powerful ministers ready "to convict her of damnable heresies." The narrator's portrait of these men is distinctly unflattering—they freely use their power and position as ministers and lawyers to intimidate Hutchinson, but without success.

The narrator continues by describing Hutchinson's ensuing appearance before "the supreme civil tribunal" (similar to a state Supreme Court) by legal authorities (the Elders of the church and state) and presided over by John Winthrop, the founder of Massachusetts Bay Colony. The narrator's tone changes in this part of the story to more direct satire and even ridicule: "It is a place of humble aspect where the Elders of the people are met, sitting in judgment upon the disturber of Israel." Hutchinson becomes a stand-in for all of womankind that threatens established (male) power: "In the midst, and in the centre of all eyes, we see the Woman." From this point to the end of the story, the narrator depicts Hutchinson as a smart, formidable foe who refuses to stand down, speaking openly, eloquently, and vigorously in her defense. Ironically, according to the narrator, Hutchinson's intellect and keen understanding of the church's lust for power proved her accusers' charges. She is indeed a threat to the established order of Puritan society and is subsequently exiled to Rhode Island.

"Mrs. Hutchinson"

by Nathaniel Hawthorne

First published in the Salem *Gazette,* "Mrs. Hutchinson" is Hawthorne's treatment of Anne Hutchinson, a radical Puritan minister of the early-to-mid 1600s.

Nathaniel Hwthorne, "Mrs. Hutchinson," 1830.

Hutchinson is mentioned in the first chapter of *The Scarlet Letter*, where Hawthorne writes about the rose bush that inexplicably grows next to the prison where Hester Prynne is doing time:

"But whether it had merely survived out of the stern old wilderness, so long after the dall of the gigantic pines and oaks that originally overshadowed it, — or whether, as there is fair authority for believing. it had sprung up under the footsteps of the sainted Anne Hutchinson, as she entered the prison door, — we shall not take upon us to determine."

Also, many critics find a spiritual and artistic progenitor of Hester Prynne in Hutchinson. After the jump, the full text of Nathaniel Hawthorne's "Mrs. Hutchinson."

THE character of this female suggests a train of thought which will form as natural an introduction to her story as most of the prefaces to Gay's Fables or the tales of Prior, besides that the general soundness of the moral may excuse any want of present applicability. We will not look for a living resemblance of Mrs. Hutchinson, though the search might not be altogether fruitless.–But there are portentous indications, changes gradually taking place in the habits and feelings of the gentle sex, which seem to threaten our posterity with many of those public women, whereof one was a burthen too grievous for our fathers. The press, however, is now the medium through which feminine ambition chiefly manifests itself; and we will not anticipate the period, (trusting to be gone hence ere it arrive,) when fair orators shall be as numerous as the fair authors of our own day. The hastiest glance may show, how much of the texture and body of cis-Atlantic literature is the work of those slender fingers, from which only a light and fanciful embroidery has heretofore been required, that might sparkle upon the garment without enfeebling the web. Woman's intellect should never give the tone to that of man, and even her morality is not exactly the material for masculine virtue. A false liberality which mistakes the strong division lines of Nature for arbitrary distinctions, and a courtesy, which might polish criticism but should never soften it, have done their best to add a girlish feebleness to the tottering infancy of our literature. The evil is likely to be a growing one. As yet, the great body of American women are a domestic race; but when a continuance of ill-judged incitements shall have turned their hearts away from the fireside, there are obvious circumstances which will render female pens more numerous and more prolific than those of men, though but equally encouraged; and (limited of course by the scanty support of the public, but increasing indefinitely within those limits) the ink-staned Amazons will expel their rivals by actual pressure, and petticoats wave triumphant over all the field. But, allowing that such forebodings are slightly exaggerated, is it good for woman's self that the path of feverish hope, of tremulous success, of bitter and ignominious disappointment, should be left wide open to her? Is the prize worth her having if she win it? Fame does not increase the peculiar respect which men pay to female excellence, and there is a delicacy, (even in rude bosoms, where few would think to find it) that perceives, or fancies, a sort of impropriety in the display of woman's naked mind to the gaze of the world, with indications by which its inmost secrets may be searched out. In fine, criticism should examine with a stricter, instead of a more indulgent eye, the merits of females at its bar, because they are to justify themselves for an irregularity which men do not commit in appearing there; and woman, when she feels the impulse of genius like a command of Heaven within her, should be aware that she is relinquishing a part of the loveliness of her sex, and obey the inward voice with sorrowing reluctance, like the Arabian maid who bewailed the gift of Prophecy. Hinting thus imperfectly at sentiments which may be developed on a future occasion, we proceed to consider the celebrated subject of this sketch.

Mrs. Hutchinson was a woman of extraordinary talent and strong imagination, whom the latter quality, following the general direction taken by the enthusiasm of the times, prompted to stand forth as a reformer in religion. In her native country, she had shown symptoms of irregular and daring thought, but, chiefly by the influence of a favorite pastor, was restrained from open indiscretion. On the removal of this clergyman, becoming dissatisfied with the ministry under which she lived, she was drawn in by the great tide of Puritan emigration, and visited Massachusetts within a few years after its first settlement. But she bore trouble in her own bosom, and could find no peace in this chosen land.–She soon began to promulgate strange and dangerous opinions, tending, in the peculiar situation of the colony, and from the principles which were its basis and indispensable for its temporary support, to eat into its very existence. We shall endeavor to give a more practical idea of this part of her course.

It is a summer evening. The dusk has settled heavily upon the woods, the waves, and the Trimontane peninsula, increasing that dismal aspect of the embryo town which was said to have drawn tears of despondency from Mrs. Hutchinson, though she believed that her mission thither was divine. The houses, straw-thatched and lowly roofed, stand irregularly along streets that are yet roughened by the roots of the trees, as if the forest, departing at the approach of man, had left its reluctant foot prints behind. Most of the dwellings are lonely and silent, from a few we may hear the reading of some sacred text, or the quiet voice of prayer; but nearly all the sombre life of the scene is collected near the extremity at the village. A crowd of hooded women, and of men in steeple hats and close cropt hair, are assembled at the door and open windows of a house newly built. An earnest expression glows in every face, and some press inward as if the bread of life were to be dealt forth, and they feared to lose their share, while others would fain hold them back, but enter with them since they may not be restrained. We also will go in, edging through the thronged doorway to an apartment which occupies the whole breadth of the house. At the upper end, behind a table on which are placed the Scriptures and two glimmering lamps, we see a woman, plainly attired as befits her ripened years, her hair, complexion, and eyes are dark, the latter somewhat dull and hearty, but kindling up with a gradual brightness. Let us look round upon the hearers. At her right hand, his countenance suiting well with the gloomy light which discovers it, stands Vane the youthful governor, preferred by a hasty judgment of the people over all the wise and hoary heads that had preceded him to New-England. In his mysterious eyes we may read a dark enthusiasm, akin to that of the woman whose cause he has espoused, combined with a shrewd worldly foresight, which tells him that her doctrines will be productive of change and tumult, the elements of his power and delight. On her left, yet slightly drawn back so as to evince a less decided support, is Cotton, no young and hot enthusiast, but a mild, grave man in the decline of life, deep in all the learning of the age, and sanctified in heart and made venerable in feature by the long exercise of his holy profession. He also is deceived by the strange fire now laid upon the altar, and he alone among his brethren is excepted in the denunciation of the new Apostle, as sealed and set apart by Heaven to the work of the ministry. Others of the priesthood stand full in front of the woman, striving to beat her down with brows of wrinkled iron, and whispering sternly and significantly among themselves, as she unfolds her seditious doctrines and grows warm in their support. Foremost is Hugh Peters, full of holy wrath, and scarce containing himself from rushing forward to convict her of damnable heresies; there also is Ward, meditating a reply of empty puns, and quaint antitheses, and tinkling jests that puzzle us with nothing but a sound. The audience are variously affected, but none indifferent. On the foreheads of the aged, the mature, and strong-minded, you may generally read steadfast disapprobation, though here and there is one, whose faith seems shaken in those whom he had trusted for years; the females, on the other hand, are shuddering and weeping, and at times they cast a desolate look of fear around them; while the young men lean forward, fiery and impatient, fit instruments for whatever rash deed may be suggested. And what is the eloquence that gives rise to all these passions? The woman tells them, (and cites texts from the Holy Book to prove her words,) that they have put their trust in unregenerated and uncommissioned men, and have followed them into the wilderness for naught. Therefore their hearts are turning from those whom they had chosen to lead them to Heaven, and they feel like children who have been enticed far from home, and see the features of their guides change all at once, assuming a fiendish shape in some frightful solitude.

These proceedings of Mrs. Hutchinson could not long be endured by the provincial government. The present was a most remarkable case, in which religious freedom was wholly inconsistent with public safety, and where the principles of an illiberal age indicated the very course which must have been pursued by worldly policy and enlightened wisdom. Unity of faith was the star that had guided these people over the deep, and a diversity of sects would either have scattered them from the land to which they had as yet so few attachments, or perhaps have excited a diminutive civil war among those who had come so far to worship together. The opposition to what may be termed the established church had now lost its chief support, by the removal of Vane from office and his departure for England, and Mr. Cotton began to have that light in regard to his errors, which will sometimes break in upon the wisest and most pious men, when their opinions are unhappily discordant with those of the Powers that be. A Synod, the first in New England, was speedily assembled, and pronounced its condemnation of the obnoxious doctrines. Mrs. Hutchinson was next summoned before the supreme civil tribunal, at which, however, the most eminent of the clergy were present, and appear to have taken a very active part as witnesses and advisers. We shall here resume the more picturesque style of narration.

It is a place of humble aspect where the Elders of the people are met, sitting in judgment upon the disturber of Israel. The floor of the low and narrow hall is laid with planks hewn by the axe,–the beams of the roof still wear the rugged bark with which they grew up in the forest, and the hearth is formed of one broad unhammered stone, heaped with logs that roll their blaze and smote up a chimney of wood and clay. A sleety shower beats fitfully against the windows, driven by the November blast, which comes howling onward from the northern desert, the boisterous and unwelcome herald of a New England winter. Rude benches are arranged across the apartment and along its sides, occupied by men whose piety and learning might have entitled them to seats in those high Councils of the ancient Church, whence opinions were sent forth to confirm or supersede the Gospel in the belief of the whole world and of posterity.–Here are collected all those blessed Fathers of the land, who rank in our veneration next to the Evangelists of Holy Writ, and here also are many, unpurified from the fiercest errors of the age and ready to propagate the religion of peace by violence. In the highest place sits Winthrop, a man by whom the innocent and the guilty might alike desire to be judged, the first confiding in his integrity and wisdom, the latter hoping in his mildness. Next is Endicott, who would stand with his drawn sword at the gate of Heaven, and resist to the death all pilgrims thither, except they travelled his own path. The infant eyes of one in this assembly beheld the faggots blazing round the martyrs, in bloody Mary's time; in later life he dwelt long at Leyden, with the first who went from England for conscience sake; and now, in his weary age, it matters little where he lies down to die. There are others whose hearts were smitten in the high meridian of ambitious hope, and whose dreams still tempt them with the pomp of the old world and the din of its crowded cities, gleaming and echoing over the deep. In the midst, and in the centre of all eves, we see the Woman. She stands loftily before her judges, with a determined brow, and, unknown to herself, there is a flash of carnal pride half hidden in her eye, as she surveys the many learned and famous men whom her doctrines have put in fear. They question her, and her answers are ready and acute; she reasons with them shrewdly, and brings scripture in support of every argument; the deepest controversialists of that scholastic day find here a woman, whom all their trained and sharpened intellects are inadequate to foil. But by the excitement of the contest, her heart is made to rise and swell within her, and she bursts forth into eloquence. She tells them of the long unquietness which she had endured in England, perceiving the corruption of the church, and yearning for a purer and more perfect light, and how, in a day of solitary prayer, that light was given; she claims for herself the peculiar power of distinguishing between the chosen of man and the Sealed of Heaven, and affirms that her gifted eye can see the glory round the foreheads of the Saints, sojourning in their mortal state. She declares herself commissioned to separate the true shepherds from the false, and denounces present and future judgments on the land, if she be disturbed in her celestial errand. Thus the accusations are proved from her own mouth. Her judges hesitate, and some speak faintly in her defence; but, with a few dissenting voices, sentence is pronounced, bidding her go out from among them, and trouble the land no more.

Mrs. Hutchinson's adherents throughout the colony were now disarmed, and she proceeded to Rhode Island, an accustomed refuge for the exiles of Massachusetts, in all seasons o persecution. Her enemies believed that the anger of Heaven was following her, of which Governor Winthrop does no disdain to record a notable instance, very interesting in a scientific point of view, but fitter for his old and homely narrative than for modern repetition. In a little time, also, she lost her husband, who is mentioned in history only as attending her footsteps, and whom we may conclude to have been (like most husbands of celebrated women) mere insignificant appendage of his mightier wife. She now grew uneasy among the Rhode-Island colonists, whose liberality towards her, at an era when literality was not esteemed a Christian virtue, probably arose from a comparative insolicitude on religious matters, more distasteful to Mrs. Hutchinson than even the uncompromising narrowness of the Puritans. Her final movement was to lead her family within the limits of the Dutch Jurisdiction, where, having felled the trees of a virgin soil, she became herself the virtual head, civil and ecclesiastical, of a little colony.

Perhaps here she found the repose, hitherto so vainly sought. Secluded from all whose faith she could not govern, surrounded by the dependents over whom she held an unlimited influence, agitated by none of the tumultuous billows which were left swelling behind her, we may suppose, that, in the stillness of Nature, her heart was stilled. But her impressive story was to have an awful close. Her last scene is as difficult to be portrayed as a shipwreck, where the shrieks of the victims die unheard along a desolate sea, and a shapeless mass of agony is all that can be brought home to the imagination. The savage foe was on the watch for blood. Sixteen persons assembled at the evening prayer; in the deep midnight, their cry rang through the forest; and daylight dawned upon the lifeless clay of all but one. It was a circumstance not to be unnoticed by our stem ancestors, in considering the fate of her who had so troubled their religion, that an infant daughter, the sole survivor amid the terrible destruction of her mother's household, was bred in a barbarous faith, and never learned the way to the Christian's Heaven. Yet we will hope, that there the mother and the child have met.

Critical Thinking

In typical style, Hawthorne ends the story on an ambivalent, even ambiguous note: how are we to regard Hutchinson? Was she too smart for her own good?

If she is a representative of Woman, what are the qualities of women that threaten the status quo?

In terms of criminal justice, to what extent does gender bias play a role in the justice system, especially when women actively resist implicit social and cultural roles?

Do we judge women more harshly than men when they transgress implicit (and sometimes explicit) gender codes?

Do legal authorities today (law enforcement officers, prosecutors, for example) use intimidation tactics to try and force defendants to confess to their crimes?

Chapter 2

Criminal Behavior

Routine Activities Theory

"The Purloined Letter"

by Edgar Allan Poe

Edgar Allan Poe (1809–1849) is one of America's most famous authors, known for his gothic and supernatural tales and for founding the modern detective story. Indeed, he influenced, among others, Sir Arthur Conan Doyle and his creation of Sherlock Holmes, literature's greatest detective. "The Purloined Letter" (1844) was first published in the literary annual *The Gift for 1845* and subsequently reprinted in journals and newspapers. It is the third story featuring Poe's detective (the first in literary history), C. Auguste Dupin. Similar to "The Murders in the Rue Morgue" and "The Mystery of Marie Roget," this tale pits Dupin's intellectual detecting skills against the overconfident but curious Prefect of the Parisian police, Monsieur G—, as related by an unnamed first-person narrator.

The tale begins with Dupin recounting his previous successes when Monsieur G— arrives to describe the strange, seemingly unsolvable case of a purloined letter and engage Dupin's opinion. A prominent woman's letter has been stolen from her apartment by an unscrupulous government official who plans to blackmail the woman in exchange for keeping the letter's contents secret. The owner of the letter has sought the Prefect's help to get the letter back, but to no avail. Responding to Dupin's inquiries, Monsieur G— details the actions that he and his police officers have so far undertaken to retrieve the letter, including searching the blackmailer's residence and workplace thoroughly, but without success. Frustrated and dumbfounded by the minister's cunning, the Prefect offers to pay the person who finds the letter fifty thousand francs. In a stunning move, Dupin accepts the offer, stating that he will indeed retrieve the letter. The narrator wonders how Dupin could locate the letter after the Prefect's and the Parisian police's search. For the remainder of the tale, he details how he retrieves the letter, contrasting his skills against those of the police, who, he notes, "are exceedingly able in their way. They are persevering, ingenious, cunning, and thoroughly versed in the knowledge which their duties seem chiefly to demand." However, they lack the skills that will become ubiquitous to the detective story and to modern policing, including psychological profiling, analysis of personality and motives, and logical reasoning. As you read the story, consider how modern policing has evolved since Poe wrote this story.

"The Purloined Letter"

by Edgar Allan Poe

Nil sapientiae odiosius acumine nimio

—Seneca.

At Paris, just after dark one gusty evening in the autumn of 18—, I was enjoying the twofold luxury of meditation and a meerschaum, in company with my friend C. Auguste Dupin, in his little back library, or book-closet, au troisieme, No. 33, Rue Dunot, Faubourg St. Germain. For one hour at least we had maintained a profound silence; while each, to any casual observer, might have seemed intently and exclusively occupied with the curling eddies of smoke that oppressed the atmosphere of the chamber. For myself, however, I was mentally discussing certain topics which had formed matter for conversation between us at an earlier period of the evening; I mean the affair of the Rue Morgue, and the mystery attending the murder of Marie Roget. I looked upon it, therefore, as something of a coincidence, when the door of our apartment was thrown open and admitted our old acquaintance, Monsieur G—, the Prefect of the Parisian police.

We gave him a hearty welcome; for there was nearly half as much of the entertaining as of the contemptible about the man, and we had not seen him for several years. We had been sitting in the dark, and Dupin now arose for the purpose of lighting a lamp, but sat down again, without doing so, upon G.'s saying that he had called to consult us, or rather to ask the opinion of my friend, about some official business which had occasioned a great deal of trouble.

"If it is any point requiring reflection," observed Dupin, as he forbore to enkindle the wick, "we shall examine it to better purpose in the dark."

"That is another of your odd notions," said the Prefect, who had a fashion of calling every thing "odd" that was beyond his comprehension, and thus lived amid an absolute legion of "oddities."

"Very true," said Dupin, as he supplied his visitor with a pipe, and rolled towards him a comfortable chair.

"And what is the difficulty now?" I asked. "Nothing more in the assassination way, I hope?"

Source: Edgar Allan Poe, "The Purloined Letter," 1845.

"Oh no; nothing of that nature. The fact is, the business is very simple indeed, and I make no doubt that we can manage it sufficiently well ourselves; but then I thought Dupin would like to hear the details of it, because it is so excessively odd."

"Simple and odd," said Dupin.

"Why, yes; and not exactly that, either. The fact is, we have all been a good deal puzzled because the affair is so simple, and yet baffles us altogether."

"Perhaps it is the very simplicity of the thing which puts you at fault," said my friend.

"What nonsense you do talk!" replied the Prefect, laughing heartily.

"Perhaps the mystery is a little too plain," said Dupin.

"Oh, good heavens! who ever heard of such an idea?"

"A little too self-evident."

"Ha! ha! ha! —ha! ha! ha! —ho! ho! ho!" —roared our visitor, profoundly amused, "oh, Dupin, you will be the death of me yet!"

"And what, after all, is the matter on hand?" I asked.

"Why, I will tell you," replied the Prefect, as he gave a long, steady, and contemplative puff, and settled himself in his chair. "I will tell you in a few words; but, before I begin, let me caution you that this is an affair demanding the greatest secrecy, and that I should most probably lose the position I now hold, were it known that I confided it to any one.

"Proceed," said I.

"Or not," said Dupin.

"Well, then; I have received personal information, from a very high quarter, that a certain document of the last importance, has been purloined from the royal apartments. The individual who purloined it is known; this beyond a doubt; he was seen to take it. It is known, also, that it still remains in his possession."

"How is this known?" asked Dupin.

"It is clearly inferred," replied the Prefect, "from the nature of the document, and from the nonappearance of certain results which would at once arise from its passing out of the robber's possession; —that is to say, from his employing it as he must design in the end to employ it."

"Be a little more explicit," I said.

"Well, I may venture so far as to say that the paper gives its holder a certain power in a certain quarter where such power is immensely valuable." The Prefect was fond of the cant of diplomacy.

"Still I do not quite understand," said Dupin.

"No? Well; the disclosure of the document to a third person, who shall be nameless, would bring in question the honor of a personage of most exalted station; and this fact gives the holder of the document an ascendancy over the illustrious personage whose honor and peace are so jeopardized."

"But this ascendancy," I interposed, "would depend upon the robber's knowledge of the loser's knowledge of the robber. Who would dare—"

"The thief," said G., is the Minister D—, who dares all things, those unbecoming as well as those becoming a man. The method of the theft was not less ingenious than bold. The document in question —a letter, to be frank —had been received by the personage robbed while alone in the royal boudoir. During its perusal she was suddenly interrupted by the entrance of the other exalted personage from whom especially it was her wish to conceal it. After a hurried and vain endeavor to thrust it in a drawer, she was forced to place it, open as it was, upon a table. The address, however, was uppermost, and, the contents thus unexposed, the letter escaped notice. At this juncture enters the Minister D—. His lynx eye immediately perceives the paper, recognises the handwriting of the address, observes the confusion of the personage addressed, and fathoms her secret. After some business transactions, hurried through in his ordinary manner, he produces a letter somewhat similar to the one in question, opens it, pretends to read it, and then places it in close juxtaposition to the other. Again he converses, for some fifteen minutes, upon the public affairs. At length, in taking leave, he takes also from the table the letter to which he had no claim. Its rightful owner saw, but, of course, dared not call attention to the act, in the presence of the third personage who stood at her elbow. The minister decamped; leaving his own letter —one of no importance —upon the table."

"Here, then," said Dupin to me, "you have precisely what you demand to make the ascendancy complete —the robber's knowledge of the loser's knowledge of the robber."

"Yes," replied the Prefect; "and the power thus attained has, for some months past, been wielded, for political purposes, to a very dangerous extent. The personage robbed is more thoroughly convinced, every day, of the necessity of reclaiming her letter. But this, of course, cannot be done openly. In fine, driven to despair, she has committed the matter to me."

"Than whom," said Dupin, amid a perfect whirlwind of smoke, "no more sagacious agent could, I suppose, be desired, or even imagined."

"You flatter me," replied the Prefect; "but it is possible that some such opinion may have been entertained."

"It is clear," said I, "as you observe, that the letter is still in possession of the minister; since it is this possession, and not any employment of the letter, which bestows the power. With the employment the power departs."

"True," said G. "and upon this conviction I proceeded. My first care was to make thorough search of the minister's hotel; and here my chief embarrassment lay in the necessity of searching without his knowledge. Beyond all things, I have been warned of the danger which would result from giving him reason to suspect our design."

"But," said I, "you are quite au fait in these investigations. The Parisian police have done this thing often before."

"Oh yes; and for this reason I did not despair. The habits of the minister gave me, too, a great advantage. He is frequently absent from home all night. His servants are by no means numerous. They sleep at a distance from their master's apartment, and, being chiefly Neapolitans, are readily made drunk. I have keys, as you know, with which I can open any chamber or cabinet in Paris. For three months a night has not passed, during the greater part of which I have not been engaged, personally, in ransacking the D— Hotel. My honor is interested, and, to mention a great secret, the reward is enormous. So I did not abandon the search until I had become fully satisfied that the thief is a more astute man than myself. I fancy that I have investigated every nook and corner of the premises in which it is possible that the paper can be concealed."

"But is it not possible," I suggested, "that although the letter may be in possession of the minister, as it unquestionably is, he may have concealed it elsewhere than upon his own premises?"

"This is barely possible," said Dupin. "The present peculiar condition of affairs at court, and especially of those intrigues in which D— is known to be involved, would render the instant availability of the document —its susceptibility of being produced at a moment's notice —a point of nearly equal importance with its possession."

"Its susceptibility of being produced?" said I.

"That is to say, of being destroyed," said Dupin.

"True," I observed; "the paper is clearly then upon the premises. As for its being upon the person of the minister, we may consider that as out of the question."

"Entirely," said the Prefect. "He has been twice waylaid, as if by footpads, and his person rigorously searched under my own inspection.

"You might have spared yourself this trouble," said Dupin. "D—, I presume, is not altogether a fool, and, if not, must have anticipated these waylayings, as a matter of course."

"Not altogether a fool," said G., "but then he's a poet, which I take to be only one remove from a fool."

"True," said Dupin, after a long and thoughtful whiff from his meerschaum, "although I have been guilty of certain doggerel myself."

"Suppose you detail," said I, "the particulars of your search."

"Why the fact is, we took our time, and we searched every where. I have had long experience in these affairs. I took the entire building, room by room; devoting the nights of a whole week to each. We examined, first, the furniture of each apartment. We opened every possible drawer; and I presume you know that, to a properly trained police agent, such a thing as a secret drawer is impossible. Any man is a dolt who permits a 'secret' drawer to escape him in a search of this kind. The thing is so plain. There is a certain amount of bulk —of space —to be accounted for in every cabinet. Then we have accurate rules. The fiftieth part of a line could not escape us. After the cabinets we took the chairs. The cushions we probed with the fine long needles you have seen me employ. From the tables we removed the tops."

"Why so?"

"Sometimes the top of a table, or other similarly arranged piece of furniture, is removed by the person wishing to conceal an article; then the leg is excavated, the article deposited within the cavity, and the top replaced. The bottoms and tops of bedposts are employed in the same way."

"But could not the cavity be detected by sounding?" I asked.

"By no means, if, when the article is deposited, a sufficient wadding of cotton be placed around it. Besides, in our case, we were obliged to proceed without noise."

"But you could not have removed —you could not have taken to pieces all articles of furniture in which it would have been possible to make a deposit in the manner you mention. A letter may be compressed into a thin spiral roll, not differing much in shape or bulk from a large knitting-needle, and in this form it might be inserted into the rung of a chair, for example. You did not take to pieces all the chairs?"

"Certainly not; but we did better —we examined the rungs of every chair in the hotel, and, indeed, the jointings of every description of furniture, by the aid of a most powerful microscope. Had there been any traces of recent disturbance we should not have failed to detect it instantly. A single grain of gimlet-dust, for example, would have been as obvious as an apple. Any disorder in the glueing —any unusual gaping in the joints —would have sufficed to insure detection."

"I presume you looked to the mirrors, between the boards and the plates, and you probed the beds and the bed-clothes, as well as the curtains and carpets."

"That of course; and when we had absolutely completed every particle of the furniture in this way, then we examined the house itself. We divided its entire surface into compartments, which we numbered, so that none might be missed; then we scrutinized each individual square inch throughout the premises, including the two houses immediately adjoining, with the microscope, as before."

"The two houses adjoining!" I exclaimed; "you must have had a great deal of trouble."

"We had; but the reward offered is prodigious.

"You include the grounds about the houses?"

"All the grounds are paved with brick. They gave us comparatively little trouble. We examined the moss between the bricks, and found it undisturbed."

"You looked among D—'s papers, of course, and into the books of the library?"

"Certainly; we opened every package and parcel; we not only opened every book, but we turned over every leaf in each volume, not contenting ourselves with a mere shake, according to the fashion of some of our police officers. We also measured the thickness of every book-cover, with the most accurate admeasurement, and applied to each the most jealous scrutiny of the microscope. Had any of the bindings been recently meddled with, it would have been utterly impossible that the fact should have escaped observation. Some five or six volumes, just from the hands of the binder, we carefully probed, longitudinally, with the needles."

"You explored the floors beneath the carpets?"

"Beyond doubt. We removed every carpet, and examined the boards with the microscope."

"And the paper on the walls?"

"Yes.

"You looked into the cellars?"

"We did."

"Then," I said, "you have been making a miscalculation, and the letter is not upon the premises, as you suppose.

"I fear you are right there," said the Prefect. "And now, Dupin, what would you advise me to do?"

"To make a thorough re-search of the premises."

"That is absolutely needless," replied G—. "I am not more sure that I breathe than I am that the letter is not at the Hotel."

"I have no better advice to give you," said Dupin. "You have, of course, an accurate description of the letter?"

"Oh yes!" —And here the Prefect, producing a memorandum-book, proceeded to read aloud a minute account of the internal, and especially of the external appearance of the missing document. Soon after finishing the perusal of this description, he took his departure, more entirely depressed in spirits than I had ever known the good gentleman before.

In about a month afterwards he paid us another visit, and found us occupied very nearly as before. He took a pipe and a chair and entered into some ordinary conversation. At length I said,—

"Well, but G—, what of the purloined letter? I presume you have at last made up your mind that there is no such thing as overreaching the Minister?"

"Confound him, say I —yes; I made the reexamination, however, as Dupin suggested —but it was all labor lost, as I knew it would be."

"How much was the reward offered, did you say?" asked Dupin.

"Why, a very great deal —a very liberal reward —I don't like to say how much, precisely; but one thing I will say, that I wouldn't mind giving my individual check for fifty thousand francs to any one who could obtain me that letter. The fact is, it is becoming of more and more importance every day; and the reward has been lately doubled. If it were trebled, however, I could do no more than I have done."

"Why, yes," said Dupin, drawlingly, between the whiffs of his meerschaum, "I really —think, G—, you have not exerted yourself—to the utmost in this matter. You might —do a little more, I think, eh?"

"How? —In what way?"

"Why —puff, puff —you might —puff, puff —employ counsel in the matter, eh? —puff, puff, puff. Do you remember the story they tell of Abernethy?"

"No; hang Abernethy!"

"To be sure! hang him and welcome. But, once upon a time, a certain rich miser conceived the design of spunging upon this Abernethy for a medical opinion. Getting up, for this purpose, an ordinary conversation in a private company, he insinuated his case to the physician, as that of an imaginary individual.

"'We will suppose,' said the miser, 'that his symptoms are such and such; now, doctor, what would you have directed him to take?'

"'Take!' said Abernethy, 'why, take advice, to be sure.'"

"But," said the Prefect, a little discomposed, "I am perfectly willing to take advice, and to pay for it. I would really give fifty thousand francs to any one who would aid me in the matter."

"In that case," replied Dupin, opening a drawer, and producing a check-book, "you may as well fill me up a check for the amount mentioned. When you have signed it, I will hand you the letter."

I was astounded. The Prefect appeared absolutely thunderstricken. For some minutes he remained speechless and motionless, less, looking incredulously at my friend with open mouth, and eyes that seemed starting from their sockets; then, apparently in some measure, he seized a pen, and after several pauses and vacant stares, finally filled up and signed a check for fifty thousand francs, and handed it across the table to Dupin. The latter examined it carefully and deposited it in his pocket-book; then, unlocking an escritoire, took thence a letter and gave it to the Prefect. This functionary grasped it in a perfect agony of joy, opened it with a trembling hand, cast a rapid glance at its contents, and then, scrambling and struggling to the door, rushed at length unceremoniously from the room and from the house, without having uttered a syllable since Dupin had requested him to fill up the check.

When he had gone, my friend entered into some explanations.

"The Parisian police," he said, "are exceedingly able in their way. They are persevering, ingenious, cunning, and thoroughly versed in the knowledge which their duties seem chiefly to demand. Thus, when G— detailed to us his mode of searching the premises at the Hotel D—, I felt entire confidence in, his having made a satisfactory investigation —so far as his labors extended."

"So far as his labors extended?" said I.

"Yes," said Dupin. "The measures adopted were not only the best of their kind, but carried out to absolute perfection. Had the letter been deposited within the range of their search, these fellows would, beyond a question, have found it."

I merely laughed —but he seemed quite serious in all that he said.

"The measures, then," he continued, "were good in their kind, and well executed; their defect lay in their being inapplicable to the case, and to the man. A certain set of highly ingenious resources are, with the Prefect, a sort of Procrustean bed, to which he forcibly adapts his designs. But he perpetually errs by being too deep or too shallow, for the matter in hand; and many a schoolboy is a better reasoner than he. I knew one about eight years of age, whose success at guessing in the game of 'even and odd' attracted universal admiration. This game is simple, and is played with marbles. One player holds in his hand a number of these toys, and demands of another whether that number is even or odd. If the guess is right, the guesser wins one; if wrong, he loses one. The boy to whom I allude won all the marbles of the school. Of course he had some principle of guessing; and this lay in mere observation and admeasurement of the astuteness of his opponents. For example, an arrant simpleton is his opponent, and, holding up his closed hand, asks, 'are they even or odd?' Our schoolboy replies, 'odd,' and loses; but upon the second trial he wins, for he then says to himself, the simpleton had them even upon the first trial, and his amount of cunning is just sufficient to make him have them odd upon the second; I will therefore guess odd'; —he guesses odd, and wins. Now, with a simpleton a degree above the first, he would have reasoned thus: 'This fellow finds that in the first instance I guessed odd, and, in the second, he will propose to himself upon the first impulse, a simple variation from even to odd, as did the first simpleton; but then a second thought will suggest that this is too simple a variation, and finally he will decide upon putting it even as before. I will therefore guess even' guesses even, and wins. Now this mode of reasoning in the schoolboy, whom his fellows termed "lucky," —what, in its last analysis, is it?"

"It is merely," I said, "an identification of the reasoner's intellect with that of his opponent."

"It is," said Dupin;" and, upon inquiring of the boy by what means he effected the thorough identification in which his success consisted, I received answer as follows: 'When I wish to find out how wise, or how stupid, or how good, or how wicked is any one, or what are his thoughts at the moment, I fashion the expression of my face, as accurately as possible, in accordance with the expression of his, and then wait to see what thoughts or sentiments arise in my mind or heart, as if to match or correspond with the expression.' This response of the schoolboy lies at the bottom of all the spurious profundity which has been attributed to Rochefoucauld, to La Bougive, to Machiavelli, and to Campanella."

"And the identification," I said, "of the reasoner's intellect with that of his opponent, depends, if I understand you aright upon the accuracy with which the opponent's intellect is admeasured."

"For its practical value it depends upon this," replied Dupin; and the Prefect and his cohort fall so frequently, first, by default of this identification, and, secondly, by ill-admeasurement, or rather through non-admeasurement, of the intellect with which they are engaged. They consider only their own ideas of ingenuity; and, in searching for anything hidden, advert only to the modes in which they would have hidden it. They are right in this much —that their own ingenuity is a faithful representative of that of the mass; but when the cunning of the individual felon is diverse in character from their own, the felon foils them, of course. This always happens when it is above their own, and very usually when it is below. They have no variation of principle in their investigations; at best, when urged by some unusual emergency —by some extraordinary reward —they extend or exaggerate their old modes of practice, without touching their principles. What, for example, in this case of D—, has been done to vary the principle of action? What is all this boring, and probing, and sounding, and scrutinizing with the microscope, and dividing the surface of the building into registered square inches —what is it all but an exaggeration of the application of the one principle or set of principles of search, which are based upon the one set of notions regarding human ingenuity, to which the Prefect, in the long routine of his duty, has been accustomed? Do you not see he has taken it for granted that all men proceed to conceal a letter, —not exactly in a gimlet-hole bored in a chair-leg —but, at least, in some hole or corner suggested by the same tenor of thought which would urge a man to secrete a letter in a gimlet-hole bored in a chair-leg? And do you not see also, that such recherches nooks for concealment are adapted only for ordinary occasions, and would be adopted only by ordinary intellects; for, in all cases of concealment, a disposal of the article concealed —a disposal of it in this recherche manner, —is, in the very first instance, presumable and presumed; and thus its discovery depends, not at all upon the acumen, but altogether upon the mere care, patience, and determination of the seekers; and where the case is of importance —or, what amounts to the same thing in the policial eyes, when the reward is of magnitude, —the qualities in question have never been known to fall. You will now understand what I meant in suggesting that, had the purloined letter been hidden anywhere within the limits of the Prefect's examination —in other words, had the principle of its concealment been comprehended within the principles of the Prefect —its discovery would have been a matter altogether beyond question. This functionary, however, has been thoroughly mystified; and the remote source of his defeat lies in the supposition that the Minister is a fool, because he has acquired renown as a poet. All fools are poets; this the Prefect feels; and he is merely guilty of a non distributio medii in thence inferring that all poets are fools."

"But is this really the poet?" I asked. "There are two brothers, I know; and both have attained reputation in letters. The Minister I believe has written learnedly on the Differential Calculus. He is a mathematician, and no poet."

"You are mistaken; I know him well; he is both. As poet and mathematician, he would reason well; as mere mathematician, he could not have reasoned at all, and thus would have been at the mercy of the Prefect."

"You surprise me," I said, "by these opinions, which have been contradicted by the voice of the world. You do not mean to set at naught the well-digested idea of centuries. The mathematical reason has long been regarded as the reason par excellence.

"'Il y a a parier,'" replied Dupin, quoting from Chamfort, "'que toute idee publique, toute convention recue, est une sottise, car elle a convenu au plus grand nombre.' The mathematicians, I grant you, have done their best to promulgate the popular error to which you allude, and which is none the less an error for its promulgation as truth. With an art worthy a better cause, for example, they have insinuated the term 'analysis' into application to algebra. The French are the originators of this particular deception; but if a term is of any importance —if words derive any value from applicability —then 'analysis' conveys 'algebra' about as much as, in Latin, 'ambitus' implies 'ambition,' 'religio' religion or 'homines honesti,' a set of honorable men."

"You have a quarrel on hand, I see," said I, "with some of the algebraists of Paris; but proceed."

"I dispute the availability, and thus the value, of that reason which is cultivated in any especial form other than the abstractly logical. I dispute, in particular, the reason educed by mathematical study. The mathematics are the science of form and quantity; mathematical reasoning is merely logic applied to observation upon form and quantity. The great error lies in supposing that even the truths of what is called pure algebra, are abstract or general truths. And this error is so egregious that I am confounded at the universality with which it has been received. Mathematical axioms are not axioms of general truth. What is true of relation —of form and quantity —is often grossly false in regard to morals, for example. In this latter science it is very usually untrue that the aggregated parts are equal to the whole. In chemistry also the axiom falls. In the consideration of motive it falls; for two motives, each of a given value, have not, necessarily, a value when united, equal to the sum of their values apart. There are numerous other mathematical truths which are only truths within the limits of relation. But the mathematician argues, from his finite truths, through habit, as if they were of an absolutely general applicability —as the world indeed imagines them to be. Bryant, in his very learned 'Mythology,' mentions an analogous source of error, when he says that 'although the Pagan fables are not believed, yet we forget ourselves continually, and make inferences from them as existing realities.' With the algebraists, however, who are Pagans themselves, the 'Pagan fables' are believed, and the inferences are made, not so much through lapse of memory, as through an unaccountable addling of the brains. In short, I never yet encountered the mere mathematician who could be trusted out of equal roots, or one who did not clandestinely hold it as a point of his faith that x squared $+ px$ was absolutely and unconditionally equal to q. Say to one of these gentlemen, by way of experiment, if you please, that you believe occasions may occur where x squared $+ px$ is not altogether equal to q, and, having made him understand what you mean, get out of his reach as speedily as convenient, for, beyond doubt, he will endeavor to knock you down.

I mean to say," continued Dupin, while I merely laughed at his last observations, "that if the Minister had been no more than a mathematician, the Prefect would have been under no necessity of giving me this check. I knew him, however, as both mathematician and poet, and my measures were adapted to his capacity, with reference to the circumstances by which he was surrounded. I knew him as a courtier, too, and as a bold intriguant. Such a man, I considered, could not fall to be aware of the ordinary policial modes of action. He could not have failed to anticipate —and events have proved that he did not fail to anticipate —the waylayings to which he was subjected. He must have foreseen, I reflected, the secret investigations of his premises. His frequent absences from home at night, which were hailed by the Prefect as certain aids to his success, I regarded only as ruses, to afford opportunity for thorough search to the police, and thus the sooner to impress them with the conviction to which G—, in fact, did finally arrive —the conviction that the letter was not upon the premises. I felt, also, that the whole train of thought, which I was at some pains in detailing to you just now, concerning the invariable principle of policial action in searches for articles concealed —I felt that this whole train of thought would necessarily pass through the mind of the Minister. It would imperatively lead him to despise all the ordinary nooks of concealment. He could not, I reflected, be so weak as not to see that the most intricate and remote recess of his hotel would be as open as his commonest closets to the eyes, to the probes, to the gimlets, and to the microscopes of the Prefect. I saw, in fine, that he would be driven, as a matter of course, to simplicity, if not deliberately induced to it as a matter of choice. You will remember, perhaps, how desperately the Prefect laughed when I suggested, upon our first interview, that it was just possible this mystery troubled him so much on account of its being so very self-evident."

"Yes," said I, "I remember his merriment well. I really thought he would have fallen into convulsions."

"The material world," continued Dupin, "abounds with very strict analogies to the immaterial; and thus some color of truth has been given to the rhetorical dogma, that metaphor, or simile, may be made to strengthen an argument, as well as to embellish a description. The principle of the vis inertiae, for example, seems to be identical in physics and metaphysics. It is not more true in the former, that a large body is with more difficulty set in motion than a smaller one, and that its subsequent momentum is commensurate with this difficulty, than it is, in the latter, that intellects of the vaster capacity, while more forcible, more constant, and more eventful in their movements than those of inferior grade, are yet the less readily moved, and more embarrassed and full of hesitation in the first few steps of their progress. Again: have you ever noticed which of the street signs, over the shop doors, are the most attractive of attention?"

"I have never given the matter a thought," I said.

"There is a game of puzzles," he resumed, "which is played upon a map. One party playing requires another to find a given word —the name of town, river, state or empire —any word, in short, upon the motley and perplexed surface of the chart. A novice in the game generally seeks to embarrass his opponents by giving them the most minutely lettered names; but the adept selects such words as stretch, in large characters, from one end of the chart to the other. These, like the over-largely lettered signs and placards of the street, escape observation by dint of being excessively obvious; and here the physical oversight is precisely analogous with the moral inapprehension by which the intellect suffers to pass unnoticed those considerations which are too obtrusively and too palpably self-evident. But this is a point, it appears, somewhat above or beneath the understanding of the Prefect. He never once thought it probable, or possible, that the Minister had deposited the letter immediately beneath the nose of the whole world, by way of best preventing any portion of that world from perceiving it.

"But the more I reflected upon the daring, dashing, and discriminating ingenuity of D—; upon the fact that the document must always have been at hand, if he intended to use it to good purpose; and upon the decisive evidence, obtained by the Prefect, that it was not hidden within the limits of that dignitary's ordinary search —the more satisfied I became that, to conceal this letter, the Minister had resorted to the comprehensive and sagacious expedient of not attempting to conceal it at all.

"Full of these ideas, I prepared myself with a pair of green spectacles, and called one fine morning, quite by accident, at the Ministerial hotel. I found D— at home, yawning, lounging, and dawdling, as usual, and pretending to be in the last extremity of ennui. He is, perhaps, the most really energetic human being now alive —but that is only when nobody sees him.

"To be even with him, I complained of my weak eyes, and lamented the necessity of the spectacles, under cover of which I cautiously and thoroughly surveyed the apartment, while seemingly intent only upon the conversation of my host.

"I paid special attention to a large writing-table near which he sat, and upon which lay confusedly, some miscellaneous letters and other papers, with one or two musical instruments and a few books. Here, however, after a long and very deliberate scrutiny, I saw nothing to excite particular suspicion.

"At length my eyes, in going the circuit of the room, fell upon a trumpery filigree card-rack of pasteboard, that hung dangling by a dirty blue ribbon, from a little brass knob just beneath the middle of the mantelpiece. In this rack, which had three or four compartments, were five or six visiting cards and a solitary letter. This last was much soiled and crumpled. It was torn nearly in two, across the middle —as if a design, in the first instance, to tear it entirely up as worthless, had been altered, or stayed, in the second. It had a large black seal, bearing the D— cipher very conspicuously, and was addressed, in a diminutive female hand, to D—, the minister, himself. It was thrust carelessly, and even, as it seemed, contemptuously, into one of the upper divisions of the rack.

"No sooner had I glanced at this letter, than I concluded it to be that of which I was in search. To be sure, it was, to all appearance, radically different from the one of which the Prefect had read us so minute a description. Here the seal was large and black, with the D— cipher; there it was small and red, with the ducal arms of the S— family. Here, the address, to the Minister, was diminutive and feminine; there the superscription, to a certain royal personage, was markedly bold and decided; the size alone formed a point of correspondence. But, then, the radicalness of these differences, which was excessive; the dirt; the soiled and torn condition of the paper, so inconsistent with the true methodical habits of D—, and so suggestive of a design to delude the beholder into an idea of the worthlessness of the document; these things, together with the hyperobtrusive situation of this document, full in the view of every visitor, and thus exactly in accordance with the conclusions to which I had previously arrived; these things, I say, were strongly corroborative of suspicion, in one who came with the intention to suspect.

"I protracted my visit as long as possible, and, while I maintained a most animated discussion with the Minister, on a topic which I knew well had never failed to interest and excite him, I kept my attention really riveted upon the letter. In this examination, I committed to memory its external appearance and arrangement in the rack; and also fell, at length, upon a discovery which set at rest whatever trivial doubt I might have entertained. In scrutinizing the edges of the paper, I observed them to be more chafed than seemed necessary. They presented the broken appearance which is manifested when a stiff paper, having been once folded and pressed with a folder, is refolded in a reversed direction, in the same creases or edges which had formed the original fold. This discovery was sufficient. It was clear to me that the letter had been turned, as a glove, inside out, redirected, and re-sealed. I bade the Minister good morning, and took my departure at once, leaving a gold snuff-box upon the table.

"The next morning I called for the snuff-box, when we resumed, quite eagerly, the conversation of the preceding day. While thus engaged, however, a loud report, as if of a pistol, was heard immediately beneath the windows of the hotel, and was succeeded by a series of fearful screams, and the shoutings of a mob. D— rushed to a casement, threw it open, and looked out. In the meantime, I stepped to the card-rack, took the letter, put it in my pocket, and replaced it by a fac-simile, (so far as regards externals,) which I had carefully prepared at my lodgings; imitating the D— cipher, very readily, by means of a seal formed of bread.

"The disturbance in the street had been occasioned by the frantic behavior of a man with a musket. He had fired it among a crowd of women and children. It proved, however, to have been without ball, and the fellow was suffered to go his way as a lunatic or a drunkard. When he had gone, D-came from the window, whither I had followed him immediately upon securing the object in view. Soon afterwards I bade him farewell. The pretended lunatic was a man in my own pay.

"But what purpose had you," I asked, in replacing the letter by a fac-simile? Would it not have been better, at the first visit, to have seized it openly, and departed?"

"D—," replied Dupin, "is a desperate man, and a man of nerve. His hotel, too, is not without attendants devoted to his interests. Had I made the wild attempt you suggest, I might never have left the Ministerial presence alive. The good people of Paris might have heard of me no more. But I had an object apart from these considerations. You know my political prepossessions. In this matter, I act as a partisan of the lady concerned. For eighteen months the Minister has had her in his power. She has now him in hers; since, being unaware that the letter is not in his possession, he will proceed with his exactions as if it was. Thus will he inevitably commit himself, at once, to his political destruction. His downfall, too, will not be more precipitate than awkward. It is all very well to talk about the facilis descensus Averni; but in all kinds of climbing, as Catalani said of singing, it is far more easy to get up than to come down. In the present instance I have no sympathy —at least no pity —for him who descends. He is the monstrum horrendum, an unprincipled man of genius. I confess, however, that I should like very well to know the precise character of his thoughts, when, being defied by her whom the Prefect terms 'a certain personage,' he is reduced to opening the letter which I left for him in the card-rack."

"How? did you put any thing particular in it?"

"Why —it did not seem altogether right to leave the interior blank —that would have been insulting. D—, at Vienna once, did me an evil turn, which I told him, quite good-humoredly, that I should remember. So, as I knew he would feel some curiosity in regard to the identity of the person who had outwitted him, I thought it a pity not to give him a clue. He is well acquainted with my MS., and I just copied into the middle of the blank sheet the words—

—Un dessein si funeste, S'il n'est digne d'Atree, est digne de Thyeste.

They are to be found in Crebillon's 'Atree.'"

Critical Thinking

How does Routine Activities theory explain the crime being investigated by Dupin?

What methods do police use to solve crimes that are similar to those Dupin employs?

To what extent do police departments rely on profilers, forensic psychologists, and others to solve crimes and understand criminal motives?

Sociological Theories of Crime: Subcultural Theory

"Some of Us Have Been Threatening Our Friend Colby"
by Donald Barthelme

A one-time reporter for the *Houston Post* newspaper and later one of the founders of the creative writing program of the University of Houston, Donald Barthelme (1931–1989) became known for his absurdist tinge and humor. "Some of Us Have Been Threatening Our Friend Colby" offers both while also illustrating the concept of subcultures found in society.

Subcultures are a smaller cultural group found within a larger culture. Their members may have different interests or values that distinguish them from the larger culture itself. The Goth subculture and the hip-hop subculture are but two examples. When a subculture favors criminal activity, it may be defined as a deviant subculture.

Criminology theories related to the causes of delinquency and their connection to various subcultures are sometimes labeled as subculture theories. Some theories included under this umbrella are Albert Cohen's delinquent subculture theory, Richard Cloward and Lloyd Ohlin's differential opportunity theory, Walter Miller's lower-class focal concerns theory, Marvin Wolfgang and Franco Ferracuti's theory of the subculture of violence, and Gresham Sykes and David Matza's theories of neutralization and subterranean values.

Some theorists have also claimed that there is a distinctive police subculture, with early researchers seeing a subculture with a variety of negative attributes (hostility to the public, secrecy, group solidarity, and a code of silence, for example) while later researchers saw a more nuanced and even favorable view that included concepts such as competence and morality. With a more diverse police force drawn from the full spectrum of a contemporary American community, identifying stereotypical characteristics that would indicate a policing subculture may be problematic.

When reading Barthelme's short story, we see examples of a deviant subculture with the group determining that Colby had "gone too far"—one assumes in violation of the group's own standards—along with Colby's eventual acceptance of his guilt and punishment by his associates. His punishment, death by hanging, is seen as a potential violation of the norms of the greater society that "was almost certainly against the law," yet the group determined the crime and the crime's punishment outside of the norms of that society.

Though this is a humorous story seen as a bit ludicrous by many, former FBI special agent Joseph Pistone described a similar incident in his biography *Donnie Brasco*. While undercover with the New York mob, he successfully infiltrated the Bonanno crime family, becoming an associate of one of the bosses in the organization, Dominck "Sonny Black" Napolitano. After the undercover operation was terminated and the Bonanno's were informed that Donnie Brasco was, in reality, an FBI agent, the Bonanno family called for Sonny Black's murder in retribution for allowing the FBI to infiltrate the crime family. Upon being ordered to the meeting, Sonny arranged for his personal jewelry and keys to his apartment to be given to a friend, knowing that he would not be returning. A year later Sonny's body was recovered; he was reputedly murdered by Bonanno associates.

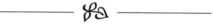

"Some of Us Had Been Threatening Our Friend Colby"
by Donald Barthelme

Some of us had been threatening our friend Colby for a long time, because of the way he had been behaving. And now he'd gone too far, so we decided to hang him. Colby argued that just because he had gone too far (he did not deny that he had gone too far) did not mean that he should be subjected to hanging. Going too far, he said, was something everybody did sometimes. We didn't pay much attention to this argument. We asked him what sort of music he would like played at the hanging. He said he'd think about it but it would take him a while to decide. I pointed out that we'd have to know soon, because Howard, who is a conductor would have to hire and rehearse the musicians and he couldn't begin until he knew what the music was going to be. Colby said he'd always been fond of Ives's Fourth Symphony. Howard said that this was a "delaying tactic" and that everybody knew that the Ives was almost impossible to perform and would involve weeks of rehearsal, and that the size of the orchestra and chorus would put us way over the music budget. "Be reasonable," he said to Colby. Colby said he'd try to think of something a little less exacting.

Hugh was worried about the wording of the invitations. What if one of them fell into the hands of the authorities? Hanging Colby was doubtless against the law, and if the authorities learned in advance what the plan was they would very likely come in and try to mess everything up. I said that although hanging Colby was almost certainly against the law, we had a perfect *moral* right to do so because he was *our* friend, *belonged* to us in various important senses, and he had after all gone too far. We agreed that the invitations would be worded in such a way that the person invited could not know for sure what he was being invited to. We decided to refer to the event as "An Event Involving Mr. Colby Williams." A handsome script was selected from a catalogue and we picked a cream-colored paper. Magnus said he'd see to having the invitations printed, and wondered whether we should serve drinks. Colby said he thought drinks would be nice but was worried about the expense. We told him kindly that the expense didn't matter, that we were after all his dear friends and if a group of his dear friends couldn't get together and do the thing with a little bit of *éclat*, why, what was the world coming to? Colby asked if he would be able to have drinks, too, before the event. We said, "Certainly."

The next item of business was the gibbet. None of us knew too much about gibbet design, but Tomás, who is an architect, said he'd look it up in old books and draw the plans. The important thing, as far as he recollected, was that the trapdoor function perfectly. He said that just roughly, counting labor and materials, it shouldn't run us more than four hundred dollars. "Good God!" Howard said. He said what was Tomás figuring on, rosewood? No, just a good grade of pine, Tomás said. Victor asked if un-painted pine wouldn't look kind of "raw," and Tomás replied that he thought it could be stained a dark walnut without too much trouble.

I said that although I thought the whole thing ought to be done really well and all, I also thought four hundred dollars for a gibbet, on top of the expense for the drinks, invitations, musicians, and everything, was a bit steep, and why didn't we just use a tree–a nice-looking oak, or something? I pointed out that since it was going to be a June hanging the trees would be in glorious leaf and that not only would a tree add a kind of "natural" feeling but it was also strictly traditional, especially in the West. Tomás, who had been sketching gibbets on the backs of envelopes, reminded us that an outdoor hanging always had to contend with the threat of rain. Victor said he liked the idea of doing it outdoors, possibly on the bank of a river, but noted that we would have to hold it some distance from the city, which presented the problem of getting the guests, musicians, etc., to the site and then back to town.

At this point, everybody looked at Harry, who runs a car-and-truck-rental business. Harry said he thought he could round up enough limousines to take care of that end but that the drivers would have to be paid. The drivers, he pointed out, wouldn't be friends of Colby's and couldn't be expected to donate their services, any more than the bartender or the musicians. He said that he had about ten limousines, which he used mostly for funerals, and that he could probably obtain another dozen by calling around to friends of his in the trade. He said also that if we did it outside, in the open air, we'd better figure on a tent or awning of some kind to cover at least the principals and the orchestra, because if the hanging was being rained on he thought it would look kind of dismal. As between gibbet and tree, he said, he had no particular preferences and he really thought that the choice ought to be left up to Colby, since it was his hanging. Colby said that everybody went too far, sometimes, and weren't we being a little Draconian? Howard said rather sharply that all that had already been discussed, and which did he want, gibbet or tree? Colby asked if he could have a firing squad. No, Howard said, he could not. Howard said a firing squad would just be an ego trip for Colby, the blindfold and last-cigarette bit, and that Colby was in enough hot water already without trying to "upstage" everyone with unnecessary theatrics. Colby said he was sorry, he hadn't meant it that way, he'd take the tree. Tomás crumpled up the gibbet sketches he'd been making, in disgust.

Then the question of the hangman came up. Pete said did we really need a hangman? Because if we used a tree, the noose could be adjusted to the appropriate level and Colby could just jump off something—a chair or stool or something. Besides, Pete said, he very much doubted if there were any free-lance hangmen wandering around the country, now that capital punishment has been done away with absolutely, temporarily, and that we'd probably have to fly one in from England or one of the South American countries, and even if we did that how could we know in advance that the man was a professional, a real hangman, and not just some money-hungry amateur who might bungle the job and shame us all, in front of everybody? We all agreed then that Colby should just jump off something and that a chair was not what he should jump off of, because that would look, we felt, extremely tacky—some old kitchen chair sitting out there under our beautiful tree. Tomás, who is quite modern in outlook and not afraid of innovation, proposed that Colby be standing on a large round rubber ball ten feet in diameter. This, he said, would afford a sufficient "drop" and would also roll out of the way if Colby suddenly changed his mind after jumping off. He reminded us that by not using a regular hangman we were placing an awful lot of the responsibility for the success of the affair on Colby himself, and that although he was sure Colby would perform creditably and not disgrace his friends at the last minute, still, men have been known to get a little irresolute at times like that, and the ten-foot-round rubber ball, which could probably be fabricated rather cheaply, would insure a "bang-up" production right down to the wire.

At the mention of "wire," Hank, who had been silent all this time, suddenly spoke up and said he wondered if it wouldn't be better if we used wire instead of rope—more efficient and in the end kinder to Colby, he suggested. Colby began looking a little green, and I didn't blame him, because there is something extremely distasteful in thinking about being hanged with wire instead of rope—it gives you sort of a revulsion, when you think about it. I thought it was really quite unpleasant of Hank to be sitting there talking about wire, just when we had solved the problem of what Colby was going to jump off of so neatly, with Tomás's idea about the rubber ball, so I hastily said that wire was out of the question, because it would injure the tree—cut into the branch it was tied to when Colby's full weight hit it—and that in these days of increased respect for the environment, we didn't want that, did we? Colby gave me a grateful look, and the meeting broke up.

Everything went off very smoothly on the day of the event (the music Colby finally picked was standard stuff, Elgar, and it was played very well by Howard and his boys). It didn't rain, the event was well attended, and we didn't run out of Scotch, or anything. The ten-foot rubber ball had been painted a deep green and blended in well with the bucolic setting. The two things I remember best about the whole episode are the grateful look Colby gave me when I said what I said about the wire, and the fact that nobody has ever gone too far again.

Critical Thinking

Can you think how one's friends and associates can lead an individual to commit a crime?

Can you identify any examples where people put themselves in harm's way because of the expectations of the subculture?

What might a parent do to minimize the potential for a child to become involved in a deviant subculture?

Are stereotypical views of police and policing an accurate interpretation of a police subculture?

Sociological Theories of Crime: General Theory of Crime

"My Last Duchess" and "Porphyria's Lover"

by Robert Browning

Robert Browning (1812–1889) was an English Victorian poet known for his poetic dramatic monologues—the creation of a persona, or a character distinct from the poet, who reveals his/her personality and temperament through speaking in the poem to a listener in a narrative style.

The personas in two of Browning's poems are murderers whose entitlement, arrogance, lack of self-control, and impulsiveness could exemplify the proposition of the general theory of crime. Browning's murderers believe themselves outside societal and moral constraints. In "My Last Duchess" (1842), a duke addresses an emissary for a count who is considering offering his daughter to the duke as a future wife. The duke implies that he ordered his last wife killed because she dared to be happy and smile at others besides himself.

"My Last Duchess"

by Robert Browning

FERRARA

That's my last Duchess painted on the wall,
Looking as if she were alive. I call
That piece a wonder, now; Fra Pandolf's hands
Worked busily a day, and there she stands.
Will't please you sit and look at her? I said
"Fra Pandolf" by design, for never read
Strangers like you that pictured countenance,
The depth and passion of its earnest glance,
But to myself they turned (since none puts by

Source: Robert Browning, "My Last Duchess," 1842.

The curtain I have drawn for you, but I)
And seemed as they would ask me, if they durst,
How such a glance came there; so, not the first
Are you to turn and ask thus. Sir, 'twas not
Her husband's presence only, called that spot
Of joy into the Duchess' cheek; perhaps
Fra Pandolf chanced to say, "Her mantle laps
Over my lady's wrist too much," or "Paint
Must never hope to reproduce the faint
Half-flush that dies along her throat." Such stuff
Was courtesy, she thought, and cause enough
For calling up that spot of joy. She had
A heart—how shall I say?— too soon made glad,
Too easily impressed; she liked whate'er
She looked on, and her looks went everywhere.
Sir, 'twas all one! My favour at her breast,
The dropping of the daylight in the West,
The bough of cherries some officious fool
Broke in the orchard for her, the white mule
She rode with round the terrace—all and each
Would draw from her alike the approving speech,
Or blush, at least. She thanked men—good! but thanked
Somehow—I know not how—as if she ranked
My gift of a nine-hundred-years-old name
With anybody's gift. Who'd stoop to blame
This sort of trifling? Even had you skill
In speech—which I have not—to make your will
Quite clear to such an one, and say, "Just this
Or that in you disgusts me; here you miss,
Or there exceed the mark"—and if she let
Herself be lessoned so, nor plainly set
Her wits to yours, forsooth, and made excuse—
E'en then would be some stooping; and I choose
Never to stoop. Oh, sir, she smiled, no doubt,
Whene'er I passed her; but who passed without
Much the same smile? This grew; I gave commands;
Then all smiles stopped together. There she stands
As if alive. Will't please you rise? We'll meet
The company below, then. I repeat,
The Count your master's known munificence
Is ample warrant that no just pretense
Of mine for dowry will be disallowed;
Though his fair daughter's self, as I avowed

At starting, is my object. Nay, we'll go
Together down, sir. Notice Neptune, though,
Taming a sea-horse, thought a rarity,
Which Claus of Innsbruck cast in bronze for me!

Critical Thinking

Why do you think the duke so clearly admits to the emissary the duchess's failings and the consequences for her behavior?

Does he appear to have remorse for his actions?

Details in Browning's poems reveal much about the personas. For example, what does the duke's captivation with the painting and the statue indicate about him?

Porphyria's Lover

by Robert Browning

The rain set early in to-night,
    The sullen wind was soon awake,
It tore the elm-tops down for spite,
    And did its worst to vex the lake:
    I listened with heart fit to break.
When glided in Porphyria; straight
    She shut the cold out and the storm,
And kneeled and made the cheerless grate
    Blaze up, and all the cottage warm;
    Which done, she rose, and from her form
Withdrew the dripping cloak and shawl,
    And laid her soiled gloves by, untied
Her hat and let the damp hair fall,
    And, last, she sat down by my side
    And called me. When no voice replied,
She put my arm about her waist,
    And made her smooth white shoulder bare,
And all her yellow hair displaced,
    And, stooping, made my cheek lie there,
    And spread, o'er all, her yellow hair,
Murmuring how she loved me — she
    Too weak, for all her heart's endeavour,
To set its struggling passion free
    From pride, and vainer ties dissever,
    And give herself to me for ever.
But passion sometimes would prevail,
    Nor could to-night's gay feast restrain
A sudden thought of one so pale
    For love of her, and all in vain:
    So, she was come through wind and rain.
Be sure I looked up at her eyes
    Happy and proud; at last I knew
Porphyria worshipped me; surprise
    Made my heart swell, and still it grew
    While I debated what to do.

Source: Robert Browning, "Porphyria's Lover," 1842.

That moment she was mine, mine, fair,
    Perfectly pure and good: I found
A thing to do, and all her hair
    In one long yellow string I wound
    Three times her little throat around,
And strangled her. No pain felt she;
    I am quite sure she felt no pain.
As a shut bud that holds a bee,
    I warily oped her lids: again
    Laughed the blue eyes without a stain.
And I untightened next the tress
    About her neck; her cheek once more
Blushed bright beneath my burning kiss:
    I propped her head up as before,
    Only, this time my shoulder bore
Her head, which droops upon it still:
    The smiling rosy little head,
So glad it has its utmost will,
    That all it scorned at once is fled,
    And I, its love, am gained instead!
Porphyria's love: she guessed not how
    Her darling one wish would be heard.
And thus we sit together now,
    And all night long we have not stirred,
    And yet God has not said a word!

Critical Thinking

The man in "Porphyria's Lover" (1836) narrates his act of murder more specifically than the duke does. Once again, the reader is permitted inside a criminal mind, this time as the victim is strangled with her own hair. The persona implies that Porphyria had defied her family by coming to his cottage but that she was only temporarily his. This realization appears to fuel his desperation. Note references in the poem to time and measurements of time.

What "darling wish" of Porphyria is now fulfilled, according to her murderer? Is the murderer's remorse suggested by the last line of the poem?

Given the impulsivity and apparent randomness of the fictional crimes characterized in Browning's poems, how could these murders have been prevented?

Could these murderers be rehabilitated?

Sociological Theories of Crime:
Differential Association and Learning Theory

"Barn Burning"
by William Faulkner

William Faulkner (1897–1962) is one of America's finest novelists, celebrated for his contributions to American literature in general and Southern literature in particular, with *The Sound and the Fury, As I Lay Dying, Light in August,* and *Absalom, Absalom!* regarded as his best work. Awarded the Nobel Prize in Literature in 1949, he was born in Oxford, Mississippi. Faulkner's fictional Yoknapatawpha County in Mississippi, a microcosm of the South he knew so well, is the setting for several of his novels, and the Snopes family the subject of a novel trilogy (both the county and the family also figure in "Barn Burning"). His experimentation with stream of consciousness narrative, cadence, and diction are also hallmarks of his writing. Within his fictional setting and experimental style, Faulkner explored the moral and racial implications of southern history, particularly after the Civil War and failed Reconstruction, with his characters struggling to re-establish order as they feel caught between the Old (pre-Civil War) and New Worlds.

First published in 1939 in *Harper's Magazine,* "Barn Burning" explores Sarty Snopes' struggle to reconcile family loyalty (especially to his father) with a higher form of justice. The Snopes clan represents the indigent poverty and displacement that many white southerners faced as the South made an uncertain, sometimes turbulent and violent transition from an agrarian to an industrial society. The story, told in third person from the point of view of ten-year-old Sarty, opens in a country store where the county Justice of the Peace is holding court. Sarty's father, Abner Snopes, has been accused of burning a man's barn. Sarty is asked to testify, and he is ridden with anxiety because he knows his father expects him to lie out of family loyalty. Although there isn't enough proof to find Abner guilty, the Justice urges him to leave the area as soon as possible. Abner and Sarty leave the store and find the rest of the family waiting in a grove across the road. The narrator describes a family in abject poverty living in an impoverished South, tenant farmers constantly moving from place to place (at least twelve times), and subject to Abner's dictatorial, often violent temper. We also hear Sarty's internal thoughts. He is anxious and worried about his father, hoping that he will no longer give in to his obsession with fire and its destructive power. However, when the family camps for a night on the way to another house, Abner confronts Sarty and accuses him of disloyalty. He strikes his son, reminding him that bloodlines are more important than society's system of justice.

When the Snopeses arrive at their next farm, Abner takes Sarty to visit the man Abner will be working for. Although somewhat dilapidated after the Civil War, the plantation house in which Major de Spain and his family reside is still grand, bigger and wealthier than anything

Sarty has ever seen. He hopes, in vain, that his father will change. Instead, Abner steps in horse droppings, pushes past the black butler, and soils the expensive rug (imported from France) inside the house's entrance. The mistress orders Abner to leave, and later he shares his resentment of de Spain's wealth with Sarty. Later that evening, Major de Spain brings the rug to Abner and orders him to clean it, declaring that he will deduct the cost of the rug from Abner's corn crops. Following this humiliation, Sarty is terrified anew that his father will resort to burning de Spain's barn in revenge, even after the local Justice of the Peace revises the penalty initially imposed by de Spain.

Despite his hopes that his father will change, Sarty realizes that his father plans to burn de Spain's barn. Faced with supporting his father or acceding to a higher form of justice, he escapes from Abner's clutches and runs to de Spain's plantation, warning him that his father plans to burn the barn. As he watches the plantation's men riding toward his father, Sarty hears three gun shots. Knowing what has happened, Sarty decides his father must have been brave, yet the story ends on a more hopeful, if ambiguous, note: Sarty is free and moving forward.

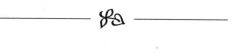

"Barn Burning"
by William Faulkner

The store in which the Justice of the Peace's court was sitting smelled of cheese. The boy, crouched on his nail keg at the back of the crowded room, knew he smelled cheese, and more: from where he sat he could see the ranked shelves close-packed with the solid, squat, dynamic shapes of tin cans whose labels his stomach read, not from the lettering which meant nothing to his mind but from the scarlet devils and the silver curve of fish—this, the cheese which he knew he smelled and the hermetic meat which his intestines believed he smelled coming in intermittent gusts momentary and brief between the other constant one, the smell and sense just a little of fear because mostly of despair and grief, the old fierce pull of blood. He could not see the table where the Justice sat and before which his father and his father's enemy (*our enemy* he thought in that despair; *ourn! mine and hisn both! He's my father!*) stood, but he could hear them, the two of them that is, because his father had said no word yet:

"But what proof have you, Mr. Harris?"

"I told you. The hog got into my corn. I caught it up and sent it back to him. He had no fence that would hold it. I told him so, warned him. The next time I put the hog in my pen. When he came to get it I gave him enough wire to patch up his pen. The next time I put the hog up and kept it. I rode down to his house and saw the wire I gave him still rolled on to the spool in his yard. I told him he could have the hog when he paid me a dollar pound fee. That evening a nigger came with the dollar and got the hog. He was a strange nigger. He said, 'He say to tell you wood and hay kin burn.' I said, 'What?' 'That whut he say to tell you,' the nigger said, 'Wood and hay kin burn.' That night my barn burned. I got the stock out but I lost the barn."

"Where is the nigger? Have you got him?"

"He was a strange nigger, I tell you. I don't know what became of him."

"But that's not proof. Don't you see that's not proof?"

"Get that boy up here. He knows." For a moment the boy thought too that the man meant his older brother until Harris said, "Not him. The little one. The boy," and, crouching, small for his age, small and wiry like his father, in patched and faded jeans even too small for him, with straight, uncombed, brown hair and eyes gray and wild as storm scud, he saw the men between himself and the table part and become a lane of grim faces, at the end of which he saw the Justice, a shabby, collarless, graying man in spectacles, beckoning him. He felt no floor under his bare feet; he seemed to walk beneath the palpable weight of the grim turning faces. His father, stiff in his black Sunday coat donned not for the trial but for the moving, did not even look at him. *He aims for me to lie,* he thought, again with that frantic grief and despair. *And I will have to do hit.*

"What's your name, boy?" the Justice said.

"Colonel Sartoris Snopes," the boy whispered.

"Hey?" the Justice said. "Talk louder. Colonel Sartoris? I reckon anybody named for Colonel Sartoris in this country can't help but tell the truth, can they?" The boy said nothing. *Enemy! Enemy!* he thought; for a moment he could not even see, could not see that the Justice's face was kindly nor discern that his voice was troubled when he spoke to the man named Harris: "Do you want me to question this boy?" But he could hear, and during those subsequent long seconds while there was absolutely no sound in the crowded little room save that of quiet and intent breathing it was as if he had swung outward at the end of a grape vine, over a ravine, and at the top of the swing had been caught in a prolonged instant of mesmerized gravity, weightless in time.

"No!" Harris said violently, explosively. "Damnation! Send him out of here!" Now time, the fluid world, rushed beneath him again, the voices coming to him again through the smell of cheese and sealed meat, the fear and despair and the old grief of blood:

"This case is closed. I can't find against you, Snopes, but I can give you advice. Leave this country and don't come back to it."

His father spoke for the first time, his voice cold and harsh, level, without emphasis: "I aim to. I don't figure to stay in a country among people who . . ." he said something unprintable and vile, addressed to no one.

"That'll do," the Justice said. "Take your wagon and get out of this country before dark. Case dismissed."

His father turned, and he followed the stiff black coat, the wiry figure walking a little stiffly from where a Confederate provost's man's musket ball had taken him in the heel on a stolen horse thirty years ago, followed the two backs now, since his older brother had appeared from somewhere in the crowd, no taller than the father but thicker, chewing tobacco steadily, between the two lines of grim-faced men and out of the store and across the worn gallery and down the sagging steps and among the dogs and half-grown boys in the mild May dust, where as he passed a voice hissed:

"Barn burner!"

Again he could not see, whirling; there was a face in a red haze, moonlike, bigger than the full moon, the owner of it half again his size, he leaping in the red haze toward the face, feeling no blow, feeling no shock when his head struck the earth, scrabbling up and leaping again, feeling no blow this time either and tasting no blood, scrabbling up to see the other boy in full flight and himself already leaping into pursuit as his father's hand jerked him back, the harsh, cold voice speaking above him: "Go get in the wagon."

It stood in a grove of locusts and mulberries across the road. His two hulking sisters in their Sunday dresses and his mother and his sister in calico and sunbonnets were already in it, sitting on and among the sorry residue of the dozen and more movings which even the boy could remember—the battered stove, the broken beds and chairs, the clock inlaid with mother-of-pearl, which would not run, stopped at some fourteen minutes past two o'clock of a dead and forgotten day and time, which had been his mother's dowry. She was crying, though when she saw him she drew her sleeve across her face and began to descend from the wagon. "Get back," the father said.

"He's hurt. I got to get some water and wash his . . ."

"Get back in the wagon," his father said. He got in too, over the tail-gate. His father mounted to the seat where the older brother already sat and struck the gaunt mules two savage blows with the peeled willow, but without heat. It was not even sadistic; it was exactly that same quality which in later years would cause his descendants to over-run the engine before putting a motor car into motion, striking and reining back in the same movement. The wagon went on, the store with its quiet crowd of grimly watching men dropped behind; a curve in the road hid it. *Forever* he thought. *Maybe he's done satisfied now, now that he has . . .* stopping himself, not to say it aloud even to himself. His mother's hand touched his shoulder.

"Does hit hurt?" she said.

"Naw," he said. "Hit don't hurt. Lemme be."

"Can't you wipe some of the blood off before hit dries?"

"I'll wash tonight," he said. "Lemme be, I tell you."

The wagon went on. He did not know where they were going. None of them ever did or ever asked, because it was always somewhere, always a house of sorts waiting for them a day or two days or even three days away. Likely his father had already arranged to make a crop on another farm before he . . . Again he had to stop himself. He (the father) always did. There was something about his wolflike independence and even courage when the advantage was at least neutral which impressed strangers, as if they got from his latent ravening ferocity not so much a sense of dependability as a feeling that his ferocious conviction in the rightness of his own actions would be of advantage to all whose interest lay with his.

That night they camped, in a grove of oaks and beeches where a spring ran. The nights were still cool and they had a fire against it, of a rail lifted from a nearby fence and cut into lengths—a small fire, neat, niggard almost, a shrewd fire; such fires were his father's habit and custom always, even in freezing weather. Older, the boy might have remarked this and wondered why not a big one; why should not a man who had not only seen the waste and extravagance of war, but who had in his blood an inherent voracious prodigality with material not his own, have burned everything in sight? Then he might have gone a step farther and thought that that was the reason: that niggard blaze was the living fruit of nights passed during those four years in the woods hiding from all men, blue or gray, with his strings of horses (captured horses, he called them). And older still, he might have divined the true reason: that the element of fire spoke to some deep main-spring of his father's being, as the element of steel or of powder spoke to other men, as the one weapon for the preservation of integrity, else breath were not worth the breathing, and hence to be regarded with respect and used with discretion.

But he did not think this now and he had seen those same niggard blazes all his life. He merely ate his supper beside it and was already half asleep over his iron plate when his father called him, and once more he followed the stiff back, the stiff and ruthless limp, up the slope and on to the starlit road where, turning, he could see his father against the stars but without face or depth—a shape black, flat, and bloodless as though cut from tin in the iron folds of the frockcoat which had not been made for him, the voice harsh like tin and without heat like tin:

"You were fixing to tell them. You would have told him." He didn't answer. His father struck him with the flat of his hand on the side of the head, hard but without heat, exactly as he had struck the two mules at the store, exactly as he would strike either of them with any stick in order to kill a horse fly, his voice still without heat or anger: "You're getting to be a man. You got to learn. You got to learn to stick to your own blood or you ain't going to have any blood to stick to you. Do you think either of them, any man there this morning, would? Don't you know all they wanted was a chance to get at me because they knew I had them beat? Eh?" Later, twenty years later, he was to tell himself, "If I had said they wanted only truth, justice, he would have hit me again." But now he said nothing. He was not crying. He just stood there. "Answer me," his father said.

"Yes," he whispered. His father turned.

"Get on to bed. We'll be there tomorrow."

Tomorrow they were there. In the early afternoon the wagon stopped before a paintless two-room house identical almost with the dozen others it had stopped before even in the boy's ten years, and again, as on the other dozen occasions, his mother and aunt got down and began to unload the wagon, although his two sisters and his father and brother had not moved.

"Likely hit ain't fitten for hawgs," one of the sisters said.

"Nevertheless, fit it will and you'll hog it and like it," his father said. "Get out of them chairs and help your Ma unload."

The two sisters got down, big, bovine, in a flutter of cheap ribbons; one of them drew from the jumbled wagon bed a battered lantern, the other a worn broom. His father handed the reins to the older son and began to climb stiffly over the wheel. "When they get unloaded, take the team to the barn and feed them." Then he said, and at first the boy thought he was still speaking to his brother: "Come with me."

"Me?" he said.

"Yes," his father said. "You."

"Abner," his mother said. His father paused and looked back—the harsh level stare beneath the shaggy, graying, irascible brows.

"I reckon I'll have a word with the man that aims to begin tomorrow owning me body and soul for the next eight months."

They went up the road. A week ago—or before last night, that is—he would have asked where they were going, but not now. His father had struck him before last night but never before had he paused afterward to explain why; it was as if the blow and the following calm, outrageous voice still rang, repercussed, divulging nothing to him save the terrible handicap of being young, the light weight of his few years, just heavy enough to prevent his soaring free of the world as it seemed to be ordered but not heavy enough to keep him footed solid in it, to resist it and try to change the course of its events.

Presently he could see the grove of oaks and cedars and the other flowering trees and shrubs where the house would be, though not the house yet. They walked beside a fence massed with honeysuckle and Cherokee roses and came to a gate swinging open between two brick pillars, and now, beyond a sweep of drive, he saw the house for the first time and at that instant he forgot his father and the terror and despair both, and even when he remembered his father again (who had not stopped) the terror and despair did not return. Because, for all the twelve movings, they had so-journed until now in a poor country, a land of small farms and fields and houses, and he had never seen a house like this before. *Hit's big as a courthouse* he thought quietly, with a surge of peace and joy whose reason he could not have thought into words, being too young for that: *They are safe from him. People whose lives are a part of this peace and dignity are beyond his touch, he no more to them than a buzzing wasp capable of stinging for a little moment but that's all; the spell of this peace and dignity rendering even the barns and stable and cribs which belong to it impervious to the puny flames he might contrive . . .* this, the peace and joy, ebbing for an instant as he looked again at the stiff black back, the stiff and implacable limp of the figure which was not dwarfed by the house, for the reason that it had never looked big anywhere and which now, against the serene columned backdrop, had more than ever that impervious quality of something cut ruthlessly from tin, depthless, as though, sidewise to the sun, it would cast no shadow. Watching him, the boy remarked the absolutely un-deviating course which his father held and saw the stiff foot come squarely down in a pile of fresh droppings where a horse had stood in the drive and which his father could have avoided by a simple change of stride. But it ebbed only for a moment, though he could not have thought this into words either, walking on in the spell of the house, which he could even want but without envy, without sorrow, certainly never with that ravening and jealous rage which unknown to him walked in the ironlike black coat before him: *Maybe he will feel it too. Maybe it will even change him now from what maybe he couldn't help but be.*

They crossed the portico. Now he could hear his father's stiff foot as it came down on the boards with clocklike finality, a sound out of all proportion to the displacement of the body it bore and which was not dwarfed either by the white door before it, as though it had attained to a sort of vicious ravening minimum not to be dwarfed by anything—the flat, wide, black hat, the formal coat of broadcloth which had once been black but which had now that friction-glazed greenish cast of the bodies of old house flies, the lifted sleeve which was too large, the lifted hand like a curled claw. The door opened so promptly that the boy knew the Negro must have been watching them all the time, an old man with neat grizzled hair, in a linen jacket, who stood barring the door with his body, saying, "Wipe yo foots, white man, fo you come in here. Major ain't home nohow."

"Get out of my way, nigger," his father said, without heat too, flinging the door back and the Negro also and entering, his hat still on his head. And now the boy saw the prints of the stiff foot on the doorsill and saw them appear on the pale rug behind the machinelike deliberation of the foot which seemed to bear (or transmit) twice the weight which the body compassed. The Negro was shouting "Miss Lula! Miss Lula!" somewhere behind them, then the boy, deluged as though by a warm wave by a suave turn of carpeted stair and a pendant glitter of chandeliers and a mute gleam of gold frames, heard the swift feet and saw her too, a lady—perhaps he had never seen her like before either—in a gray, smooth gown with lace at the throat and an apron tied at the waist and the sleeves turned back, wiping cake or biscuit dough from her hands with a towel as she came up the hall, looking not at his father at all but at the tracks on the blond rug with an expression of incredulous amazement.

"I tried," the Negro cried. "I tole him to . . ."

"Will you please go away?" she said in a shaking voice. "Major de Spain is not at home. Will you please go away?"

His father had not spoken again. He did not speak again. He did not even look at her. He just stood stiff in the center of the rug, in his hat, the shaggy iron-gray brows twitching slightly above the pebble-colored eyes as he appeared to examine the house with brief deliberation. Then with the same deliberation he turned; the boy watched him pivot on the good leg and saw the stiff foot drag round the arc of the turning, leaving a final long and fading smear. His father never looked at it, he never once looked down at the rug. The Negro held the door. It closed behind them, upon the hysteric and indistinguishable woman-wail. His father stopped at the top of the steps and scraped his boot clean on the edge of it. At the gate he stopped again. He stood for a moment, planted stiffly on the stiff foot, looking back at the house. "Pretty and white, ain't it?" he said. "That's sweat. Nigger sweat. Maybe it ain't white enough yet to suit him. Maybe he wants to mix some white sweat with it."

Two hours later the boy was chopping wood behind the house within which his mother and aunt and the two sisters (the mother and aunt, not the two girls, he knew that; even at this distance and muffled by walls the flat loud voices of the two girls emanated an incorrigible idle inertia) were setting up the stove to prepare a meal, when he heard the hooves and saw the linen-clad man on a fine sorrel mare, whom he recognized even before he saw the rolled rug in front of the Negro youth following on a fat bay carriage horse—a suffused, angry face vanishing, still at full gallop, beyond the corner of the house where his father and brother were sitting in the two tilted chairs; and a moment later, almost before he could have put the axe down, he heard the hooves again and watched the sorrel mare go back out of the yard, already galloping again. Then his father began to shout one of the sisters' names, who presently emerged backward from the kitchen door dragging the rolled rug along the ground by one end while the other sister walked behind it.

"If you ain't going to tote, go on and set up the wash pot," the first said.

"You, Sarty!" the second shouted. "Set up the wash pot!" His father appeared at the door, framed against that shabbiness, as he had been against that other bland perfection, impervious to either, the mother's anxious face at his shoulder.

"Go on," the father said. "Pick it up." The two sisters stooped, broad, lethargic; stooping, they presented an incredible expanse of pale cloth and a flutter of tawdry ribbons.

"If I thought enough of a rug to have to git hit all the way from France I wouldn't keep hit where folks coming in would have to tromp on hit," the first said. They raised the rug.

"Abner," the mother said. "Let me do it."

"You go back and get dinner," his father said. "I'll tend to this."

From the woodpile through the rest of the afternoon the boy watched them, the rug spread flat in the dust beside the bubbling wash pot, the two sisters stooping over it with that profound and lethargic reluctance, while the father stood over them in turn, implacable and grim, driving them though never raising his voice again. He could smell the harsh homemade lye they were using; he saw his mother come to the door once and look toward them with an expression not anxious now but very like despair; he saw his father turn, and he fell to with the axe and saw from the corner of his eye his father raise from the ground a flattish fragment of field stone and examine it and return to the pot, and this time his mother actually spoke: "Abner. Abner. Please don't. Please, Abner."

Then he was done too. It was dusk; the whippoorwills had already begun. He could smell coffee from the room where they would presently eat the cold food remaining from the mid-afternoon meal, though when he entered the house he realized they were having coffee again probably because there was a fire on the hearth, before which the rug now lay spread over the backs of the two chairs. The tracks of his father's foot were gone. Where they had been were now long, water-cloudy scoriations resembling the sporadic course of a Lilliputian mowing machine.

It still hung there while they ate the cold food and then went to bed, scattered without order or claim up and down the two rooms, his mother in one bed, where his father would later lie, the older brother in the other, himself, the aunt, and the two sisters on pallets on the floor. But his father was not in bed yet. The last thing the boy remembered was the depthless, harsh silhouette of the hat and coat bending over the rug and it seemed to him that he had not even closed his eyes when the silhouette was standing over him, the fire almost dead behind it, the stiff foot prodding him awake. "Catch up the mule," his father said.

When he returned with the mule his father was standing in the black door, the rolled rug over his shoulder. "Ain't you going to ride?" he said.

"No. Give me your foot."

He bent his knee into his father's hand, the wiry, surprising power flowed smoothly, rising, he rising with it, on to the mule's bare back (they had owned a saddle once; the boy could re-member it though not when or where) and with the same effortlessness his father swung the rug up in front of him. Now in the starlight they retraced the afternoon's path, up the dusty road rife with honeysuckle, through the gate and up the black tunnel of the drive to the lightless house, where he sat on the mule and felt the rough warp of the rug drag across his thighs and vanish.

"Don't you want me to help?" he whispered. His father did not answer and now he heard again that stiff foot striking the hollow portico with that wooden and clocklike deliberation, that outrageous overstatement of the weight it carried. The rug, hunched, not flung (the boy could tell that even in the darkness) from his father's shoulder, struck the angle of wall and floor with a sound unbelievably loud, thunderous, then the foot again, unhurried and enormous; a light came on in the house and the boy sat, tense, breathing steadily and quietly and just a little fast, though the foot itself did not increase its beat at all, descending the steps now; now the boy could see him.

"Don't you want to ride now?" he whispered. "We kin both ride now," the light within the house altering now, flaring up and sinking. *He's coming down the stairs now,* he thought. He had already ridden the mule up beside the horse block; presently his father was up behind him and he doubled the reins over and slashed the mule across the neck, but before the animal could begin to trot the hard, thin arm came round him, the hard, knotted hand jerking the mule back to a walk.

In the first red rays of the sun they were in the lot, putting plow gear on the mules. This time the sorrel mare was in the lot before he heard it at all, the rider collarless and even bareheaded, trembling, speaking in a shaking voice as the woman in the house had done, his father merely looking up once before stooping again to the hame he was buckling, so that the man on the mare spoke to his stooping back:

"You must realize you have ruined that rug. Wasn't there anybody here, any of your women . . ." He ceased, shaking, the boy watching him, the older brother leaning now in the stable door, chewing, blinking slowly and steadily at nothing apparently. "It cost a hundred dollars. But you never had a hundred dollars. You never will. So I'm going to charge you twenty bushels of corn against your crop. I'll add it in your contract and when you come to the commissary you can sign it. That won't keep Mrs. de Spain quiet but maybe it will teach you to wipe your feet off before you enter her house again."

Then he was gone. The boy looked at his father, who still had not spoken or even looked up again, who was now adjusting the logger-head in the hame.

"Pap," he said. His father looked at him—the inscrutable face, the shaggy brows beneath which the gray eyes glinted coldly. Suddenly the boy went toward him, fast, stopping as suddenly. "You done the best you could!" he cried. "If he wanted hit done different why didn't he wait and tell you how? He won't git no twenty bushels! He won't git none! We'll get hit and hide hit! I kin watch . . ."

"Did you put the cutter back in that straight stock like I told you?"

"No, sir," he said.

"Then go do it."

That was Wednesday. During the rest of that week he worked steadily, at what was within his scope and some which was beyond it, with an industry that did not need to be driven nor even commanded twice; he had this from his mother, with the difference that some at least of what he did he liked to do, such as splitting wood with the half-size axe which his mother and aunt had earned, or saved money somehow, to present him with at Christmas. In company with the two older women (and on one afternoon, even one of the sisters), he built pens for the shoat and the cow which were a part of his father's contract with the landlord, and one afternoon, his father being absent, gone somewhere on one of the mules, he went to the field.

They were running a middle buster now, his brother holding the plow straight while he handled the reins, and walking beside the straining mule, the rich black soil shearing cool and damp against his bare ankles, he thought *Maybe this is the end of it. Maybe even that twenty bushels that seems hard to have to pay for just a rug will be a cheap price for him to stop forever and always from being what he used to be*; thinking, dreaming now, so that his brother had to speak sharply to him to mind the mule: *Maybe he even won't collect the twenty bushels. Maybe it will all add up and balance and vanish—corn, rug, fire; the terror and grief, the being pulled two ways like between two teams of horses—gone, done with for ever and ever.*

Then it was Saturday; he looked up from beneath the mule he was harnessing and saw his father in the black coat and hat. "Not that," his father said. "The wagon gear." And then, two hours later, sitting in the wagon bed behind his father and brother on the seat, the wagon accomplished a final curve, and he saw the weathered paintless store with its tattered tobacco— and patent-medicine posters and the tethered wagons and saddle animals below the gallery. He mounted the gnawed steps behind his father and brother, and there again was the lane of quiet, watching faces for the three of them to walk through. He saw the man in spectacles sitting at the plank table and he did not need to be told this was a Justice of the Peace; he sent one glare of fierce, exultant, partisan defiance at the man in collar and cravat now, whom he had seen but twice before in his life, and that on a galloping horse, who now wore on his face an expression not of rage but of amazed unbelief which the boy could not have known was at the incredible circumstance of being sued by one of his own tenants, and came and stood against his father and cried at the Justice: "He ain't done it! He ain't burnt . . ."

"Go back to the wagon," his father said.

"Burnt?" the Justice said. "Do I understand this rug was burned too?"

"Does anybody here claim it was?" his father said. "Go back to the wagon." But he did not, he merely retreated to the rear of the room, crowded as that other had been, but not to sit down this time, instead, to stand pressing among the motionless bodies, listening to the voices:

"And you claim twenty bushels of corn is too high for the damage you did to the rug?"

"He brought the rug to me and said he wanted the tracks washed out of it. I washed the tracks out and took the rug back to him."

"But you didn't carry the rug back to him in the same condition it was in before you made the tracks on it."

His father did not answer, and now for perhaps half a minute there was no sound at all save that of breathing, the faint, steady suspiration of complete and intent listening.

"You decline to answer that, Mr. Snopes?" Again his father did not answer. "I'm going to find against you, Mr. Snopes. I'm going to find that you were responsible for the injury to Major de Spain's rug and hold you liable for it. But twenty bushels of corn seems a little high for a man in your circumstances to have to pay. Major de Spain claims it cost a hundred dollars. October corn will be worth about fifty cents. I figure that if Major de Spain can stand a ninety-five-dollar loss on something he paid cash for, you can stand a five-dollar loss you haven't earned yet. I hold you in damages to Major de Spain to the amount of ten bushels of corn over and above your contract with him, to be paid to him out of your crop at gathering time. Court adjourned."

It had taken no time hardly, the morning was but half begun. He thought they would return home and perhaps back to the field, since they were late, far behind all other farmers. But instead his father passed on behind the wagon, merely indicating with his hand for the older brother to follow with it, and crossed the road toward the blacksmith shop opposite, pressing on after his father, overtaking him, speaking, whispering up at the harsh, calm face beneath the weathered hat: "He won't git no ten bushels neither. He won't git one. We'll . . ." until his father glanced for an instant down at him, the face absolutely calm, the grizzled eyebrows tangled above the cold eyes, the voice almost pleasant, almost gentle:

"You think so? Well, we'll wait till October anyway."

The matter of the wagon—the setting of a spoke or two and the tightening of the tires—did not take long either, the business of the tires accomplished by driving the wagon into the spring branch behind the shop and letting it stand there, the mules nuzzling into the water from time to time, and the boy on the seat with the idle reins, looking up the slope and through the sooty tunnel of the shed where the slow hammer rang and where his father sat on an upended cypress bolt, easily, either talking or listening, still sitting there when the boy brought the dripping wagon up out of the branch and halted it before the door.

"Take them on to the shade and hitch," his father said. He did so and returned. His father and the smith and a third man squatting on his heels inside the door were talking, about crops and animals; the boy, squatting too in the amoniac dust and hoof-parings and scales of rust, heard his father tell a long and unhurried story out of the time before the birth of the older brother even when he had been a professional horsetrader. And then his father came up beside him where he stood before a tattered last year's circus poster on the other side of the store, gazing rapt and quiet at the scarlet horses, the incredible poisings and convolution of tulle and tights and the painted leers of comedians, and said, "It's time to eat."

But not at home. Squatting beside his brother against the front wall, he watched his father emerge from the store and produce from a paper sack a segment of cheese and divide it carefully and deliberately into three with his pocket knife and produce crackers from the same sack. They all three squatted on the gallery and ate, slowly, without talking; then in the store again, they drank from a tin dipper tepid water smelling of the cedar bucket and of living beech trees. And still they did not go home. It was a horse lot this time, a tall rail fence upon and along which men stood and sat and out of which one by one horses were led, to be walked and trotted and then cantered back and forth along the road while the slow swapping and buying went on and the sun began to slant westward, they—the three of them—watching and listening, the older brother with his muddy eyes and his steady, inevitable tobacco, the father commenting now and then on certain of the animals, to no one in particular.

It was after sundown when they reached home. They ate supper by lamplight, then, sitting on the doorstep, the boy watched the night fully accomplish, listening to the whippoorwills and the frogs, when he heard his mother's voice: "Abner! No! No! Oh, God. Oh, God. Abner!" and he rose, whirled, and saw the altered light through the door where a candle stub now burned in a bottle neck on the table and his father, still in the hat and coat, at once formal and burlesque as though dressed carefully for some shabby and ceremonial violence, emptying the reservoir of the lamp back into the five-gallon kerosene can from which it had been filled, while the mother tugged at his arm until he shifted the lamp to the other hand and flung her back, not savagely or viciously, just hard, into the wall, her hands flung out against the wall for balance, her mouth open and in her face the same quality of hopeless despair as had been in her voice. Then his father saw him standing in the door.

"Go to the barn and get that can of oil we were oiling the wagon with," he said. The boy did not move. Then he could speak.

"What . . ." he cried. "What are you . . ."

"Go get that oil," his father said. "Go."

Then he was moving, running, outside the house, toward the stable: this the old habit, the old blood which he had not been permitted to choose for himself, which had been bequeathed him willy nilly and which had run for so long (and who knew where, battening on what of outrage and savagery and lust) before it came to him. *I could keep on,* he thought. *I could run on and on and never look back, never need to see his face again. Only I can't. I can't,* the rusted can in his hand now, the liquid sploshing in it as he ran back to the house and into it, into the sound of his mother's weeping in the next room, and handed the can to his father.

"Ain't you going to even send a nigger?" he cried. "At least you sent a nigger before!"

This time his father didn't strike him. The hand came even faster than the blow had, the same hand which had set the can on the table with almost excruciating care flashing from the can toward him too quick for him to follow it, gripping him by the back of his shirt and on to tiptoe before he had seen it quit the can, the face stooping at him in breathless and frozen ferocity, the cold, dead voice speaking over him to the older brother who leaned against the table, chewing with that steady, curious, sidewise motion of cows:

"Empty the can into the big one and go on. I'll catch up with you."

"Better tie him up to the bedpost," the brother said.

"Do like I told you," the father said. Then the boy was moving, his bunched shirt and the hard, bony hand between his shoulder-blades, his toes just touching the floor, across the room and into the other one, past the sisters sitting with spread heavy thighs in the two chairs over the cold hearth, and to where his mother and aunt sat side by side on the bed, the aunt's arms about his mother's shoulders.

"Hold him," the father said. The aunt made a startled movement. "Not you," the father said. "Lennie. Take hold of him. I want to see you do it." His mother took him by the wrist. "You'll hold him better than that. If he gets loose don't you know what he is going to do? He will go up yonder." He jerked his head toward the road. "Maybe I'd better tie him."

"I'll hold him," his mother whispered.

"See you do then." Then his father was gone, the still foot heavy and measured upon the boards, ceasing at last.

Then he began to struggle. His mother caught him in both arms, he jerking and wrenching at them. He would be stronger in the end, he knew that. But he had no time to wait for it. "Lemme go!" he cried. "I don't want to have to hit you!"

"Let him go!" the aunt said. "If he don't go, before God, I am going up there myself!"

"Don't you see I can't?" his mother cried. "Sarty! Sarty! No! No! Help me, Lizzie!"

Then he was free. His aunt grasped at him but it was too late. He whirled, running, his mother stumbled forward on to her knees behind him, crying to the nearer sister: "Catch him, Net! Catch him!" But that was too late too, the sister (the sisters were twins, born at the same time, yet either of them now gave the impression of being, encompassing as much living meat and volume and weight as any other two of the family) not yet having begun to rise form the chair, her head, face, alone merely turned, presenting to him in the flying instant an astonishing expanse of young female features untroubled by any surprise even, wearing only an expression of bovine interest. Then he was out of the room, out of the house, in the mild dust of the starlit road and the heavy rifeness of honeysuckle, the pale ribbon un-spooling with terrific slowness under his running feet, reaching the gate at last and turning in, running, his heart and lungs drumming, on up the drive toward the lighted house, the lighted door. He did not knock, he burst in, sobbing for breath, incapable for the moment of speech; he saw the astonished face of the Negro in the linen jacket without knowing when the Negro had appeared.

"De Spain!" he cried, panted. "Where's . . ." then he saw the white man too emerging from a white door down the hall. "Barn!" he cried. "Barn!"

"What?" the white man said. "Barn?"

"Yes!" the boy cried. "Barn!"

"Catch him!" the white man shouted.

But it was too late this time too. The Negro grasped his shirt, but the entire sleeve, rotten with washing, carried away, and he was out that door too and in the drive again, and had actually never ceased to run even while he was screaming into the white man's face.

Behind him the white man was shouting, "My horse! Fetch my horse!" and he thought for an instant of cutting across the park and climbing the fence into the road, but he did not know the park nor how high the vine-massed fence might be and he dared not risk it. So he ran on down the drive, blood and breath roaring; presently he was in the road again though he could not see it. He could not hear either: the galloping mare was almost upon him before he heard her, and even then he held his course, as if the very urgency of his wild grief and need must in a moment more find him wings, waiting until the ultimate instant to hurl himself aside and into the weed-choked roadside ditch as the horse thundered past and on, for an instant in furious silhouette against the stars, the tranquil early summer night sky which, even before the shape of the horse and rider vanished, strained abruptly and violently upward: a long, swirling roar incredible and soundless, blotting the stars, and he springing up and into the road again, running again, knowing it was too late yet still running even after he heard the shot and, an instant later, two shots, pausing now without knowing he had ceased to run, crying "Pap! Pap!," running again before he knew he had begun to run, stumbling, tripping over something and scrabbling up again without ceasing to run, looking backward over his shoulder at the glare as he got up, running on among the invisible trees, panting, sobbing, "Father! Father!"

At midnight he was sitting on the crest of a hill. He did not know it was midnight and he did not know how far he had come. But there was no glare behind him now and he sat now, his back toward what he had called home for four days anyhow, his face toward the dark woods which he would enter when breath was strong again, small, shaking steadily in the chill darkness, hugging himself into the remainder of his thin, rotten shirt, the grief and despair now no longer terror and fear but just grief and despair. *Father. My father,* he thought. "He was brave!" he cried suddenly, aloud but not loud, no more than a whisper: "He was! He was in the war! He was in Colonel Sartoris' cav'ry!" not knowing that his father had gone to that war a private in the fine old European sense, wearing no uniform, admitting the authority of and giving fidelity to no man or army or flag, going to war as Malbrouck himself did: for booty—it meant nothing and less than nothing to him if it were enemy booty or his own.

The slow constellations wheeled on. It would be dawn and then sun-up after a while and he would be hungry. But that would be tomorrow and now he was only cold, and walking would cure that. His breathing was easier now and he decided to get up and go on, and then he found that he had been asleep because he knew it was almost dawn, the night almost over. He could tell that from the whippoorwills. They were everywhere now among the dark trees below him, constant and inflectioned and ceaseless, so that, as the instant for giving over to the day birds drew nearer and nearer, there was no interval at all between them. He got up. He was a little stiff, but walking would cure that too as it would the cold, and soon there would be the sun. He went on down the hill, toward the dark woods within which the liquid silver voices of the birds called unceasing—the rapid and urgent beating of the urgent and quiring heart of the late spring night. He did not look back.

Critical Thinking

How does Abner Snopes view the world around him, and what motivates him to destroy property via fire? How does he define morality and justice?

How and why are the Snopeses marginalized and condemned to abject poverty?

Reread Sarty's interior monologues (the italicized parts of the story). How and why are his motivations and view of the world different from his father's?

When and why does Sarty realize his father's actions are wrong?

Will Sarty have a different future than the one his father imagined for him?

Does the story exemplify differential association or learning theory? Why or why not?

Sociological Theories of Crime: Social Control Theory

"For All the Rude People"

by Jack Ritchie (John George Reitci)

John Reitci (1922–1983), a prolific American short story writer and World War II army veteran, published over 500 stories during his writing career. One, "The Absence of Emily," received the Edgar Award for Best Short Story in 1982 from the Mystery Writers of America, after Reitci had been previously nominated in 1976 for "The Many-Flavored Crime" and "Nobody Tells Me Anything" a year later.

"For All the Rude People" introduces the reader to Mr. Turner, a terminally ill individual who "had no family, no close friends. And four months to live." Throughout the story he murders a number of people, all rude at one time or another. Criminological theory historically asked the question as to why people commit crimes, but in this case, and in social control theory, we are introduced to a different question: why do people not commit crime? Social control theory posits that we all would be criminals but for having bonds to society that inhibits us from deviant behavior. Earlier theorists such as Emile Durkheim and his idea that society would always have a certain amount of deviants that provided examples to others of the moral boundaries of a community and Albert Reiss, Jr.'s concepts of deviant behavior developing from the breakdown of personal internal controls or the conflict with external rules gave a foundation to Travis Hirschi's own version of social control theory, sometimes referred to as social bonding theory. Others included Walter Reckless and his ideas of a positive self-concept serving as a defense against deviance and David Matza and Gresham Sykes' theory regarding neutralization techniques used by delinquents to internally justify their actions (and suspend their bonds to community norms) by denying responsibility ("I didn't mean to do it.") or denying a victim's injury ("They weren't really hurt."), for example.

In Mr. Turner's case the bonds to society are quite limited; he has no family, no friends and little need for a job. With no attachment to peers, no further involvement in work, no commitment to family, and no belief in acknowledging society's rules as fair—society's rules meant that "we suffer wrongs with meekness, we endure them because to eliminate them might cause even more pain. . ."—social control theory would postulate that Mr. Turner is an individual with a potential for deviance.

In later years Hirschi, working with Michael Gottfredson, would develop a new iteration of social control theory with their "general theory of crime," called by some self-control theory, believing that juveniles with low self-control who are raised with ineffective child rearing skills are at greater risk for committing criminal acts throughout life than individuals with high self-control.

"For All the Rude People"

by Jack Ritchie

"How old are you?" I asked!

His eyes were on the revolver I was holding. "Look, mister, there's not much in the cash register, but take it all. I won't make no trouble."

"I am not interested in your filthy money. How old are you?"

He was puzzled. "Forty-two."

I clicked my tongue. "What a pity. From your point of view, at least. You might have lived another twenty or thirty years if you had just taken the slight pains to be polite."

He didn't understand.

"I am going to kill you," I said, "because of the four-cent stamp and because of the cherry candy."

He did not know what I meant by the cherry candy, but he did know about the stamp.

Panic raced into his face. "You must be crazy. You can't kill me just because of that."

"But I can."

And I did.

When Dr. Briller told me that I had but four months to live, I was, of course, perturbed. "Are you positive you haven't mixed up the X-rays? I've heard of such things."

"I'm afraid not, Mr. Turner."

I gave it more earnest thought. "The laboratory reports. Perhaps my name was accidentally attached to the wrong . . ."

He shook his head slowly. "I double-checked. I always do that in cases like these. Sound medical practice, you know."

It was late afternoon and the time when the sun is tired. I rather hoped that when my time came to actually die, it might be in the morning. Certainly more cheerful.

"In cases like this," Dr. Briller said, "a doctor is faced with a dilemma. Shall he or shall he not tell his patient? I always tell mine. That enables them to settle their affairs and to have a fling, so to speak." He pulled a pad of paper toward him. "Also I'm writing a book. What do you intend doing with your remaining time?"

"I really don't know. I've just been thinking about it for a minute or two, you know."

"Of course," Briller said. "No immediate rush. But when you do decide, you will let me know, won't you? My book concerns the things that people do with their remaining time when they know just when they're going to die."

He pushed aside the pad. "See me every two or three weeks. That way we'll be able to measure the progress of your decline."

Briller saw me to the door. "I already have written up twenty-two cases like yours." He seemed to gaze into the future.

"Could be a best seller, you know."

I have always lived a bland life. Not an unintelligent one, but bland.

I have contributed nothing to the world–and in that I have much in common with almost every soul on earth–but on the other hand I have not taken away anything either. I have, in short, asked merely to be left alone. Life is difficult enough without undue association with people.

What can one do with the remaining four months of a bland life?

I have no idea how long I walked and thought on that subject, but eventually I found myself on the long curving bridge that sweeps down to join the lake drive. The sounds of mechanical music intruded themselves upon my mind and I looked down.

A circus, or very large carnival, lay below.

It was the world of shabby magic, where the gold is gilt, where the top-hatted ringmaster is as much a gentleman as the medals on his chest are authentic, and where the pink ladies on horseback are hard-faced and narrow-eyed. It was the domain of the harsh-voiced vendors and the short-change.

I have always felt that the demise of the big circus may be counted as one of the cultural advances of the twentieth century, yet I found myself descending the footbridge and in a few moments I was on the midway between the rows of stands where human mutations are exploited and exhibited for the entertainment of all children.

Eventually, I reached the big top and idly watched the bored ticket-taker in his elevated box at one side of the main entrance.

A pleasant-faced man leading two little girls approached him and presented several cardboard rectangles which appeared to be passes.

The ticket-taker ran his finger down a printed list at his side. His eyes hardened and he scowled down at the man and the children for a moment. Then slowly and deliberately he tore the passes to bits and let the fragments drift to the ground. "These are no damn good," he said.

The man below him flushed. "I don't understand."

"You didn't leave the posters up," the ticket-taker snapped. "Beat it, crumb!"

The children looked up at their father, their faces puzzled. Would he do something about this?

He stood there and the white of anger appeared on his face. He seemed about to say something, but then he looked down at the children. He closed his eyes for a moment as though to control his anger, and then he said, "Come on, kids.

Let's go home."

He led them away, down the midway, and the children looked back, bewildered, but saying nothing.

I approached the ticket-taker. "Why did you do that?"

He glanced down. "What's it to you?"

"Perhaps a great deal."

He studied me irritably. "Because he didn't leave up the posters."

"I heard that before. Now explain it."

He exhaled as though it cost him money. "Our advance man goes through a town two weeks before we get there. He leaves posters advertising the show any place he can–grocery stores, shoe shops, meat markets–any place that will paste them in the window and keep them there until the show comes to town. He hands out two or three passes for that. But what some of these jokers don't know is that we check up. If the posters aren't still up when we hit town, the passes are no good."

"I see," I said dryly. "And so you tear up the passes in their faces and in front of their children. Evidently that man removed the posters from the window of his little shop too soon. Or perhaps he had those passes given to him by a man who removed the posters from his window."

"What's the difference? The passes are no good."

"Perhaps there is no difference in that respect. But do you realize what you have done?"

His eyes were narrow, trying to estimate me and any power I might have.

"You have committed one of the most cruel of human acts," I said stiffly. "You have humiliated a man before his children. You have inflicted a scar that will remain with him and them as long as they live. He will take those children home and it will be a long, long way. And what can he say to them?"

"Are you a cop?"

"I am not a cop. Children of that age regard their father as the finest man in the world. The kindest, the bravest. And now they will remember that a man had been bad to their father–and he had been unable to do anything about it."

"So I tore up his passes. Why didn't he buy tickets? Are you a city inspector?"

"I am not a city inspector. Did you expect him to buy tickets after that humiliation? You left the man with no recourse whatsoever. He could not buy tickets and he could not create a well-justified scene because the children were with him.

He could do nothing. Nothing at all, but retreat with two children who wanted to see your miserable circus and now they cannot."

I looked down at the foot of his stand. There were the fragments of many more dreams–the debris of other men who had committed the capital crime of not leaving their posters up long enough. "You could at least have said, 'I'm sorry, sir. But your passes are not valid.' And then you could have explained politely and quietly why."

"I'm not paid to be polite." He showed yellow teeth. "And mister, I like tearing up passes. It gives me a kick."

And there it was. He was a little man who had been given a little power and he used it like a Caesar.

He half rose. "Now get the hell out of here, mister, before I come down there and chase you all over the lot."

Yes. He was a man of cruelty, a two-dimensional animal born without feeling and sensitivity and fated to do harm as long as he existed. He was a creature who should be eliminated from the face of the earth.

If only I had the power to . . .

I stared up at the twisted face for a moment more and then turned on my heel and left. At the top of the bridge I got a bus and rode to the sports shop at Thirty-seventh.

I purchased a .32 caliber revolver and a box of cartridges.

Why do we not murder? Is it because we do not feel the moral justification for such a final act? Or is it more because we fear the consequences if we are caught–the cost to us, to our families, to our children?

And so we suffer wrongs with meekness, we endure them because to eliminate them might cause us even more pain than we already have.

But I had no family, no close friends. And four months to live.

The sun had set and the carnival lights were bright when I got off the bus at the bridge. I looked down at the midway and he was still in his box.

How should I do it? I wondered. Just march up to him and shoot him as he sat on his little throne?

The problem was solved for me. I saw him replaced by another man—apparently his relief. He lit a cigarette and strolled off the midway toward the dark lake front.

I caught up with him around a bend concealed by bushes. It was a lonely place, but close enough to the carnival so that its sounds could still reach me.

He heard my footsteps and turned. A tight smile came to his lips and he rubbed the knuckles of one hand. "You're asking for it, mister."

His eyes widened when he saw my revolver.

"How old are you?" I asked.

"Look, mister," he said swiftly, "I only got a couple of tens in my pocket."

"How old are you?" I repeated.

His eyes flicked nervously. "Thirty-two."

I shook my head sadly. "You could have lived into your seventies. Perhaps forty more years of life, if only you had taken the simple trouble to act like a human being."

His face whitened. "Are you off your rocker, or something?"

"A possibility."

I pulled the trigger.

The sound of the shot was not as loud as I had expected, or perhaps it was lost against the background of the carnival noises.

He staggered and dropped to the edge of the path and he was quite dead.

I sat down on a nearby park bench and waited.

Five minutes. Ten. Had no one heard the shot?

I became suddenly conscious of hunger. I hadn't eaten since noon. The thought of being taken to a police station and being questioned for any length of time seemed unbearable. And I had a headache, too.

I tore a page from my pocket notebook and began writing:

A careless word may be forgiven. But a lifetime of cruel rudeness may cannot. This man deserves to die.

I was about to sign my name, but then I decided that my initials would be sufficient for the time being. I did not want to be apprehended before I had a good meal and some aspirins.

I folded the page and put it into the dead ticket-taker's breast pocket.

I met no one as I returned up the path and ascended the footbridge. I walked to Weschler's, probably the finest restaurant in the city. The prices are, under normal circumstances, beyond me, but I thought that this time I could indulge myself.

After dinner, I decided an evening bus ride might be in order. I rather enjoyed that form of city excursion and, after all, my freedom of movement would soon become restricted.

The driver of the bus was an impatient man and clearly his passengers were his enemies. However, it was a beautiful night and the bus was not crowded.

At Sixty-eighth Street, a fragile white-haired woman with cameo features waited at the curb. The driver grudgingly brought his vehicle to a stop and opened the door.

She smiled and nodded to the passengers as she put her foot on the first step, and one could see that her life was one of gentle happiness and very few bus rides.

"Well!" the driver snapped. "Is it going to take you all day to get in?"

She flushed and stammered. "I'm sorry." She presented him with a five-dollar bill.

He glared. "Don't you have any change?"

The flush deepened. "I don't think so. But I'll look."

The driver was evidently ahead of his schedule and he waited.

And one other thing was clear. He was enjoying this.

She found a quarter and held it up timorously.

"In the box!" he snapped.

She dropped it into the box.

The driver moved his vehicle forward jerkily and she almost fell. Just in time she managed to catch hold of a strap.

Her eyes went to the passengers, as though to apologize for herself–for not having moved faster, for not having immediate change, for almost falling. The smile trembled and she sat down.

At Eighty-second, she pulled the buzzer cord, rose, and made her way forward.

The driver scowled over his shoulder as he came to a stop. "Use the rear door. Don't you people ever learn to use the rear door?"

I am all in favor of using the rear door. Especially when a bus is crowded. But there were only a half a dozen passengers on this bus and they read their newspapers with frightened neutrality.

She turned, her face pale, and left by the rear door.

The evening she had had, or the evening she was going to have, had now been ruined. Perhaps many more evenings, with the thought of it.

I rode the bus to the end of the line.

I was the only passenger when the driver turned it around and parked.

It was a deserted, dimly lit corner, and there were no waiting passengers at the small shelter at the curb. The driver glanced at his watch, lit his cigarette, and then noticed me. "If you're taking the ride back, mister, put another quarter in the box. No free riders here."

I rose from my seat and walked slowly to the front of the bus. "How old are you?"

His eyes narrowed. "That's none of your business."

"About thirty-five, I'd imagine," I said. "You'd have had another thirty years or more ahead of you." I produced the revolver.

He dropped the cigarette. "Take the money," he said.

"I'm not interested in money. I'm thinking about a gentle lady and perhaps the hundreds of other gentle ladies and the kind harmless men and the smiling children. You are a criminal. There is no justification for what you do to them. There is no justification for your existence."

And I killed him.

I sat down and waited.

After ten minutes, I was still alone with the corpse.

I realized that I was sleepy. Incredibly sleepy. It might be better if I turned myself in to the police after a good night's sleep.

I wrote my justification for the driver's demise on a sheet of note paper, added my initials, and put the page in his pocket.

I walked four blocks before I found a taxi and took it to my apartment building.

I slept soundly and perhaps I dreamed. But if I did, my dreams were pleasant and innocuous, and it was almost nine before I woke.

After a shower and a leisurely breakfast, I selected my best suit. I remembered I had not yet paid that month's telephone bill. I made out a check and addressed an envelope. I discovered that I was out of stamps. But no matter, I would get one on the way to the police station.

I was almost there when I remembered the stamp. I stopped in at a corner drugstore. It was a place I had never entered before.

The proprietor, in a semi-medical jacket, sat behind the soda fountain reading a newspaper and a salesman was making notations in a large order book.

The proprietor did not look up when I entered and he spoke to the salesman. "They've got his fingerprints on the notes, they've got his handwriting, and they've got his initials. What's wrong with the police?"

The salesman shrugged. "What good are fingerprints if the murderer doesn't have his in the police files? The same goes for the handwriting if you got nothing to compare it with. And how many thousand people in the city got the initials L. T.?" He closed the book. "I'll be back next week."

When he was gone, the druggist continued reading the newspaper.

I cleared my throat.

He finished reading a long paragraph and then looked up. "Well?"

"I'd like a four-cent stamp, please."

It appeared almost as though I had struck him. He stared at me for fifteen seconds and then he left his stool and slowly made his way to the rear of the store toward a small barred window.

I was about to follow him, but a display of pipes at my elbow caught my attention.

After a while I felt eyes upon me and looked up.

The druggist stood at the far end of the store, one hand on his hip and the other disdainfully holding the single stamp. "Do you expect me to bring it to you?"

And now I remembered a small boy of six who had had five pennies. Not just one, this time, but five, and this was in the days of penny candies.

He had been entranced by the display in the showcase–the fifty varieties of sweet things, and his mind had revolved in a pleasant indecision. The red whips? The licorice? The grab bags? But not the candy cherries. He didn't like those.

And then he had become conscious of the druggist standing beside the display case–tapping one foot. The druggist's eyes had smoldered with irritation–no, more than that–with anger. "Are you going to take all day for your lousy nickel?"

He had been a sensitive boy and he had felt as though he had received a blow. His precious five pennies were now nothing. This man despised them. And this man despised him.

He pointed numbly and blindly. "Five cents of that."

When he left the store he had found that he had the candy cherries.

But that didn't really matter. Whatever it had been, he couldn't have eaten it.

Now I stared at the druggist and the four-cent stamp and the narrow hatred for anyone who did not contribute directly to his profits. I had no doubt that he would fawn if I purchased one of his pipes.

But I thought of the four-cent stamp, and the bag of cherry candy I had thrown away so many years ago.

I moved toward the rear of the store and took the revolver out of my pocket. "How old are you?"

When he was dead, I did not wait longer than necessary to write a note. I had killed for myself this time and I felt the need of a drink.

I went several doors down the street and entered a small bar. I ordered a brandy and water.

After ten minutes, I heard the siren of a squad car.

The bartender went to the window. "It's just down the street." He took off his jacket. "Got to see what this is all about. If anybody comes in, tell them I'll be right back." He put the bottle of brandy on the bar. "Help yourself, but tell me how many."

I sipped the brandy slowly and watched the additional squad cars and finally the ambulance appear.

The bartender returned after ten minutes and a customer followed at his heels. "A short beer, Joe."

"This is my second brandy," I said.

Joe collected my change. "The druggist down the street got himself murdered. Looks like it was by the man who kills people because they're not polite."

The customer watched him draw a beer. "How do you figure that? Could have been just a holdup."

Joe shook his head. "No. Fred Masters—he's got the TV shop across the street—found the body and he read the note."

The customer put a dime on the bar. "I'm not going to cry about it. I always took my business someplace else. He acted as though he was doing you a favor every time he waited on you."

Joe nodded. "I don't think anybody in the neighborhood's going to miss him. He always made a lot of trouble."

I had been about to leave and return to the drugstore to give myself up, but now I ordered another brandy and took out my notebook. I began making a list of names.

It was surprising how one followed another. They were bitter memories, some large, some small, some I had experienced and many more that I had witnessed—perhaps felt more than the victims.

Names. And that warehouseman. I didn't know his name, but I must include him.

I remembered the day and Miss Newman. We were her sixth-graders and she had taken us on another one of her excursions—this time to the warehouses along the river, where she was going to show us "how industry works."

She always planned her tours and she always asked permission of the places we visited, but this time she strayed or became lost and we arrived at the warehouse—she and the thirty children who adored her.

And the warehouseman had ordered her out. He had used language we did not understand, but we sensed its intent, and he had directed it against us and Miss Newman.

She was small and she had been frightened and we retreated. And Miss Newman did not report to school the next day or any day after that and we learned that she had asked for a transfer.

And I, who loved her, too, knew why. She could not face us after that.

Was he still alive? He had been in his twenties then, I imagined.

When I left the bar a half an hour later, I realized I had a great deal of work to do.

The succeeding days were busy ones and, among others, I found the warehouseman. I told him why he was dying, because he did not even remember.

And when that was done, I dropped into a restaurant not far away.

The waitress eventually broke off her conversation with the cashier and strode to my table. "What do you want?"

I ordered a steak and tomatoes.

The steak proved to be just about what one could expect in such a neighborhood. As I reached for my coffee spoon, I accidentally dropped it to the floor. I picked it up. "Waitress, would you mind bringing me another spoon, please?"

She stalked angrily to my table and snatched the spoon from my hand. "You got the shakes, or something?"

She returned in a few minutes and was about to deposit a spoon, with considerable emphasis, upon my table.

But then a sudden thought altered the harsh expression of her face. The descent of the arm diminuendoed, and when the spoon touched the tablecloth, it touched gently. Very gently.

She laughed nervously. "I'm sorry if I was sharp, mister."

It was an apology, and so I said, "That's quite all right."

"I mean that you can drop a spoon any time you want to. I'll be glad to get you another."

"Thank you." I turned to my coffee.

"You're not offended, are you, mister?" she asked eagerly.

"No. Not at all."

She snatched a newspaper from an empty neighboring table. "Here, sir, you can read this while you eat. I mean, it's on the house. Free."

When she left me, the wide-eyed cashier stared at her. "What's with all that, Mable?"

Mable glanced back at me with a trace of uneasiness. "You can never tell who he might be. You better be polite these days."

As I ate I read, and an item caught my eye. A grown man had heated pennies in a frying pan and had tossed them out to some children who were making trick-or-treat rounds before Halloween. He had been fined a miserable twenty dollars.

I made a note of his name and address.

Dr. Briller finished his examination. "You can get dressed now, Mr. Turner."

I picked up my shirt. "I don't suppose some new miracle drug has been developed since I was here last?"

He laughed with self-enjoyed good nature. "No, I'm afraid not." He watched me button the shirt. "By the way, have you decided what you're going to do with your remaining time?"

I had, but I thought I'd say, "Not yet."

He was faintly perturbed. "You really should, you know. Only about three months left. And be sure to let me know when you do."

While I finished dressing, he sat down at his desk and glanced at the newspaper lying there. "The killer seems to be rather busy, doesn't he?"

He turned a page. "But really the most surprising thing about the crimes seems to be the public's reaction. Have you read the Letters from the People column recently?"

"No."

"These murders appear to be meeting with almost universal approval. Some of the letter writers even hint that they might be able to supply the murderer with a few choice names themselves."

I would have to get a paper.

"Not only that," Dr. Briller said, "but a wave of politeness has struck the city."

I put on my coat. "Shall I come back in two weeks?"

He put aside the paper. "Yes. And try to look at this whole thing as cheerfully as possible. We all have to go some day."

But his day was indeterminate and presumably in the distant future.

My appointment with Dr. Briller had been in the evening, and it was nearly ten by the time I left my bus and began the short walk to my apartment building.

As I approached the last corner, I heard a shot. I turned into Milding Lane and found a little man with a revolver standing over a newly dead body on the quiet and deserted sidewalk.

I looked down at the corpse. "Goodness. A policeman."

The little man nodded. "Yes, what I've done does seem a little extreme, but you see he was using a variety of language that was entirely necessary."

"Ah," I said.

The little man nodded. "I'd parked my car in front of this fire hydrant. Entirely inadvertently, I assure you. And this policeman was waiting when I returned to my car. And also he discovered that I'd forgotten my driver's license. I would not have acted as I did if he had simply written out a ticket–for I was guilty, sir, and I readily admit it–but he was not content with that. He made embarrassing observations concerning my intelligence, my eyesight, the possibility that I'd stolen the car, and finally on the legitimacy of my birth." He blinked at a fond memory. "And my mother was an angel, sir. An angel."

I remembered a time when I'd been apprehended while absentmindedly jaywalking. I would contritely have accepted the customary warning, or even a ticket, but the officer insisted upon a profane lecture before a grinning assemblage of interested pedestrians. Most humiliating.

The little man looked at the gun in his hand. "I bought this just today and actually I'd intended to use it on the superintendent of my apartment building. A bully."

I agreed. "Surly fellows."

He sighed. "But now I suppose I'll have to turn myself over to the police?"

I gave it a thought. He watched me.

He cleared his throat. "Or perhaps I should just leave a note? You see I've been reading in the newspapers about. . ."

I lent him my notebook.

He wrote a few lines, signed his initials, and deposited the slip of paper between two buttons of the dead officer's jacket.

He handed the notebook back to me. "I must remember to get one of these."

He opened the door of his car. "Can I drop you off anywhere?"

"No, thank you," I said. "It's a nice evening. I'd rather walk."

Pleasant fellow, I reflected, as I left him.

Too bad there weren't more like him.

Critical Thinking

When thinking of associates over the years, were you aware of any individuals who seemed to have low self-control? What became of them?

Can you think of anything in life that might mitigate someone's behavior so that they wouldn't be as likely to commit a crime, even if they still had low self-control as an adult?

If social bonding theory explains Mr. Turner's actions, does it necessarily explain the "little man's" actions at the end of the story?

Chapter 3

Criminal Law

Defenses—Necessity

"Rosalie Prudent"

by Guy de Maupassant

Guy de Maupassant (1850–1893) was a French writer considered one of the originators of the modern short story. Known for literary and psychological realism, as well as detailed plotting, he influenced other major writers, including O. Henry. His stories represent literary naturalism, a movement founded by other French writers such as Emile Zola. Naturalist writers emphasized the control exerted by the forces of heredity and environment over human life, and the animalistic and instinctual elements in man. Its subject matter includes lower-class situations and characters, focusing on a deterministic philosophy that frequently emphasizes the operations of blind chance. Human life is viewed as being at the mercy of uncontrollable exterior forces. "Rosalie Prudent," for example, focuses on the fate of a servant girl who, impregnated by her master's nephew, kills and then buries her twins when she realizes that poverty and her low social status will present her from caring for them. The story follows her trial for infanticide, depicting her masters' harsh condemnation of her behavior for bringing shame upon their house; the jury's and observers' shifting perceptions as Rosalie relates the circumstances of her crime; and the judge's questions that also allow Rosie to defend her actions. "Rosalie Prudent" is but one example of the necessity defense, which provides that a greater crime could have occurred or that the defendant had no reasonable alternative than the crime she committed.

———— ℘ ————

"Rosalie Prudent"

by Guy de Maupassant

There was a mystery in that affair about Rosalie Prudent, which neither the jury, nor the judge, nor the prosecuting attorney of the republic himself could understand.

The girl Rosalie was a servant at the house of the Varambot family, of Mantes. She became *enceinte*, and, unknown to her employers, had given birth to a child in the garret, during the night, and had then killed the child and buried it in the garden.

It was the ordinary story of most of the infanticides committed by servants. But one act remained inexplicable. The examination of the girl's room had resulted in the discovery of a complete *layette* for an infant, made by Rosalie herself, who had passed her nights during three months in cutting out the garments and sewing them. The grocer where she had bought her candles (paid for out of her wages), in order to perform this long task, came forward and testified to the fact of their purchase. In addition it was learned that the midwife of the town, informed by Rosalie of her condition, had given her all the advice and information necessary in case the child should be born at a time when aid was impossible to obtain. She had found a place also, at Poissy, for Rosalie Prudent, who foresaw her loss of situation, as the Varambots were severe on the subject of morality.

They appeared in court, the man and his wife, small provincials of moderate means, exasperated against the vulgar creature who had besmirched the immaculateness of their house. They would have liked to see her guillotined at once, without trial, and they overwhelmed her with insults which in their mouths became accusations.

The guilty one, a tall, handsome girl of lower Normandy, fairly well educated for her station, wept without ceasing, and made no reply to them or to anyone. The Court came to the conclusion that she had accomplished that act of barbarity in a moment of despair and insanity, since everything indicated that she had hoped to keep her infant and bring it up.

The judge tried once more to make her speak, to get her to acknowledge her crime, and having asked her with great kindness to do so, he made her understand at last that the jury sitting there to judge her did not wish her death, but were ready to pity her.

The girl appeared to be making up her mind to speak at last.

"Tell us now at first who is the father of that child," said the judge.

Until that moment she had refused obstinately to divulge this fact. Now she replied suddenly, looking straight at her employers, who had come there in a rage to calumniate her.

"It is Monsieur Joseph, the nephew of Monsieur Varambot!"

Varambot and his wife started, and both cried at the same time:

"It is false! She lies! It is infamous!"

Source: Guy De Maupassant, "Rosalie Prudent," 1886.

The judge bade them be silent, and said:

"Continue, I beg of you, and tell us how it happened."

Then the girl began to speak hurriedly, seeming to find some comfort for her poor, solitary, bruised heart in giving vent to her sorrow before these severe-looking men, whom she had taken until then for enemies and inflexible judges.

"Yes it was Monsieur Joseph Varambot—it happened when he came for his vacation last summer."

"What is the occupation of this monsieur Joseph Varambot?"

"He is underofficer in the artillery, Monsieur. He was two months at the house—two months of the summer. I wasn't thinking of anything when he began to look at me, and then to say things to me, and finally to make love to me the whole day long. I was easy, Monsieur! He told me I was a handsome girl, that I pleased him, that I was to his taste. For myself, he pleased me, to be sure. What would you have? Anyone listens to those things, when one is alone—as I am. I am alone on the earth, Monsieur. There is no one to whom I can talk—no one to whom I can tell my troubles. I have neither father, nor mother, nor brother, nor sister—no one! He seemed like a brother who had come to me when he began to talk to me. And then he asked me to go down to the river one evening, so that we might talk without making so much noise. And I went down there. Could I have known what would happen? He put his arms around my waist—of course I didn't want to,—no, no! I couldn't help it. I wanted to cry, the air was so soft and warm—it was clear moonlight—I couldn't help it! No, I swear it to you, I couldn't help it— he did what he pleased. That lasted three weeks, as long as he remained. I would have followed him to the end of the world. But he went away, and I didn't know that I was *enceinte*—I didn't! I didn't know it until the month afterward."

She began to weep so violently that they were obliged to give her time to compose herself. Then the judge spoke, in the tone of a father confessor: "Go on, my girl, go on."

She continued: "When I knew that I was *enceinte,* I told Madame Boudin, the midwife, to whom one can tell these things; and I asked her what to do in case that happened without her. And then I made the clothes, night after night, until one o'clock in the morning; and then I looked for another place, for I knew very well I should be discharged: but I wished to remain in that house until the end, in order to economize the pennies, seeing that I had no money and that I would need it for the little one."

"Then you did not wish to kill him?"

"Oh, surely not, Monsieur."

"Why did you kill him, then?"

"Here's how it happened. It came sooner than I thought it would. It took me in the kitchen as I was washing my dishes. Monsieur and Madame Varambot had retired already, so I went upstairs, without trouble, holding to the banisters. I lay down on the floor in my room, so as not to soil the bed. That lasted perhaps one hour—but it may have been two or three—I can't tell, so much pain did I have,—and then—and then it was over, and I took up my baby!

"Oh, yes! I was happy, for sure! I did everything that Madame Boudin told me, everything! Then I laid him on the bed,—and then another pain began, and it was a pain to kill anyone. If you knew what that was, you others, you wouldn't do as much I'm sure! I fell on my knees, and then on my back on the floor, and then it began all over again, and that, too, lasted one hour, or perhaps two and there I was all alone. Finally there came another little one, yes, another, two of them, like that! I took it up as I took the first one, and I put it on the bed by the side of the other. One—two! Can it be possible, I said! Two babies! And I, who earn twenty francs a month! Say—was it possible for me to take care of them? To care for one—yes, I might do that by depriving myself, but not two!

"The thought of that turned my head. What do I know about it, I? Could I choose, say! Do I know? I saw myself come to my last day! I couldn't keep two, so I put the pillow on them without knowing what I was doing—and I threw myself on the bed and upon them, too. And I stayed there, rolling and crying, until daylight, which I saw through the window. I looked at them—they were both dead under the pillow, quite dead. Then I took them under my arm, I went down the stairs, and out in the garden; I took the gardener's spade and I buried them in the ground, as deep as I could, one here and the other there, not together, so that they could not talk of their mother, if they do talk, the little dead children. Do I know?

"And then I went back to my bed, and I was so sick that I could not get up. They made the doctor come, and he understood everything. That is the truth, Monsieur the judge. Do what you want to me. I am ready."

During her speech half of the jury-men had been wiping their eyes over and over again, trying to hide their emotion. All the women in the court room were sobbing.

"At what spot in the garden did you bury the other infant?" asked the judge.

"Which one did you find?" Rosalie inquired.

"The one that was under the artichokes."

"Ah! the other is buried under the strawberries beside the well!" The poor girl began again to sob so loud that it was enough to break one's heart to hear her. The jury acquitted her.

Critical Thinking

Does Rosalie's defense meet the criteria for the necessity defense?

What details contribute to the jury's decision?

What elements of the story are naturalistic, and how do they contribute not only to the jury's response, but also to the reader's reaction to Rosalie's defense?

Policy Choices, Politics, and Ideology

"Before the Law" and "The Problem of Our Laws"
by Franz Kafka

Frank Kafka (1883–1924) was a Czech writer of novels and short stories, and considered one of the most important writers of the twentieth century. His work is notable for featuring protagonists in often surreal, bizarre, absurdist circumstances who experience feelings of alienation, existential despair, and modernist anxiety. "The Metamorphosis" is his most well-known story. "Before the Law" (1915) and "The Problem of Our Laws" (1931; posthumously) are two parables exploring the arbitrariness of laws in their construction and application, as well as their mutable existence to those who are under the law.

"Before the Law" tells an allegorical tale about a man who comes from the country to access the law, but is prevented from doing so by one of many gatekeepers. The man asks when he will be able to pass through the gate, but the gatekeeper equivocates each time he is asked: perhaps, someday, at a later time the man will get access to the law. When the man considers rushing past the gatekeeper, the gatekeeper challenges him to do so, but warns that each successive room in the building has its own gatekeeper, "each more powerful than the other." The man is troubled by his inability to secure entrance to the law, believing in equality under the law and that all should have equal opportunity to use (and benefit from) it. The man spends the rest of his life before the first gatekeeper, repeating his request to gain entrance and meeting the same obstacles. He dies just as he makes his final request.

        ℬ

"Before the Law"
by Franz Kafka

Before the Law stands a doorkeeper. To this doorkeeper there comes a man from the country and prays for admittance to the Law. But the doorkeeper says that he cannot grant admittance at the moment." The man thinks it over and then asks if he will be allowed in later. "It is possible," says the doorkeeper, "but not at the moment." Since the gate stands open, as usual, and the doorkeeper steps to one side, the man stoops to peer through the gateway into the interior. Observing that, the doorkeeper laughs and says: "If you are so drawn to it, just try to go in despite my veto. But take note: I am powerful. And I am only the least of the doorkeepers. From hall to hall there is one doorkeeper after another, each more powerful than the last. The third doorkeeper is already so terrible that even I cannot bear to look at him." These are difficulties the man from the country has not expected; the Law, he thinks, should surely be accessible at all times and to everyone, but as he now takes a closer look at the doorkeeper in his fur coat, with his big sharp nose and long, thin, black Tartar beard, he decides that it is better to wait until he gets permission to enter. The doorkeeper gives him a stool and lets him sit down at one side of the door. There he sits for days and years. He makes many attempts to be admitted, and wearies the doorkeeper by his importunity. The doorkeeper frequently has little interviews with him, asking him questions about his home and many other things, but the questions are put indifferently, as great lords put them, and always finish with the statement that he cannot be let in yet. The man, who has furnished himself with many things for his journey, sacrifices all he has, however valuable, to bribe the doorkeeper. The doorkeeper accepts everything, but always with the remark: "I am only taking it to keep you from thinking you may have omitted anything." During these many years the man fixes his attention almost continuously on the doorkeeper. He forgets the other doorkeepers, and this first one seems to him the sole obstacle preventing access to the Law. He curses his bad luck, in his early years boldly and loudly; later, as he grows old, he only grumbles to himself. He becomes childish, and since in his yearlong contemplation of the doorkeeper he has come to know even the fleas in his fur collar, he begs the fleas as well to help him and to change the doorkeeper's mind. At length his eyesight begins to fail, and he does not know whether the world is really darker or whether his eyes are only deceiving him. Yet in his darkness he is now aware of a radiance that streams inextinguishably from the gateway of the Law. Now he has not very long to live. Before he dies, all his experiences in these long years gather themselves in his head to one point, a question he has not yet asked the doorkeeper. He waves him nearer, since he can no longer raise his stiffening body. The doorkeeper has to bend low toward him, for the difference in height between them has altered much to the man's disadvantage. "What do you want to know now?" asks the doorkeeper; "you are insatiable!" "Everyone strives to reach the Law," says the man, "so how does it happen that for all these many years no one but myself has ever begged for admittance?" The doorkeeper recognizes that the man has reached his end, and, to let his failing senses catch the words, roars in his ear: "No one else could ever be admitted here, since this gate was made only for you. I am now going to shut it."

Similarly, "The Problem of Our Laws" considers the arbitrary construction and application of ancient laws not written down but assumed to be in existence both by the people who are subject to them (not the nobility) and the people who wield them (the nobility). Kafka asserts that such laws are not actually known or even exist in tangible form. They only exist as "a matter of presumption" accepted by the people, but are deliberately kept secret by the "nobles" as the means to stay in power. In short, according to Kafka, "The Law is whatever the nobles do." Thus, "The Law" is arbitrary and unequal in its application, and the people do not challenge such laws because they are accepted as "tradition." Only when the people claim the law for themselves will the nobility disappear according to Kafka. Such a claim can only be made, he argues, when the people believe they are worthy to be entrusted with the law and no longer believe the nobility are morally and legally superior.

"The Problem of Our Laws"
by Franz Kafka

Our laws are not generally known; they are kept secret by the small group of nobles who rule us. We are convinced that these ancient laws are scrupulously administered; nevertheless it is an extremely painful thing to be ruled by laws that one does not know. I am not thinking of possible discrepancies that may arise in the interpretation of the laws, or of the disadvantages involved when only a few and not the whole people are allowed to have a say in their interpretation. These disadvantages are perhaps of no great importance. For the laws are very ancient; their interpretation has been the work of centuries, and has itself doubtless acquired the status of law; and though there is still a possible freedom of interpretation left, it has now become very restricted. Moreover the nobles have obviously no cause to be influenced in their interpretation by personal interests inimical to us, for the laws were made to the advantage of the nobles from the very beginning, they themselves stand above the laws, and that seems to be why the laws were entrusted exclusively into their hands. Of course, there is wisdom in that—who doubts the wisdom of the ancient laws?—but also hardship for us; probably that is unavoidable.

The very existence of these laws, however, is at most a matter of presumption. There is a tradition that they exist and that they are a mystery confided to the nobility, but it is not and cannot be more than a mere tradition sanctioned by age, for the essence of a secret code is that it should remain a mystery. Some of us among the people have attentively scrutinized the doings of the nobility since the earliest times and possess records made by our forefathers—records which we have conscientiously continued—and claim to recognize amid the countless number of facts certain main tendencies which permit of this or that historical formulation; but when in accordance with these scrupulously tested and logically ordered conclusions we seek to adjust ourselves somewhat for the present or the future, everything becomes uncertain, and our work seems only an intellectual game, for perhaps these laws that we are trying to unravel do not exist at all. There is a small party who are actually of this opinion and who try to show that, if any law exists, it can only be this: The Law is whatever the nobles do. This party see everywhere only the arbitrary acts of the nobility, and reject the popular tradition, which according to them possesses only certain trifling and incidental advantages that do not offset its heavy drawbacks, for it gives the people a false, deceptive, and overconfident security in confronting coming events. This cannot be gainsaid, but the overwhelming majority of our people account for it by the fact that the tradition is far from complete and must be more fully inquired into, that the material available, prodigious as it looks, is still too meager, and that several centuries will have to pass before it becomes really adequate. This view, so comfortless as far as the present is concerned, is lightened only by the belief that a time will eventually come when the tradition and our research into it will jointly reach their conclusion, and as it were gain a breathing space, when everything will have become clear, the law will belong to the people, and the nobility will vanish. This is not maintained in any spirit of hatred against the nobility; not at all, and by no one. We are more inclined to hate ourselves, because we have not yet shown ourselves worthy of being entrusted with the laws. And that is the real reason why the party who believe that there is no law have remained so few—although their doctrine is in certain ways so attractive, for it unequivocally recognizes the nobility and its right to go on existing.

Actually one can express the problem only in a sort of paradox: Any party that would repudiate not only all belief in the laws, but the nobility as well, would have the whole people behind it; yet no such party can come into existence, for nobody would dare to repudiate the nobility. We live on this razor's edge. A writer once summed the matter up in this way: The sole visible and indubitable law that is imposed upon us is the nobility, and must we ourselves deprive ourselves of that one law?

Critical Thinking

Although the United States' laws are tangible—written down, legislated, revised—to what extent do citizens feel these laws are arbitrary, applied unequally, and actually unjust?

Does our country have an equivalent noble class that benefits or is excused from laws to which everyone else is held accountable?

What people, based on their experiences within the judicial system, feel barred from access to the law and fair adjudication of such laws, as the man does in "Before the Law"?

Section 2

The Policing of Crime

Chapter 4

The Policing of Crime

History of Policing in the United States

"Andy the Night-Watch," "The Town Marshal," and "Jack McGuire" from *Spoon River Anthology*

by Edgar Lee Masters

In writing *Spoon River Anthology* Edgar Lee Masters (1868–1950) touched upon a variety of criminal justice topics in his poetry. The epigraphs "Andy the Night-Watch", "The Town Marshal," and "Jack McGuire" offer a view of local law enforcement in the early 1900s. For much of American history, dating to colonial times, the night watch was the primary preventive policing force only being slowly replaced in the mid to late 1800s by the introduction of the modern police organizations modeled after the British Metropolitan Police. In Masters' epigraph one finds a night watch functional in western Illinois as late as the onset of World War I.

"Andy the Night-Watch"
by Edgar Lee Masters

IN my Spanish cloak,
And old slouch hat,
And overshoes of felt,

Edgar Lee Masters, "Andy the Night-Watch," *Spoon River Anthology*, 1916.

And Tyke, my faithful dog,
And my knotted hickory cane,
I slipped about with a bull's-eye lantern
From door to door on the square,
As the midnight stars wheeled round,
And the bell in the steeple murmured
From the blowing of the wind;
And the weary steps of old Doc Hill
Sounded like one who walks in sleep,
And a far-off rooster crew.
And now another is watching Spoon River
As others watched before me.
And here we lie, Doc Hill and I
Where none breaks through and steals,
And no eye needs to guard.

Critical Thinking

Why would a community such as the apocryphal Spoon River still have a night watch when cities such as Chicago and St. Louis had police departments responsible for addressing criminal activity?

Can you think of any contemporary examples of a night watch?

"The Town Marshal" introduces another individual responsible for community social control. While some think of a town marshal in a western setting such as Dodge City or Abilene, the position has been in use for many years prior to American expansion westward. The epigraph shows what were considered appropriate qualifications for a law enforcement position in the early twentieth century—primarily "righteous, strong, (and) courageous."

"The Town Marshal"
by Edgar Lee Masters

THE Prohibitionists made me Town Marshal
When the saloons were voted out,
Because when I was a drinking man,
Before I joined the church, I killed a Swede
At the saw-mill near Maple Grove.
And they wanted a terrible man,
Grim, righteous, strong, courageous,
And a hater of saloons and drinkers,
To keep law and order in the village.
And they presented me with a loaded cane
With which I struck Jack McGuire
Before he drew the gun with which he killed me.
The Prohibitionists spent their money in vain
To hang him, for in a dream
I appeared to one of the twelve jurymen
And told him the whole secret story.
Fourteen years were enough for killing me.

Edgar Lee Masters, "The Town Marshal," *Spoon River Anthology,* 1916.

Critical Thinking

Unarmed as many officers were at the time except with a wooden "cane" loaded with lead allowing it to be used as a sap or truncheon, the marshal would be gunned down after assaulting a drunk. The marshal also brought a bias to his policing, having also been hired for his hatred of saloons and drinkers.

Do you believe his prejudice determined his initial reaction to Jack McGuire?

What other bias might a modern officer bring to the job from his background prior to entering law enforcement?

How might an agency prevent that bias from unduly impacting his actions?

The epigraph "Jack McGuire" exemplifies the bargains that can be made in the courtroom with many of the members of the court working group (judge, prosecutor, defense attorney) being of the same profession and social class, associating with each other professionally and possibly socially, allowing extra-judicial factors to influence a decision. A Texas judge, for example, was having an intimate relationship with a prosecutor handling a death penalty case yet the state Supreme Court failed to overturn the conviction after the relationship became public.

"Jack McGuire"

by Edgar Lee Masters

THEY would have lynched me
Had I not been secretly hurried away
To the jail at Peoria.
And yet I was going peacefully home,
Carrying my jug, a little drunk,
When Logan, the marshal, halted me,
Called me a drunken hound and shook me,
And, when I cursed him for it, struck me
With that Prohibition loaded cane—
All this before I shot him.
They would have hanged me except for this:
My lawyer, Kinsey Keene, was helping to land
Old Thomas Rhodes for wrecking the bank,
And the judge was a friend of Rhodes
And wanted him to escape,
And Kinsey offered to quit on Rhodes
For fourteen years for me.
And the bargain was made. I served my time
And learned to read and write.

Source: Edgar Lee Masters, "Jack McGuire," *Spoon River Anthology,* 1916.

Critical Thinking

"Jack McGuire" was facing a lynching by the town's citizens and even though smuggled out he still was confronting a murder conviction and the requisite hanging. Yet his attorney struck a bargain with the sentencing judge not to investigate a friend of the judge in exchange for a minimal sentence for McGuire.

Did the bargain between McGuire's attorney and the judge allow for a fair sentence versus what would otherwise have happened?

How could one prevent such a bargain?

Logan, the Town Marshal, believed the sentence was influenced by a juror's dream. Many people think they know why a decision is made in a criminal or civil case, yet they do not have all the facts. Which reason do you believe, the Marshal's or Jack's, and why?

Can you think of any other examples of people believing a false reason or theory for some decision or incident in history?

Policing in the South: Conflict Theory, Mob Violence, Vigilantism, Lynch Mob

"A Party Down at the Square"

by Ralph Ellison

Ralph Ellison (1913–1994) was an African American novelist and short story author best known for his novel *Invisible Man*. He was born and raised in the Midwest United States.

"A Party Down at the Square" (undated circa 1940) is a story of the burning of a black man in the square of a small town in Alabama. Note that this unlawful mob action is taking place right in front of the courthouse and within sight of a moldy bronze statue of a Confederate general. During Reconstruction and into the twentieth century, lynching in the South, in particular, was not an uncommon occurrence. Sometimes these murders, usually of a black man or boy, would be executed by small groups in rural areas, but other times they were public events, entertainment, carried out in the open and attended by many townspeople. The black man's offense might be as slight as having looked a white woman in the eyes or as unjust as being wrongly accused of rape. These suspected men were not given a trial but instead were tried, convicted, and executed by prominent white citizens, sometimes those who were deputized. The impunity with which these mobs conducted their lynching is indicated by photographic postcards of hanging bodies sent after the event by proud bystanders, bragging about their participation. Rarely were the perpetrators brought to justice.

In Ellison's story, Jeb Wilson, present at the lynching, procures some of the murdered man's bones as a souvenir. That horrific practice was also not unusual and showed the total disregard of the public for the person lynched. In this story the black man's offense is never revealed, suggesting that he is considered guilty regardless.

At the end of the story Ellison includes an observation of the boy that might indicate a motivation for lynching that is linked to class and economics: "The other day I was down to Brinkley's store, and a white cropper said it didn't do no good to kill the niggers 'cause things don't get no better. He looked hungry as hell. Most of the croppers look hungry. You'd be surprised how hungry white folks can look. Somebody said that he'd better shut his damn mouth, and he shut up." Poor whites, in particular, believed that lynching would insure white prosperity. This hungry farmer's doubt as to the efficacy of lynching is silenced by his fellow farmers, who as lawbreakers believe that conformity and a code of silence are imperative. Ed shames his nephew's squeamishness in an effort to indoctrinate him into the practice of lynching.

———————— 𝒫ℯ ————————

"A Party Down at the Square"
by Ralph Ellison

I don't know what started it. A bunch of men came by my Uncle Eds place and said there was going to be a party down at the Square, and my uncle hollered for me to come on and I ran with them through the dark and rain and there we were at the Square. When we got there everybody was mad and quiet and standing around looking at the nigger. Some of the men had guns, and one man kept goosing the nigger in his pants with the barrel of a shotgun, saying he ought to pull the trigger, but he never did. It was right in front of the courthouse, and the old clock in the tower was striking twelve. The rain was falling cold and freezing as it fell. Everybody was cold, and the nigger kept wrapping his arms around himself trying to stop the shivers.

Then one of the boys pushed through the circle and snatched off the nigger's shirt, and there he stood, with his black skin all shivering in the light from the fire, and looking at us with a scaired look on his face and putting his hands in his pants pockets Folks started yelling to hurry up and kill the nigger. Somebody yelled: "Take your hands out of your pockets, nigger, we gonna have plenty heat in a minnit." But the nigger didn't hear him and kept his hands where they were.

I tell you the rain was cold. I had to stick my hands in my pockets they got so cold. The fire was pretty small, and they put some logs around the platform they had the nigger on and then threw on some gasoline, and you could see the lames light up the whole Square. It was late and the streetlights had been off for a long time. It was so bright that the bronze statue of the general standing there in the Square was like something alive. The shadows playing on his moldy green face made him seem to be smiling down at the nigger.

They threw on more gas, and it made the Square bright like it gets when the lights are turned on or when the sun is setting red. All the wagons and cars were standing around the curbs. Not like Saturday though – the niggers weren't there. Not a single nigger was there except this Bacote nigger and they dragged him there tied to the back of Jed Wilson's truck. On Saturday there's as many niggers as white folks.

Everybody was yelling crazy 'cause they were about to set fire to the nigger, and I got to the rear of the circle and looked around the Square to try to count the cars. The shadows of the folks was flickering on the trees in the middle of the Square. I saw some birds that the noise had woke up flying through the trees. I guess maybe they thought it was morning. The ice had started the cobblestones in the street to shine where the rain was falling and freezing. I counted forty cars before I lost count. I knew folks must have been there from Phenix City by all the cars mixed in with the wagons.

God, it was a hell of a night. It was some night all right. When the noise died down I heard the nigger's voice from where I stood int eh back, so I pushed my way up front. The nigger was bleeding from his nose and ears, and I could see him all red where the dark blood was running down his black skin. He kept lifting first one foot and then the other, like a chicken on a hot stove. I looked down to the platform they had him on, and they had pushed a ring of fire up close to his feet. It must have been hot to him with the flames almost touching his big black toes. Somebody yelled for the nigger to say his prayers, but the nigger wasn't saying anything now. He just kinda moaned with his eyes shut and kept moving up and down on his feet, first one foot and then the other.

I watched the flames burning the logs up closer and closer to the nigger's feet. They were burning good now, and the rain had stopped and the wind was rising, making the flames flare higher. I looked, and there must have been thirty-five women in the crowd, and I could hear their voices clear and shrill mixed in with those of the men. Then it happened. I heard the noise about the same time everyone else did. It was like the roar of a cyclone blowing up from the gulf, and everyone was looking up into the air to see what it was. Some of the faces looked surprised and scaired, all but the nigger. He didn't even hear the noise He didn't even look up. Then the roar came closer, right above our heads and the wind was blowing higher and higher and the sound seemed to be going in circles.

Then I saw her. Through the clouds and fog I could see a red and green light on her wings. I could see them just for a second: then she rose up into the low clouds. I looked out for the beacon over the tops of the buildings in the direction of the airfield that's forty miles away, and it wasn't circling around. You usually could see it sweeping around the sky at night, but it wasn't there. Then, there she was again, like a big bird lost in the fog. I looked for the red and green lights, and they weren't there anymore. She was flying even closer to the tops of the buildings than before. The wind was blowing harder, and leaves started flying about, making funny shadows on the ground, and tree limbs were cracking and falling.

It was a storm all right. The pilot must have thought he was over the landing field. Maybe he thought the fire in the Square was put there for him to land by. Gosh, but it scaired the folks. I was scaired too. They started yelling: "He's going to land. He's going to land." And: "He's going to fall." A few started for their cars and wagons. I could hear the wagons creaking and chains jangling and cars spitting and missing as they started the engines up. Off to my right, a horse started pitching and striking his hooves against a car.

I didn't know what to do. I wanted to run, and I wanted to stay and see what was going to happen. The plane was close as hell. The pilot must have been trying to see where he was at, and her motors were drowning out all the sounds. I could even feel the vibration, and my hair felt like it was standing up under my hat. I happened to look over at the statue of the general standing with one leg before the other and leaning back on a sword, and I was fixing to run over and climb between his legs and sit there and watch when the roar stopped some, and I looked up and she was gliding just over the top of the trees in the middle of the Square.

Her motors stopped altogether and I could hear the sound of branches cracking and snapping off below her landing gear. I could see her plain now, all silver and shining in the light of the fire with TWA in black letters under her wings. She was sailing smoothly out of the Square when she hit the high power lines that follow the Birmingham highway through the town. It made a loud crash. It sounded like the wind blowing the door of a tin barn shut. She only hit with her landing gear, but I could see the sparks flying, and the wires knocked loose from the poles were spitting blue sparks and whipping around like a bunch of snakes and leaving circles of blue sparks in the darkness.

The plane had knocked five or six wires loose, and they were dangling and swinging, and every time they touched they threw off more sparks. The wind was making them swing, and when I got over there, there was a crackling and spitting screen of blue haze across the highway. I lost my hat running over, but I didn't stop to look for it. I was among the first and I could hear the others pounding behind me across the grass of the Square. They were yelling to beat all hell, and they came up fast, pushing and shoving, and someone got pushed against a swinging wire. It made a sound like when a blacksmith drops a red hot horseshoe into a barrel of water, and the steam comes up. I could smell th flesh burning. The first time I'd ever smelled it. I got up close and it was a woman. It must have killed her right off. She was lying in a puddle stiff as a board, with pieces of glass insulators that the plane had knocked off the poles lying all around her. Her white dress was torn, and I saw one of her tits hanging out in the water and her thighs. Some woman screamed and fainted and almost fell on a wire, but a man caught her. The sheriff and his men were yelling and driving folks back with guns shining in their hands, and everything was lit up blue by the sparks. The shock had turned the woman almost as black as the nigger. I was trying to see if she wasn't blue too, or if it was just the sparks, and the sheriff drove me away. As I backed off trying to see, I heard the motors of the plane start up again somewhere off to the right in the clouds.

The clouds were moving fast in the wind and the wind was blowing the smell of something burning over to me. I turned around, and the crowd was headed back to the nigger. I could see him standing there in the middle of the flames. The wind was making the flames brighter every minute. The crowd was running. I ran too. I ran back across the grass with the crowd. It wasn't so large now that so many had gone when the plane came. I tripped and fell over the limb of a tree lying in the grass and bit my lip. It ain't well yet I bit it so bad. I could taste the blood in my mouth as I ran over. I guess that's what made me sick. When I got there, the fire had caught the nigger's pants, and the folks were standing around watching, but not too close on account of the wind blowing the flames. Somebody hollered, "Well, nigger, it ain't so cold now." And the nigger looked up with his great white eyes looking like they was 'bout to pop out of his head, and I had enough. I didn't want to see anymore. I wanted to run somewhere and puke, but I stayed. I stayed right there in the front of the crowd and looked.

The nigger tried to say something I couldn't hear for the roar of the wind in the fire, and I strained my ears. Jed Wilson hollered, "What you say there, nigger?" And it came back through the flames in his nigger voice: "Will somebody please cut my throat like a Christian?" And Jed hollered back, "Sorry, but ain't no Christians around tonight. Ain't no Jew-boys neither. We're just one hundred percent Americans."

Then the nigger was silent. Folks started laughing at Jed. Jed's right popular with the folks, and next year, my uncle says, they plan to run him for sheriff. The heat was too much for me, and the smoke was making my eyes to smart. I was trying to back away when Jed reached down and brought up a can of gasoline and threw it in the fire on the nigger. I could see the flames catching the gas in a puff as it went in in a silver sheet and some of it reached the nigger, making spurts of blue fire all over his chest.

Well, that nigger was tough. I have to give it to that nigger; he was really tough. He had started to burn like a house afire and was making the smoke smell like burning hides. The fire was up around his head, and the smoke was so thick and black we couldn't see him. And him not moving – we thought he was dead. Then he started out. The fire had burned the ropes they had tied him with, and he started jumping and kicking about like he was blind, and you could smell his skin burning. He kicked so hard that the platform, which was burning too, fell in, and he rolled out of the fire at my feet. I jumped back so he wouldn't get on me, I'll never forget it. Every time I eat barbeque I'll remember that never forget it. Every time I eat barbeque I'll remember that nigger. His back was just like a barbecued hog. I could see the prints of his ribs where they start around from his backbone and curve down and around. It was a sight to see, that nigger's back. He was right at my feet, and somebody behind pushed me and almost made me step on him, and he was still burning.

I didn't step on him though, and Jed and somebody else pushed him back into the burning planks and logs and poured on more gas. I wanted to leave, but the folks were yelling and I couldn't move except to look around and see the statue. A branch the wind had broken was resting on his hat. I tried to push out and get away because my guts were gone, and all I got was spit and hot breath in my face from the woman and two men standing directly behind me. So I had to turn back around. The nigger rolled out of the fire again. He wouldn't stay put. It was on the other side this time. I couldn't see him very well through the flames and smoke. They got some tree limbs and held him there this time and he stayed there till he was ashes. I guess he stayed there. I know he burned to ashes because I saw Jed a week later, and he laughed and showed me some white finger bones still held together with little pieces of the nigger's skin. Anyway, I left when somebody moved around to see the nigger. I pushed my way through the crowd, and a woman in the rear scratched my face as she yelled and fought to get up close.

I ran across the Square to the other side, where the sheriff and his deputies were guarding the wires that were still spitting and making a blue fog. My heart was pounding like I had been running a long ways, and I bent over and let my insides go. Everything came up and spilled in a big gush over the ground. I was sick, and tired, and weak, and cold. The wind was still high, and large drops of rain were beginning to fall. I headed down the street to my uncle's place past a store where the wind had broken a window, and glass lay over the sidewalk. I kicked it as I went by. I remember somebody's fool rooster crowing like it was morning in all that wind.

The next day I was too weak to go out, and my uncle kidded me and called me "the gutless wonder from Cincinnati." I didn't mind. He said you get used to it in time. He couldn't go out hisself. There was too much wind and rain. I got up and looked out of the window, and the rain was pouring down and dead sparrows and limbs of trees were scattered all over the yard. There had been a cyclone all right. It swept a path right through the county, and we were lucky we didn't get the full force of it.

It blew for three days steady, and put the town in a hell of a shape. The wind blew sparks and set fire to the white-and-green-rimmed house on Jackson Avenue that had the big concrete lions in the yard and burned it down to the ground. They had to kill another nigger who tried to run out of the county after they burned this Bacote nigger. My Uncle Ed said they always have to kill niggers in pairs to keep the other niggers in place. I don't know though, the folks seem a little skittish of the niggers. They all came back, but they act pretty sullen. They look mean as hell when you pass them down at the store. The other day I was down to Brinkley's store, and a white cropper said it didn't do no good to kill the niggers 'cause things don't get no better. He looked hungry as hell. Most of the croppers look hungry. You'd be surprised how hungry white folks can look. Somebody said that he'd better shut his damn mouth, and he shut up. But from the look on his face he won't stay shut long. He went out of the store muttering to himself and spit a big chew of tobacco right down on Brinkley's floor. Brinkley said he was sore 'cause he wouldn't let him have credit. Anyway, it didn't seem to help things. First it was the nigger and the storm, then the plane, then the woman and the wire, and now I hear the airplane line is investigating to find who set the fire that almost wrecked their plane. All that in one night, and all of it but the storm over one nigger. It was some night all right. It was some party too. I was right there, see. I was right there watching it all. It was my first party and my last. God, but that nigger was tough. That Bacote nigger was some nigger!

Critical Thinking

Why do you think the black man's name in this story is never mentioned? What is the reason for the repeated use of the word "nigger" in the story?

The story is told in the first person by a young white boy from Ohio visiting his uncle Ed. How does this boy's perspective influence the readers' understanding of the story?

Why does the boy get sick and what does this represent?

Make a comparison between the boy's and the townspeople's perceptions of the black man and the "party" at the square from the beginning till the end of the story. Can you identify any change in their perceptions? What would this comparison tell you?

Note the different reaction of the townspeople to the charred white woman from the plane crash relative to their reaction to the black man's burning. When the black man asks for his Christian attackers to mercifully kill him quickly, rather than burn him, Jeb yells, "'Sorry, but ain't no Christians around tonight. Ain't no Jew-boys neither. We're just one hundred percent Americans.'" What is Jeb implying about the meaning of being American in terms of justice and mercy?

During this era, lynching was a means of intimidation and fear, a way for mob action to keep blacks weak, socially, politically, and economically. However, the story includes mention of fear on the part of whites as well: "My Uncle Ed said they always have to kill niggers in pairs to keep the other niggers in place. I don't know though, the folks seem a little skittish of the niggers." What is their fear? Can you think of any examples today where people are viewed as scapegoats because of fear of loss of jobs or change in social status quo?

How would you describe the young boy's attitude toward the unlawful action he observed and toward the victim?

Can you predict the boy's future actions regarding breaking the law?

Do hate crimes that are currently perpetrated resemble this mob action in any way?

"The Lynching of Jube Benson"
by Paul Dunbar

Paul Dunbar (1872–1906) was an African American poet, novelist, short story writer, and playwright who was born in Dayton, Ohio, to parents who were slaves in Kentucky before Emancipation.

The short story "The Lynching of Jube Benson" (1904) is set in the post-emancipation South and focuses on the mob violence of a lynching. Vigilantism was not uncommon in the South after the Civil War, often taking the form of lynching black men for the perceived crime of even looking inappropriately at white women. These killings were fueled by whites' fear of miscegenation (mixing of the black and white races). The participants perceived themselves as police, judge, and jury. Dunbar's story is almost entirely a monologue of Dr. Melville, a middle-aged white man who explains to two other men, one a reporter, his part in the lynching seven years prior of his former black friend, Jube. Notice how Melville's description of Jube changes as he approaches the act of murder. What do you think is the effect of the use of black dialect, for which Dunbar is noted? At one point Melville talks about his "false education" and its effect on his choices.

———————— ℘ ————————

"The Lynching of Jube Benson"
by Paul Laurence Dunbar

Gordon Fairfax's library held but three men, but the air was dense with clouds of smoke. The talk had drifted from one topic to another much as the smoke wreaths had puffed, floated, and thinned away. Then Handon Gay, who was an ambitious young reporter, spoke of a lynching story in a recent magazine, and the matter of punishment without trial put new life into the conversation.

"I should like to see a real lynching," said Gay rather callously.

"Well, I should hardly express it that way," said Fairfax, "but if a real, live lynching were to come my way, I should not avoid it."

"I should," spoke the other from the depths of his chair, where he had been puffing in moody silence. Judged by his hair, which was freely sprinkled with gray, the speaker might have been

Source: Paul Laurence Dunbar, "The Lynching of Jube Benson," from *The Heart of Happy Hollow*, 1904.

a man of forty–five or fifty, but his face, though lined and serious, was youthful, the face of a man hardly past thirty.

"What! you, Dr. Melville? Why, I thought that you physicians wouldn't weaken at anything."

"I have seen one such affair," said the doctor gravely, "in fact, I took a prominent part in it."

"Tell us about it," said the reporter, feeling for his pencil and note-book, which he was, nevertheless, careful to hide from the speaker.

The men drew their chairs eagerly up to the doctor's, but for a minute he did not seem to see them, but sat gazing abstractedly into the fire, then he took a long draw upon his cigar and began:

"I can see it all very vividly now. It was in the summertime and about seven years ago. I was practising at the time down in the little town of Bradford. It was a small and primitive place, just the location for an impecunious medical man, recently out of college.

"In lieu of a regular office, I attended to business in the first of two rooms which I rented from Hiram Daly, one of the more prosperous of the townsmen. Here I boarded and here also came my patients—white and black—whites from every section, and blacks from 'nigger town,' as the west portion of the place was called.

"The people about me were most of them coarse and rough, but they were simple and generous, and as time passed on I had about abandoned my intention of seeking distinction in wider fields and determined to settle into the place of a modest country doctor. This was rather a strange conclusion for a young man to arrive at, and I will not deny that the presence in the house of my host's beautiful young daughter, Annie, had something to do with my decision. She was a beautiful young girl of seventeen or eighteen, and very far superior to her surroundings. She had a native grace and a pleasing way about her that made everybody that came under her spell her abject slave. White and black who knew her loved her, and none, I thought, more deeply and respectfully than Jube Benson, the black man of all work about the place.

"He was a fellow whom everybody trusted; an apparently steadygoing, grinning sort, as we used to call him. Well, he was completely under Miss Annie's thumb and would fetch and carry for her like a faithful dog. As soon as he saw that I began to care for Annie, and anybody could see that, he transferred some of his allegiance to me and became my faithful servitor also. Never did a man have a more devoted adherent in his wooing than did I, and many a one of Annie's tasks which he volunteered to do gave her an extra hour with me. You can imagine that I liked the boy, and you need not wonder any more that as both wooing and my practice waxed apace, I was content to give up my great ambitions and stay just where I was.

"It wasn't a very pleasant thing, then, to have an epidemic of typhoid break out in the town that kept me going so that I hardly had time for the courting that a fellow wants to carry on with his sweetheart while he is still young enough to call her his girl. I fumed, but duty was duty, and I kept to my work night and day. It was now that Jube proved how invaluable he was as coadjutor. He not only took messages to Annie, but brought sometimes little ones from her to me, and he would tell me little secret things that he had overheard her say that made me throb with joy and swear at him for repeating his mistress's conversation. But, best of all, Jube was a perfect Cerberus, and no one on earth could have been more effective in keeping away or deluding the other young fellows who visited the Dalys. He would tell me of it afterwards, chuckling softly to himself. 'An,' Doctah, I say to Mistah Hemp Stevens, "'Scuse us, Mistah Stevens, but Miss Annie, she des' gone out," an' den he go outer de gate lookin' moughty lonesome. When Sam

Elkins come, I say, "Sh, Mistah Elkins, Miss Annie, she done tuk down," an' he say, "What, Jube, you don' reckon hit de—" Den he stop an' look skeert, an' I say, "I feared hit is, Mistah Elkins," an' sheks my haid ez solemn. He goes outer de gate lookin' lak his bes' frien' done daid, an' all de time Miss Annie behine de cu'tain ovah de po'ch des' a-laffin' fit to kill.'

"Jube was a most admirable liar, but what could I do? He knew that I was a young fool of a hypocrite, and when I would rebuke him for these deceptions, he would give way and roll on the floor in an excess of delighted laughter until from very contagion I had to join him—and, well, there was no need of my preaching when there had been no beginning to his repentance and when there must ensure a continuance of his wrong-doing.

"This thing went on for over three months, and then, pouf! I was down like a shot. My patients were nearly all up, but the reaction from overwork made me an easy victim of the lurking germs. Then Jube loomed up as a nurse. He put everyone else aside, and with the doctor, a friend of mine from a neighboring town, took entire charge of me. Even Annie herself was put aside, and I was cared for as tenderly as a baby. Tom, that was my physician and friend, told me all about it afterward with tears in his eyes. Only he was a big, blunt man, and his expressions did not convey all that he meant. He told me how my nigger had nursed me as if I were a sick kitten and he my mother. Of how fiercely he guarded his right to be the sole one to 'do' for me, as he called it, and how, when the crisis came, he hovered, weeping but hopeful, at my beside until it was safely passed, when they drove him, weak and exhausted, from the room. As for me, I knew little about it at the time, and cared less. I was too busy in my fight with death. To my chimerical vision there was only a black but gentle demon that came and went, alternating with a white fairy, who would insist on coming in on her head, growing larger and larger and then dissolving. But the pathos and devotion in the story lost nothing in my blunt friend's telling.

"It was during the period of a long convalescence, however, that I came to know my humble ally as he really was, devoted to the point of abjectness. There were times when, for very shame at his goodness to me, I would beg him to go away, to do something else. He would go, but before I had time to realize that I was not being ministered to, he would be back at my side, grinning and pottering just the same. He manufactured duties for the joy of performing them. He pretended to see desires in me that I never had, because he liked to pander to them, and when I became entirely exasperated and ripped out a good round oath, he chuckled with the remark, "Dah, now, you sholy is gittin' well. Nevah did hyeah a man anywhaih nigh Jo'dan's sho' cuss lak dat.'

"Why, I grew to love, him, love him, oh, yes, I loved him as well—oh, what am I saying? All human love and gratitude are damned poor things; excuse me, gentlemen, this isn't a pleasant story. The truth is usually a nasty thing to stand.

"It was not six months after that that my friendship to Jube, which he had been at such great pains to win, was put to too severe a test.

"It was in the summertime again, and, as business was slack, I had ridden over to see my friend, Dr. Tom. I had spent a good part of the day there, and it was past four o'clock when I rode leisurely into Bradford. I was in a particularly joyous mood and no premonition of the impending catastrophe oppressed me. No sense of sorrow, present or to come, forced itself upon me, even when I saw men hurrying through the almost deserted streets. When I got within sight of my home and saw a crowd surrounding it, I was only interested sufficiently to spur my horse into a jog trot, which brought me up to the throng, when something in the sullen, settled horror in the mens' faces gave a sudden, sick thrill. They whispered a word to me, and without a thought, save for Annie, the girl who had been so surely growing into my heart, I leaped from the saddle and tore my way through the people to the house.

"It was Annie, poor girl, bruised and bleeding, her face and dress torn from struggling. They were gathered round her with whites faces, and oh, with what terrible patience they were trying to gain from her fluttering lips the name of her murderer. They made way for me and I knelt at her side. She was beyond my skill, and my will merged with theirs. One thought was in our minds.

"'Who?' I asked.

"Her eyes half opened. 'That black—' She fell back into my arms dead.

"We turned and looked at each other. The mother had broken down and was weeping, but the face of the father was like iron.

"'It is enough,' he said; 'Jube has disappeared.' He went to the door and said to the expectant crowd, 'She is dead.'

"I heard the angry roar without swelling up like the noise of a flood, and then I heard the sudden movement of many feet as the men separated into searching parties, and laying the dead girl back upon her couch, I took my rifle and went out to join them.

"As if by intuition the knowledge had passed among the men that Jube Benson had disappeared, and he, by common consent, was to be the object of our search. Fully a dozen of the citizens had seen him hasten in toward the woods and noted his skulking air, but as he had grinned in his old good-natured way they had, at the time, thought nothing of it. Now, however, the diabolical reason of his slyness was apparent. He had been shrewd enough to disarm suspicion, and by now was far away. Even Mrs. Daly, who was visiting with a neighbor, had seen him stepping out by a back way, and had said with a laugh, 'I reckon that black rascal's arunning off somewhere.' Oh, if she had only known!

"'To the woods! To the woods!' that was the cry, and away we went, each with the determination not to shoot, but to bring the culprit alive into town, and then to deal with him as his crime deserved.

"I cannot describe the feelings I experienced as I went out that night to beat the woods for this human tiger. My heart smoldered within me like a coal, and I went forward under the impulse of a will that was half my own, half some more malignant power's. My throat throbbed drily, but water nor whisky would not have quenched my thirst. The thought has come to me since that now I could interpret the panther's desire for blood and sympathize with it, but then I thought nothing. I simply went forward, add watched, watched with burning eyes for a familiar form that I had looked for as often before with such different emotions.

"Luck or ill-luck, which you will, was with our party, and just as dawn was graying the sky, we came upon our quarry crouched in the corner of a fence. It was only half light, and we might have passed, but my eyes had caught sight of him, and I raised the cry. We levelled our guns and he rose and came toward us.

"'I tought you wa'n't gwine see me,' he said sullenly, 'I didn't mean no harm.'

"'Harm!'

"Some of the men took the word up with oaths, others were ominously silent.

"We gathered around him like hungry beasts, and I began to see terror dawning in his eyes. He turned to me, 'I's moughty glad you's heah, Doc,' he said, 'you ain't gwine let 'em whup me.'

"'Whip you, you hound,' I said, 'I'm going to see you hanged,' and in the excess of my passion I struck him full on the mouth. He made a motion as if to resent the blow against even such great odds, but controlled himself.

"'W'y, Doctah,' he exclaimed in the saddest voice I have ever heard, 'w'y, Doctah! I ain't stole nuffin' o' yo'n, an' I was comin' back. I only run off to see my gal, Lucy, ovah to de Centah.'

"'You lie!' I said, and my hands were busy helping others bind him upon a horse. Why did I do it? I don't know. A false education, I reckon, one false from the beginning. I saw his black face glooming there in the half light, and I could only think of him as a monster. It's tradition. At first I was told that the black man would catch me, and when I got over that, they taught me that the devil was black, and when I had recovered from the sickness of that belief, here were Jube and his fellows with faces of menacing blackness. There was only one conclusion: This black man stood for all the powers of evil, the result of whose machinations had been gathering in my mind from childhood up. But this has nothing to do with what happened.

"After firing a few shots to announce our capture, we rode back into town with Jube. The ingathering parties from all directions met us as we made our way up to the house. All was very quiet and orderly. There was no doubt that it was, as the papers would have said, a gathering of the best citizens. It was a gathering of stern, determined men, bent on a terrible vengeance.

"We took Jube into the house, into the room where the corpse lay. At the sight of it he gave a scream like an animal's and his face went the color of storm-blown water. This was enough to condemn him. We divined rather than heard his cry of 'Miss Ann, Miss Ann, oh, my God, doc, you don't t'ink I done it?'

"Hungry hands were ready. We hurried him out into the yard. A rope was ready. A tree was at hand. Well, that part was the least of it, save that Hiram Daly stepped aside to let me be the first to pull upon the rope. It was lax at first. Then it tightened, and I felt the quivering soft weight resist my muscles. Other hands joined, and Jube swung off his feet.

"No one was masked. We knew each other. Not even the culprit's face was covered, and the last I remember of him as he went into the air was a look of sad reproach that will remain with me until I meet him face to face again.

"We were tying the end of the rope to a tree, where the dead man might hang as a warning to his fellows, when a terrible cry chilled us to the marrow.

"'Cut 'im down, cut 'im down, he ain't guilty. We got de one. Cut him down, fu' Gawd's sake. Here's de man, we foun' him hidin' in de barn!'

"Jube's brother, Ben, and another Negro came rushing toward us, half dragging, half carrying a miserable-looking wretch between them. Someone cut the rope and Jube dropped lifeless to the ground.

"'Oh, my Gawd, he's daid, he's daid!' wailed the brother, but with blazing eyes he brought his captive into the center of the group, and we saw in the full light the scratched face of Tom Skinner—the worst white ruffian in town—but the face we saw was not as we were accustomed to see it, merely smeared with dirt. It was blackened to imitate a Negro's.

"God forgive me; I could not wait to try to resuscitate Jube. I knew he was already past help, so I rushed into the house and to the dead girl's side. In the excitement they had not yet washed or laid her out. Carefully, carefully, I searched underneath her broken fingernails. There was skin there. I took it out, the little curled pieces, and went with it to my office.

"There, determinedly, I examined it under a powerful glass, and read my own doom. It was the skin of a white man, and in it were embedded strands of short, brown hair or beard.

"How I went out to tell the waiting crowd I do not know, for something kept crying in my ears, 'Blood guilty! Blood guilty!'

"The men went away stricken into silence and awe. The new prisoner attempted neither denial nor plea. When they were gone, I would have helped Ben carry his brother in, but he waved me away fiercely. 'You he'ped murder my brothah, you dat was *his* frien', go 'way, go 'way! I'll tek him home myse'f.' I could only respect his wish, and he and his comrade took up the dead man and between them bore him up the street on which the sun was now shining full.

"I saw the few men who had not skulked indoors uncovered as they passed, and I—I—stood there between the two murdered ones, while all the while something in my ears kept crying, 'Blood guilty! Blood guilty!'"

The doctor's head dropped into his hands and he sat for some time in silence, which was broken by neither of the men, then he rose, saying, "Gentlemen, that was my last lynching."

Critical Thinking

How do you think Dr. Melville's background contributed to his actions?

Why does the doctor become the first to act as judge and jury concerning Jude? What was the evidence convicting Jube?

Notice the difference in the mob's treatment of Jube and of the real killer. What accounts for that?

What was the evidence convicting Tom Skinner?

Why did Skinner wear black face when committing the crime? What does that say about the community's attitude toward blacks? Is this racism applicable to today?

The response of newspapers is alluded to in the story, both by the fascination of Melville's reporter friend and by Melville's stating concerning the mob: "There was no doubt that it was, as the papers would have said, a gathering of the best citizens." What is the practice of today's media—particularly broadcast media—in reporting on crimes when race is a factor?

Can you think of examples where individuals are racially profiled by the media in their coverage? What responsibility does the media have in reporting crime?

"Bronzeville Mother Loiters in Mississippi. Meanwhile, a Mississippi Mother Burns Bacon" and "The Last Quatrain of the Ballad of Emmett Till"

by Gwendolyn Brooks

NOTE: Neither poem is included in this anthology but they may be found on the Internet at educational sites such as poemhunter.com and allpoetry.com or at your university or college library.

Gwendolyn Brooks (1917–2000) was born in Topeka, Kansas, but spent most of her childhood and all of her adult life in Chicago, Illinois. She published her first poem when she was only thirteen years old and ultimately authored more than twenty books of poetry. She was the first African American author to win the Pulitzer Prize. She also was poet laureate of the State of Illinois and the first black woman to hold the position of poetry consultant to the Library of Congress. Much of Brooks' writing was politically motivated. Such was the case with her only novel, *Maud Martha* (1950), which focuses on the life of an urban black woman.

The poem "Bronzeville Mother Loiters in Mississippi. Meanwhile, a Mississippi Mother Burns Bacon" (1960) was occasioned by a racially-motivated murder of a black child in Mississippi in 1955. When Chicago-born Emmett Till was lynched in Money, Mississippi, he was fourteen, the same age as Brooks' son at the time. Till had traveled by train from Chicago to spend the summer with his uncle and cousins (his mother was raised in Mississippi but had moved to Chicago years before, and Till's father was killed in Europe during WWII). When visiting a country store with his cousins, Till allegedly whistled at Carolyn Bryant, the white woman working there. In the 1950s South, black males, even ones as young as Till, were considered dangerously sexual, a threat to white woman. The fear of misogyny, or mixing of the races, prevailed as well. Southern womanhood was considered sacred and in need of vigilant defense by white males. To make sure that blacks knew their place, vigilante justice, in the form of lynching and torture, was carried out routinely. A few days after the interaction between Till and Bryant, Bryant's husband, Roy Bryant, and his half-brother, J. W. Milam, kidnapped Till from his bed, tortured and murdered him and threw his body in a nearby river. Two months later, September 1955, in a sweltering hot courtroom, the men were tried by an all-white male jury, who, after deliberating only an hour, acquitted the two men. Four months later, Bryant and Milam, protected against double jeopardy, accepted payment from *Look* magazine to disclose how they murdered Emmett Till.

Shaken by the Till murder, Brooks wrote "Bronzeville Mother..." in which she as a black woman reveals a unique perspective. Though the poem is in the third person, the perspective is clearly that of a white woman in Carolyn Bryant's particular circumstances. The title refers not only to the unnamed Carolyn but to the unnamed Mamie Till, Emmett Till's mother, who came from Bronzeville, a section of Chicago, to claim her son's body and attend the trial of his murderers. In the poem, the white woman cooking breakfast for her husband and two sons is burning the bacon because she is ruminating about the murder which she set into motion and for which her husband has recently been acquitted. At first enraptured by the fairy-tale rescue from the "Dark Villain," she starts to wonder if in her husband's eyes she was worth this murder, this perversion of the law and justice system. She also begins to humanize the victim, whom she recognizes as too young to be villainous. When her husband enters the kitchen, she appears afraid of him, as he angrily mutters about the northern newspaper's coverage of the trial that portrayed him as a beast. He remains defiant and then violently slaps his young son across the face for throwing molasses at this brother. The woman imagines blood pouring from her son's cheek and threatening to spread to the world. The peril of her own children, and her inability to protect them, forces her to identify with the young black boy's mother, Mamie Till. When her husband pulls her close and kisses her roughly, she is sickened, and her mind flashes back to the courtroom and the look in the other mother's eyes. The poem ends with the white woman's romantic ballad being replaced by hatred for the man who murdered in her name.

Similar to the short stories "The Lynching of Jude Benson" by Paul Dunbar and "A Party Down at the Square," by Ralph Ellison, Brooks' "Bronzeville Mother" poem humanizes a fictional lynching victim and provides a fictional white person's perspective of vigilante justice and its effect upon that person.

Critical Thinking

Do you think Brooks' representation of this white woman is a sympathetic one? Why or why not?

How does the woman's perspective of her husband change and why?

The unique element to Brooks' poem, in comparison to Dunbar's and Ellison's stories, is that it is based on an actual lynching and its actual perpetrators. Does that heighten the effect of the poem on its readers?

Also, unlike the earlier stories, Brooks' poem depicts a lynching that goes to trial, though the murderers were acquitted. Do some research about the extent of the media coverage of the Till murder to see why this particular case went to trial while others occurring in the same time period did not.

The poem "The Last Quatrain of the Ballad of Emmett Till," (1960) is Brooks' companion piece to "Bronzeville Mother Loiters in Mississippi. Meanwhile, a Mississippi Mother Burns Bacon." While "Bronzeville Mother …" focuses on the unnamed white Carolyn Bryant, "The Last Quatrain of the Ballad of Emmett Till" (1960) names the black lynching victim in the title and refers to his mother in the poem's third line. Though this latter poem's first two lines identify the setting as after the murder and the burial, the description is of Emmett Till's pretty mother kissing her dead son as if this is an action that she repeats over and over again in her mind. This could be a reference to Mamie Till's brave insistence on the open casket of the disfigured body of her son. Hundreds of mourners filed past the casket to pay their respects in Chicago.

Local and State-Level Policing: Homelessness

"The Death of the Hired Man"
by Robert Frost

Robert Frost (1874–1963) was a modern American poet who was familiar with New England farm life and often used it as the setting for his poetry. Frost won the Pulitzer Prize for poetry four times.

"The Death of the Hired Man" (1914) is a poem detailing one evening's conversation between Warren and Mary, a farmer and his wife, about Silas, an aged hired hand. The couple debate over their responsibility to Silas, who is homeless and has returned to them after an absence. Warren cites Silas's unreliability and wants to fire him, but Mary compassionately notes the farmhand's loneliness and his desire to please and make a positive difference.

"The Death of the Hired Man"
by Robert Frost

Mary sat musing on the lamp-flame at the table
Waiting for Warren. When she heard his step,
She ran on tip-toe down the darkened passage
To meet him in the doorway with the news
And put him on his guard. "Silas is back."
She pushed him outward with her through the door
And shut it after her. "Be kind," she said.
She took the market things from Warren's arms
And set them on the porch, then drew him down
To sit beside her on the wooden steps.

"When was I ever anything but kind to him?
But I'll not have the fellow back," he said.
"I told him so last haying, didn't I?

Source: Robert Frost, "The Death of the Hired Man," 1915.

'If he left then,' I said, 'that ended it.'
What good is he? Who else will harbour him
At his age for the little he can do?
What help he is there's no depending on.
Off he goes always when I need him most.
'He thinks he ought to earn a little pay,
Enough at least to buy tobacco with,
So he won't have to beg and be beholden.'
'All right,' I say, 'I can't afford to pay
Any fixed wages, though I wish I could.'
'Someone else can.' 'Then someone else will have to.'
I shouldn't mind his bettering himself
If that was what it was. You can be certain,
When he begins like that, there's someone at him
Trying to coax him off with pocket-money,—
In haying time, when any help is scarce.
In winter he comes back to us. I'm done."

"Sh! not so loud: he'll hear you," Mary said.

"I want him to: he'll have to soon or late."
"He's worn out. He's asleep beside the stove.
When I came up from Rowe's I found him here,
Huddled against the barn-door fast asleep,
A miserable sight, and frightening, too—
You needn't smile—I didn't recognize him—
I wasn't looking for him—and he's changed.
Wait till you see."

"Where did you say he'd been?"

"He didn't say. I dragged him to the house,
And gave him tea and tried to make him smoke.
I tried to make him talk about his travels
Nothing would do: he just kept nodding off."

"What did he say? Did he say anything?"

"But little."

"Anything? Mary, confess
He said he'd come to ditch the meadow for me."

"Warren!"

"But did he? I just want to know."

"Of course he did. What would you have him say?
Surely you wouldn't grudge the poor old man
Some humble way to save his self-respect.
He added, if you really care to know,
He meant to clear the upper pasture, too.
That sounds like something you have heard before?
Warren, I wish you could have heard the way
He jumbled everything. I stopped to look
Two or three times—he made me feel so queer—

To see if he was talking in his sleep.
He ran on Harold Wilson—you remember—
The boy you had in haying four years since.
He's finished school, and teaching in his college.
Silas declares you'll have to get him back.
He says they two will make a team for work:
Between them they will lay this farm as smooth!
The way he mixed that in with other things.
He thinks young Wilson a likely lad, though daft
On education—you know how they fought
All through July under the blazing sun,
Silas up on the cart to build the load,
Harold along beside to pitch it on."

"Yes, I took care to keep well out of earshot."

"Well, those days trouble Silas like a dream.
You wouldn't think they would. How some things linger!
Harold's young college boy's assurance piqued him.
After so many years he still keeps finding
Good arguments he sees he might have used.
I sympathise. I know just how it feels
To think of the right thing to say too late.
Harold's associated in his mind with Latin.
He asked me what I thought of Harold's saying
He studied Latin like the violin
Because he liked it—that an argument!
He said he couldn't make the boy believe

He could find water with a hazel prong—
Which showed how much good school had ever done him.
He wanted to go over that. But most of all
He thinks if he could have another chance
To teach him how to build a load of hay—"

"I know, that's Silas' one accomplishment.
He bundles every forkful in its place,
And tags and numbers it for future reference,
So he can find and easily dislodge it
In the unloading. Silas does that well.
He takes it out in bunches like big birds' nests.
You never see him standing on the hay
He's trying to lift, straining to lift himself."

"He thinks if he could teach him that, he'd be
Some good perhaps to someone in the world.
He hates to see a boy the fool of books.
Poor Silas, so concerned for other folk,
And nothing to look backward to with pride,
And nothing to look forward to with hope,
So now and never any different."
Part of a moon was falling down the west,
Dragging the whole sky with it to the hills.
Its light poured softly in her lap. She saw it
And spread her apron to it. She put out her hand
Among the harp-like morning-glory strings,
Taut with the dew from garden bed to eaves,
As if she played unheard some tenderness
That wrought on him beside her in the night.
"Warren," she said, he has come home to die:
You needn't be afraid he'll leave you this time."

"Home," he mocked gently.

"Yes, what else but home?
It all depends on what you mean by home.
Of course he's nothing to us, any more
Than was the hound that came a stranger to us
Out of the woods, worn out upon the trail."

"Home is the place where, when you have to go there,
They have to take you in."

"I should have called it
Something you somehow haven't to deserve."

Warren leaned out and took a step or two,
Picked up a little stick, and brought it back
And broke it in his hand and tossed it by.
"Silas has better claim on us you think
Than on his brother? Thirteen little miles
As the road winds would bring him to his door.
Silas has walked that far no doubt to-day.
Why didn't he go there? His brother's rich.
A somebody—director in the bank."

"He never told us that."

"We know it though."

"I think his brother ought to help, of course.
I'll see to that if there is need. He ought of right
To take him in, and might be willing to—
He may be better than appearances.
But have some pity on Silas. Do you think
If he had any pride in claiming kin
Or anything he looked for from his brother,
He'd keep so still about him all this time?"
"I wonder what's between them."

"I can tell you.
Silas is what he is—we wouldn't mind him—
But just the kind that kinsfolk can't abide.
He never did a thing so very bad.
He don't know why he isn't quite as good
As anybody. Worthless though he is,
He won't be made ashamed to please his brother."

"*I* can't think Si ever hurt anyone."
"No, but he hurt my heart the way he lay.
And rolled his old head on that sharp-edged chair-back.
He wouldn't let me put him on the lounge.
You must go in and see what you can do.
I made the bed up for him there to-night.
You'll be surprised at him—how much he's broken.
His working days are done; I'm sure of it."

"I'd not be in a hurry to say that."

"I haven't been. Go, look, see for yourself.
But, Warren, please remember how it is:
He's come to help you ditch the meadow.
He has a plan. You mustn't laugh at him.
He may not speak of it, and then he may.
I'll sit and see if that small sailing cloud
Will hit or miss the moon."

It hit the moon.
Then there were three there, making a dim row,
The moon, the little silver cloud, and she.

Warren returned—too soon, it seemed to her,
Slipped to her side, caught up her hand and waited.

"Warren?" she questioned.

"Dead," was all he answered.

Critical Thinking

What keeps Silas from going to his wealthy brother, who lives nearby, to ask for help as his health declines?

How might Silas's attitude toward family be relevant to some who are homeless today?

Highlighted in this poem are the themes of justice and mercy and how they may conflict, issues which police officers no doubt frequently encounter when making decisions about homeless individuals. What is law enforcement's responsibility to the community and to the homeless population?

Do these responsibilities sometimes conflict with each other?

Local and State-Level Policing: LGBT Profiling

"Café: 3 AM" (1951)

by Langston Hughes

Langston Hughes (1902–1967) was a prominent African American poet and social activist (among other roles) in the United States, most famous for his leadership of the Harlem Renaissance. Much of his poetry addresses contemporary social and political issues facing black people during the first two-thirds of the twentieth century, including double-consciousness, racism, violence (physical and mental), and surveillance. The following poems, written later in Hughes' career, address the policing of black bodies and paint a distinctively negative portrait of law enforcement.

"Café: 3 AM" (1951) is a short poem about police surveillance of lesbian, gay, bisexual, and transgender (LGBT) people. In the first verse, the speaker notes the tired and cruel looks coming from the vice squad, who view the café's patrons in homophobic terms. However, the speaker poses what is now an accepted viewpoint, that homosexuality is not a choice, but rather natural or God-given. The speaker imagines some members of the vice squad must also be lesbian or gay. (Consider that this poem was published long before the Stonewall riots of 1969.) As you read this poem, think about how police officers' implicit biases against difference (whether sexual, ethnic, racial) affect their responses to the population they are required to protect.

"Cafe: 3 AM"

by Langston Hughes

Detectives from the vice squad
with weary sadistic eyes
spotting fairies.
Degenerates,
some folks say.

But God, Nature,
or somebody
made them that way.

Police lady or Lesbian
over there?
Where?

—Langston Hughes

Critical Thinking

What are police departments' attitudes toward LGBTQ people today?

To what extent are LGBTQ officers allowed to serve openly in departments?

Would it help the LGBTQ community feel safer or have more trust in the police if they had officers serving openly? Would it improve community relations?

Local and State-Level Policing: Racial Unrest

"Death in Yorkville (James Powell, Summer, 1964)"
by Langston Hughes

"Death in Yorkville (James Powell, Summer, 1964)" describes an all-too-common situation for black people in the United States: shooting deaths by police officers. This poem refers to a violent incident that occurred in Yorkville, a predominantly white neighborhood on the Upper West Side of Manhattan, New York. James Powell, a 15-year-old black teenager, supposedly armed with a knife, was shot to death by an off-duty white police officer. Following the shooting, a riot erupted in Harlem that resulted in one death and more than 140 people being injured. The speaker connects Powell's death to his own position as a black man in the United States, currently and throughout the country's history. He considers Powell's death a modern-day lynching, another act designed to control, subjugate, and enslave black people.

———————— ✌ ————————

"Death In Yorkville"
(James Powell, Summer, 1964)
by Langston Hughes

How many bullets does it take
To kill a fifteen-year-old kid?
How many bullets does it take
To kill me?

How many centuries does it take
To bind my mind — chain my feet —
Rope my neck — lynch me —
Unfree?

From the slave chain to the lynch rope
To the bullets of Yorkville,
Jamestown, 1619 to 1963:
Emancipation Centennial —
100 years NOT free.

Civil War Centenntial: 1965
How many Centennials does it take
To kill me,
Still alive?
When the long hot summers come
Death ain't
No jive.

Critical Thinking

To what extent is this poem still relevant in 21st century America?

What recent police shootings or killings of black men have occurred, and how have black and white people reacted to these deaths?

Do black people consider themselves "free" in the United States?

What roles do Black Lives Matter and Blue Lives Matter play in the ongoing discussion about policing and police brutality in black and other nonwhite communities?

Chapter 5

Policing: Roles, Functions, and Challenges

Controversial Police Roles

"The Majesty of the Law"
by Frank O'Connor (Michael Francis O'Donovan)

NOTE: This short story is not included in this anthology but may be found on the Internet or at your university or college library.

Growing up in Ireland during the independence movement of the early twentieth century, Michael O'Donovan (1903–1966) joined the Irish Republican Army in 1918. With the Irish-British settlement of 1921 and the establishment of the Irish Free State, O'Donovan's nationalist loyalties for a united Ireland led him to fight against the new government in the Irish Civil War, eventually concluding in his imprisonment in 1922–1923. After his release he took employment in a variety of positions, eventually becoming a librarian, later taking the name of Frank (derived from his middle name) O'Connor (his mother's maiden name) to protect his livelihood from any repercussions from his potentially controversial writings.

During the Irish War for Independence the Irish police, known as the Royal Irish Constabulary (RIC), were a prime target of the rebels as they were the primary representative of the British government in many a village throughout Ireland. Originally established in the early 1800s by Sir Robert Peel, who later created the Metropolitan Police, after a rocky start they developed a generally positive relationship with the towns and villages they lived in and served by the early nineteenth century. The struggle for Irish independence changed that view with over 400 members of the Irish constabulary killed in the fighting between 1919 and 1921. The Garda Siochána with the creation of the Irish Free State, now the Republic of Ireland, replaced the RIC.

In O'Connor's story a police sergeant has come to visit Dan Bride, an old man living alone and someone he had obviously known for some time. After discussing the sergeant's family, the two of them shared some illegal whiskey and only when leaving does the sergeant tactfully inquire, almost as an afterthought, if Dan intends to pay a fine levied against him after assaulting a neighbor during an argument. Dan, as expected, informs the sergeant he has no intention of paying, for it was not so much the money as it was "giving that fellow the satisfaction of paying" knowing that his time in jail would shame his accuser among the village. At this the sergeant tactfully informs Dan of an outstanding warrant for his arrest. After Dan suggests going with the sergeant, the sergeant demurs, suggesting it was late and might it not be more convenient for Dan to wait a day whereupon Dan responds with the suggestion of "Friday" as he had other errands that day in town. Both concur and the sergeant offers the name of a friend at the jail who will look out for Dan, making him "as comfortable as if [he] were at home."

This confrontation between the duty to enforce the law and the honor of an old man might easily have led to conflict but for the recognition of the sergeant that the law could be attended to while retaining the dignity of those it served. The "majesty" of the law is ultimately realized by the actions of its servant, the sergeant.

Critical Thinking

The role of the police is one of social control, but how that control is achieved is, in many cases, left up to the discretion of the officer. If you were an officer, would you necessarily arrest everyone you encountered that had an outstanding warrant?

If not, what criteria would determine who was arrested?

If you would arrest all, whatever the reason for the warrant, does that include the volunteer firefighter you stopped for a traffic violation that received a call to a major hospital fire while in the middle of the traffic stop?

What is the reason officers are given discretion?

Order Maintenance

"Shooting an Elephant"
by George Orwell (Eric Arthur Blair)

NOTE: This short story in not included in this anthology but may be found on the Internet or at your university or college library.

Eric Blair (1903–1950), who would adopt the pen name of George Orwell upon the publication of *Down and Out in Paris and London* in 1933, is best known for his dystopian and anti-totalitarian novels *Animal Farm* (1945) and *Nineteen Eighty-Four* (1949), published shortly before his death.

Born in colonial India but raised in England, upon graduation from the boys' boarding school Eton and unable to afford to attend a university, Blair joined the Indian Imperial Police, the police force of British India. Assigned to the Burma, then administrated as a province of India, Blair spent seven years with the police in various Burmese locations. "Shooting an Elephant" along with a number of other writings were inspired by his years in Burma in police service.

"Shooting an Elephant" explores one of the obligations of policing not often recognized by the public or admired by law enforcement officers: the responsibility for order maintenance—the duty to maintain the peace and tranquility of a community. The very term "law enforcement officer" negates this crucial role of policing, focusing on the duties of crime fighting instead of encompassing the entire police role. Another term for a police officer, "peace" officer, better describes this role while also incorporating the crime control responsibilities of the position. Domestic disturbances and public demonstrations, runaways and missing persons, traffic control and motorist safety, fights and fires, the homeless and the helpless, drunks and disorderly persons, all come under the definition of order maintenance. Of about 11.3 million arrests nationwide in 2013, only 121,500 were for crimes such as murder, manslaughter, rape, or robbery. As seen in the Orwell's story, the variety of problems addressed by police also mean that for many issues the responding officer may have little to no experience in dealing with the problem but the officer is expected to respond both professionally and appropriately for the situation.

Historically this has been a crucial aspect of modern policing with police diaries from the 1800s showing that beat officers walking the neighborhoods spent most of their time addressing the minor, daily concerns of the community they served, much of it informally. Relatively little time, in comparison, was spent in dealing with crimes such as robberies, kidnappings, or homicides.

Critical Thinking

For Orwell, the idea of serving as a colonial master caused him some discord and while on leave in Britain he resigned from the Imperial Police and started his writing career. Finding his interests leaned more toward the working class than the ruling class, he would publish *Down and Out in Paris and London* in 1933 recounting his life on the margins followed by *The Road to Wigan Pier* in 1937 describing the world of British coal miners. His experiences in the Spanish Civil War and actions of the Stalinist Soviet government contributed to his two classics, *Animal Farm* and *Nineteen Eighty-Four*.

The foundation of contemporary community policing is the premise that community order maintenance issues are crucial to successful policing yet many officers are loath to work calls related to order maintenance. Are dealing with these kinds of problems important?

If in responding to the incident and it is discovered that a law may have been violated should the officer necessarily arrest someone in these cases? Why or why not?

Should officers have discretion in dealing with these issues or should it be limited by department policy?

Undercover Investigations: Ethical Issues

"Crimes of Conscience"
by Nadine Gordimer

Nadine Gordimer (1923–2014) was a South African short story writer and novelist of international repute born in a Johannesburg suburb, winning the Nobel Prize in Literature in 1991. She was also a committed political and social activist in the anti-apartheid movement who advised Nelson Mandela on his defense speech in 1964, and became a member of the African National Congress when it was deemed illegal by the South African government. Moral and racial themes, especially the effects and consequences of oppressive, institutionalized racism enforced by South Africa's apartheid regime, figure prominently in her work, including "Happy Event" and "Crimes of Conscience," both included in this anthology.

"Crimes of Conscience" (1984 and 1991), set in Johannesburg, takes place when international sanctions against South Africa's apartheid regime were at their most severe, and internal unrest included anti-apartheid uprisings and unsuccessful crackdowns by the government to quell these uprisings. This short story opens on the steps of the city's Supreme Court, where two young (and white) people meet and begin a conversation about a trial they have been observing, a trial in which the defendant has been accused of a crime of conscience against apartheid. This seemingly chance encounter between Derek Felterman, who has returned from London after a five-year absence, and Aly Ross, a social justice and anti-apartheid advocate who has spent three months in prison for her political resistance, leads to friendship and then a love affair. The reader finds out that Felterman is actually a spy hired by the state's internal security system to infiltrate Aly's network of friends for evidence of left-wing, anti-government activities. As Aly becomes more intimate with Felterman, he becomes increasingly uneasy about lying to her, resulting in a confession at the end of the story.

"Crimes of Conscience"
by Nadine Gordimer

Apparently they noticed each other at the same moment, coming down the steps of the Supreme Court on the third day of the trial. By then casual spectators who come for a look

---

at the accused—to see for themselves who will risk prison walls round their bodies for ideas in their heads—have satisfied curiosity; only those who have some special interest attend day after day. He could have been a journalist; or an aide to the representative of one of the Western powers who "observe" political trials in countries problematic for foreign policy and subject to human rights lobbying back in Western Europe and America. He wore a corduroy suit of unfamiliar cut. But when he spoke it was clear he was, like her, someone at home—he had the accent, and the casual, colloquial turn of phrase. "What a session! I don't know . . . After two hours of that . . . , feel like I'm caught in a roll of sticky tape . . . unreal . . ."

There was no mistaking her. She was a young woman whose cultivated gentleness of expression and shabby homespun style of dress, in the context in which she was encountered, suggested not transcendental mediation centre or environmental concern group or design studio, but a sign of identification with the humanity of those who had nothing and risked themselves. Her only adornment, a necklace of ostrich-shell discs stacked along a thread, moved tight at the base of her throat tendons as she smiled and agreed. "Lawyers work like that . . . I've noticed. The first few days, it's a matter of people trying each to confuse the other side."

Later in the week, they had coffee together during the court's lunch adjournment. He expressed some naive impressions of the trial, but as if fully aware of gullibility. Why did the State call witnesses who came right out and said the regime oppressed their spirits and frustrated their normal ambitions? Surely that kind of testimony favoured the Defence, when the issue was a crime of conscience? She shook fine hair, ripply as a mohair rug. "Just wait. Just wait. That's to establish credibility. To prove their involvement with the accused, their intimate knowledge of what the accused said and did, to *inculpate* the accused in what the Defence's going to deny. Don't you see?"

"Now I see." He smiled to himself. "When I was here before, I didn't take much interest in political things . . . activist politics, I suppose you'd call it? It's only since I've been back from overseas . . ."

She asked conversationally what was expected of her: how long had he been away?

"Nearly five years. Advertising then computers . . ." The dying-out of the sentence suggested the lack of interest in which these careers had petered. "Two years ago I just felt I wanted to come back. I couldn't give myself a real reason. I've been doing the same sort of work here— actually, I ran a course at the business school of a university, this year—and I'm slowly beginning to find out *why* I wanted to. To come back. It seems it's something to do with things like *this*."

She had a face that showed her mind following another's; eyebrows and mouth expressed quiet understanding.

"I imagine all this sounds rather feeble to you. I don't suppose you're someone who stands on the sidelines."

Her thin, knobbly little hands were like tools laid upon the formica counter of the coffee bar. In a moment of absence from their capability, they fiddled with the sugar sachets while she answered. "What makes you think that?"

"You seem to know so much. As if you'd been through it yourself . . . Or maybe . . . you're a law student?"

"Me? Good lord, no." After one or two swallows of coffee, she offered a friendly response. "I work for a correspondence college."

"Teacher."

Smiling again: "Teaching people I never see."

"That doesn't fit too well. You look the kind of person who's more involved."

For the first time, polite interest changed, warmed. "That's what you missed, in London? Not being involved . . .?"

At that meeting he gave her a name, and she told him hers.

The name was Derek Felterman. It was his real name. He *had* spent five years in London; he *had* worked in an advertising company and then studied computer science at an appropriate institution, and it was in London that he was recruited by someone from the Embassy who wasn't a diplomat but a representative of the internal security section of State security in his native country. Nobody knows how secret police recognize likely candidates; it is as mysterious as sexing chickens. But if the definitive characteristic sought is there to be recognized, the recruiting agent will see it, no matter how deeply the individual may hide his likely candidacy from himself.

He was not employed to infiltrate refugee circles plotting abroad. It was decided that he would come home "clean," and begin work in the political backwater of a coastal town, on a university campus. Then he was sent north to the mining and industrial centre of the country, told to get himself an ordinary commercial job without campus connections, and, as a new face, seek contacts wherever the information his employers wanted was likely to be let slip— left-wing cultural gatherings, poster-waving protest groups, the public gallery at political trials. His employers trusted him to know how to ingratiate himself; that was one of the qualities he had been fancied for, as a woman might fancy him for some other characteristic over which he had no volition—the way one corner of his mouth curled when he smiled, or the brown gloss of his eyes.

He, in turn, had quickly recognized her—first as a type, and then, the third day, when he went away from the court for verification of her in police files, as the girl who had gone secretly to visit a woman friend who was under House Arrest, and subsequently had served a three-month jail sentence for refusing to testify in a case brought against the woman for breaking her isolation ban. Aly, she had called herself. Alison Jane Ross. There was no direct connection to be found between Alison Jane Ross's interest in the present trial and the individuals on trial; but from the point of view of his avocation this did not exclude her possible involvement with a master organization or back-up group involved in continuing action of the subversive kind the charges named. Felterman literally moved in to friendship with her, carrying a heavy case of books and a portable grill. He had asked if she would come to see a play with him on Saturday night. Alas, she was moving house that Saturday; perhaps he'd like to come and help, instead? The suggestion was added, tongue-in-cheek at her own presumption. He was there on time. Her family of friends, introduced by diminutives of their names, provided a combined service of old combi, springless station-wagon, take-away food and affectionate energy to fuel and accomplish the move from a flat to a tiny house with an ancient palm tree filling a square of garden, grating its dried fronds in the wind with the sound of a giant insect rubbing its legs together. To the night-song of that creature they made love for the first time a month later. Although all the Robs, Jimbos and Ricks, as well as the Jojos, Bets and Lils, kissed and hugged their friend Aly, there seemed to be no lover about who had therefore been supplanted. On the particular, delicate path of intimacy along which she drew him or that he laid out before her, there was room only for the two of them. At the beginning of ease between them, even before they were lovers, she had come of herself to the stage of mentioning that experience of going to prison, but she talked of it always in banal surface terms—how the blankets smelled of disinfectant and the Chief Wardress's cat used to do the inspection round with its mistress. Now she did not ask him about other women, although he was moved, occasionally, in some involuntary warm welling-up complementary to that other tide—of sexual pleasure spent—to confess by the indirection of an anecdote, past affairs, women who had had their time and place. When the right moment came naturally to her, she told without shame, resentment or vanity that she had just spent a year "on her own" as something she felt she needed after living for three years with someone who, in the end, went back to his wife. Lately there had been one or two brief affairs—"Sometimes—don't you find—an old friend suddenly becomes something else . . . just for a little while, as if a face is turned to another angle . . . ? And next day, it's the same old one again. Nothing's changed."

"Friends are the most important thing for you, aren't they? I mean, everybody has friends, but you . . . You'd really do *anything*. For your friends. Wouldn't you?"

There seemed to come from her reaction rather than his words a reference to the three months she had spent in prison. She lifted the curly pelmet of hair from her forehead and the freckles faded against a flush colouring beneath: "And they for me."

"It's not just a matter of friendship, either—of course, I see that. Comrades—a band of brothers . . ."

She saw him as a child staring through a window at others playing. She leant over and took up his hand, kissed him with the kind of caress they had not exchanged before, on each eyelid.

Nevertheless her friends were a little neglected in favour of him. He would have liked to have been taken into the group more closely, but it is normal for two people involved in a passionate love affair to draw apart from others for a while. It would have looked unnatural to press to behave otherwise. It was also understood between them that Felterman didn't have much more than acquaintances to neglect; five years abroad and then two in the coastal town accounted for that. He revived for her pleasures she had left behind as a schoolgirl: took her water-skiing and climbing. They went to see indigenous people's theatre together, part of a course in the politics of culture she was giving him not by correspondence, without being aware of what she was doing and without giving it any such pompous name. She was not to be persuaded to go to a discotheque, but one of the valuable contacts he did have with her group of friends of different races and colours was an assumption that he would be with her at their parties, where she out-danced him, having been taught by blacks how to use her body to music. She was wild and nearly lovely, in this transformation, from where he drank and watched her and her associates at play. Every now and then she would come back to him: an offering, along with the food and drink she carried. As months went by, he was beginning to distinguish certain patterns in her friendships; these were extended beyond his life with her into proscribed places and among people restricted by law from contact, like the woman for whom she had gone to prison. Slowly she gained the confidence to introduce him to risk, never discussing but evidently always sensitively trying to gauge how much he really wanted to find out if "why he wanted to come back" had to do with "things like this."

It was more and more difficult to leave her, even for one night, going out late, alone under the dry, chill agitation of the old palm tree, rustling through its files. But although he knew his place had been made for him to live in the cottage with her, he had to go back to his flat that was hardly more than an office, now, unoccupied except for the chair and dusty table at which he sat down to write his reports: he could hardly write them in the house he shared with her.

She spoke often of her time in prison. She herself was the one to find openings for the subject. But even now, when they lay in one another's arms, out of reach, undiscoverable to any investigation, out of scrutiny, she did not seem able to tell of the experience what there really was in her being, necessary to be told: why she risked, for whom and what she was committed. She seemed to be waiting passionately to be given the words, the key. From him.

It was a password he did not have. It was a code that was not supplied him.

And then one night it came to him; he found a code of his own; that night he had to speak. "I've been spying on you."

Her face drew into a moment of concentration akin to the animal world, where a threatened creature can turn into a ball of spikes or take on a fearsome aspect of blown-up muscle and defensive garishness.

The moment left her face instantly as it had taken her. He had turned away before it as a man does with a gun in his back.

She shuffled across the bed on her haunches and took his head in her hands, holding him.

Critical Thinking

What crimes of conscience are committed in this story, and by whom?

Given that he is working for the government, are Felterman's actions ethical or unethical? According to whom?

Who might Gordimer be indicting for crimes of conscience in this story?

When the goal of undercover policing is to suppress political dissent, how just or ethical is that policing? In other words, consider the multiple meanings of the story's title.

Authoritarianism

"An Apology"
by Bernard Malamud

NOTE: This short story in not included in this anthology but may be found on the Internet or at your university or college library.

William Ross, a British scholar and philosopher of the mid-twentieth century, developed a moral theory of virtue that identified seven prima facie duties that are moral obligations one has a responsibility to fulfill. Those obligations, developed from what he saw as morally significant relationships, include fidelity, reparation, gratitude, non-maleficence, beneficence, self-improvement, and justice. In "An Apology" the premise of reparation through a simple apology is brought to the forefront.

Bernard Malamud (1914–1986) was a Pulitzer Prize winning novelist and short story writer who taught creative writing at Bennington College prior to retirement. Bennington was fertile ground for writers such as Shirley Jackson ("The Lottery"), who also taught there, and Ralph Ellison ("A Party down at the Square", *The Invisible Man*), who lectured there as well as serving on the college's board of trustees. Born in New York of Russian-Jewish immigrants, though teaching in rural Vermont, Malamud's Jewish heritage and urban upbringing were incorporated into much of his writing.

In "An Apology," set in New York sometime in the mid-1930s to mid-40s, a Jewish peddler is confronted by two police officers. Though one officer decides to abuse his discretion and arrest the peddler for "Resisting an officer in the performance of his duty," the peddler's unusual behavior leads to them later releasing him. During the arrest light bulbs owned by the peddler, identified by a neighbor as Bloostein, are lost when the officers commit the same offense the peddler had that led to the original confrontation between him and the officers.

Issues of authoritarianism, cynicism, solidarity, and police discretion are all reflected in the story. The original arresting officer, Lou, abused his authority when the peddler failed to show "appropriate" respect for him when questioned, and instead of recognizing that the offense wasn't of consequence and the enforcement would not further justice, he choose to arrest the peddler, charging him not for the original offence but for a catch-all charge, resisting an officer. Historically, the charge of vagrancy was used in a similar manner by police, both in America and in England.

Cynicism rears its head when one officer, Walter, questions him regarding his lost property, suggesting that Bloostein had hid it in an attempt to obtain extra light bulbs at police expense. For the police, dealing with people who lie to them every day, mistrust easily develops regarding an individual's veracity and motivation, making officers suspicious of everyone.

Though Walter did not initiate the arrest, his solidarity with his fellow officer prevented him from confronting him over the treatment of Bloostein and his original misuse of discretion in effecting the arrest. Yet it was also discretion that came to the forefront when Walter suggested that they release Bloostein and Lou readily agreed.

These characteristics can contribute to an attitude of some officers to be hesitant in offering an apology for their actions, seeing an apology as a sign of weakness or incompetence, the antithesis of the policing role as one of authority, masculinity and strength. Yet by the end of the story, Walter has offered a sincere apology to Bloostein, both in words and in action, buying replacements for the missing bulbs of the peddler. What Malamud expresses is that the apology—the reparation of Ross—achieves a twofold purpose. It restores the dignity and self-respect of the peddler, affirming that he had done nothing wrong and didn't deserve the mistreatment brought down upon him. For Walter, though, the apology also had meaning. It helped restore his own self-esteem, possibly reconnecting him to the original reason he had joined the police: to help those it need, to protect and to serve.

Reparation through something so simple as a heartfelt apology brought balance to the peddler, to Walter and, quite possibly, for an instant at least, to the morning streets of Brooklyn.

Critical Thinking

Can you think of reasons why police departments would hesitate to apologize when their officers make a mistake?

Why might an officer be hesitant to apologize after making a mistake?

After you have been personally wronged what effect does a meaningful apology have?

When one is not given, how do you then want to respond?

Cynicism

"Hardened"

by Stephen D. Rogers

With over 900 stories, plays, and poems published in his writing career, the Short Mystery Fiction Society has honored Stephen Rogers with two "Derringer" Awards. His work can cut to the essence of an idea, as seen in both "Hardened" and in his poem "Closure," both earlier published in *The Lineup: Poems on Crime.*

The poem "Hardened" reflects the callousness and its handmaiden - cynicism - that can develop in an officer after years of seeing the worst in mankind. Though most officers enter policing to help people and serve their community, the selective interaction with the public involves officers dealing with people who have a variety of problems as well as with people who resent the presence and interference of the police. For officers "everyone lies"—including their fellow officers—making them question the believability of any statements given or any emotions expressed to them by those they deal with and reinforcing any cynicism they have developed on the job and within their early training.

This insensitivity and mistrust impact the police department's own attempts at building bridges between them and the community they serve. Community policing, a philosophy of involving the community in helping determine the goals and objectives of the department on a neighborhood basis, is made harder by having officers on the street interacting in an inappropriate manner with the very public they represent.

The suspicion that everyone has an agenda that leads them to lying can limit an officer's relationship with non-police personnel as they come to suspect that there is an agenda or ulterior motive behind any kindness or pleasantry initiated by a "civilian." That, in turn, further isolates officers from those they serve, limiting their social network that normally serves as a balance against the skewed view of society one can develop while working in law enforcement. It also has the potential to carry over to an officer's family, putting stress on a relationship when a loved one is also automatically suspected of having a hidden agenda or motive for their actions. That stress then contributes to the overall stress the job itself creates and can leave no sanctuary for the officer except in associating with his or her peers, eventually developing an "us versus them" mentality.

"Hardened"

by Stephen D. Rogers

She sits cuffed to the bench
Sobbing between questions
"Where do you live?"
Moaning
"How long have you lived there?"
Wailing
"What's your telephone number?"
Crying for someone whose name
We can't quite make out

Critical Thinking

How can an officer's cynicism negatively impact an investigation? How might it actually help?

Knowing of the danger of developing a negative attitude of callousness and cynicism, what might an officer do to minimize or even prevent the problem?

Can leadership minimize cynicism? If so, how?

Police Discretion

"The Hidden Law"
by W. H. Auden

Wystan Hugh Auden (1907–1973), born and raised in England and educated at Oxford, immigrated to the United States in 1939 after having established a reputation as a writer in Britain. By 1947 he had been awarded the Pulitzer Prize in poetry for *The Age of Anxiety*. Considered one of the great poets of the twentieth century, his work has continued to inform contemporary writers.

Auden's Anglican Christianity is suggested in "The hidden Law" as the poem argues for the existence of a greater law than that law imposed by mankind. One interpretation of that hidden law referred to is what is described as natural law, sometimes suggested as divine law.

Natural law is premised on the theory that law has a moral basis and is grounded in the idea that humans have an inborn notion of what is right and wrong, which can also be cultivated by rational thought. Earlier described by Aristotle and Cicero, Thomas Aquinas would meld Christian theology with natural law, claiming that if human or positive law violates natural law, it is unjust and not necessarily valid. The Church would allude to that logic to later challenge secular authority claiming that natural law and, by extension, the Church's law, was divine.

With the Enlightenment the premises of natural law were expressed in the concept of the *social contract*, the idea that all were members of a community on equal terms and therefore all were entitled to equal rights. John Locke argued that an individual could not be subjected to governmental power without one's consent—which was incorporated later in the American Declaration of Independence:

> We hold these truths to be self-evident, that all men are created equal, that they are endowed by their Creator with certain unalienable Rights, that among these are Life, Liberty and the pursuit of Happiness.—That to secure these rights, Governments are instituted among Men, deriving their just powers from the consent of the governed . . .

Locke's original argument, which was the precursor for Jefferson's Declaration, focused on the protection of property rights (as well as health), recognizing that if property was denied, liberty was then but a sham:

> The state of nature has a law of nature to govern it, which obliges every one: and reason, which is that law, teaches all mankind, who will but consult it, that being all equal and independent, no one ought to harm another in his life, health, liberty, or possessions . . .

The development of the idea of being free by nature and being endowed with natural rights was later expressed in the Bill of Rights of the United States Constitution, which enumerated specific individual rights of the newly independent Americans.

Originally seen as moral abstractions, natural law transitioned into the concept of natural rights restraining the state, leading to constitutions then affirming those rights. The judiciary would use the concept of natural law as justification to abrogate any law that was perceived to usurp one's natural rights. The difficulty is that as few natural rights are codified, interpretations left much to be desired as various groups were excluded from the protections of natural rights throughout American history including Native Americans, blacks, and women.

For law enforcement officers, the concept of natural law offers a level of discretion to officers to interpret a given law's moral implications. Officers make moral decisions on a daily basis. Though an individual may violate the letter of the law, the decision to arrest may be grounded in an officer's own moral compass, morality determining his or her decision and not the law. Whether allowing an illegal protest instead of forcing a confrontation or not arresting a minor for petty possession of marijuana to avoid giving them a life-long criminal record, these kinds of discretionary decisions may be based on a recognition that the dignity of the individual and their unwritten natural rights as a human trumps the enforcement of any given law.

"The Hidden Law"
by W. H. Auden

The Hidden Law does not deny
Our laws of probability,
But takes the atom and the star
And human beings as they are,
And answers nothing when we lie.

It is the only reason why
No government can codify,
And verbal definitions mar
The Hidden Law.
Its utter patience will not try
To stop us if we want to die:
When we escape It in a car,
When we forget It in a bar,
These are the ways we're punished by
The Hidden Law

Critical Thinking

Can you think of a crime where not arresting someone may be morally appropriate?

Can you think of any examples where the rule of law was inappropriately enforced to the detriment of the individual and the community?

Should officers even have this kind of discretion? Why might some departments limit an officer's discretion? What might be the consequences in doing so?

Police Discretion: Friends and Family

"After Twenty Years"

by O. Henry (William Sydney Porter)

William Sydney Porter (1862–1910), known as O. Henry, was a prolific American short story writer, whose narrative style and endings are often compared to Guy de Maupassant. Like many of the naturalist and realist writers of his generation, Henry set his stories in contemporary society; featured common people as his characters, including police officers; and used rich, precise detail. New York City, among other cities, figures prominently in his work. Like other journalist-fiction writers of his time (such as Mark Twain and Stephen Crane), Henry paid close attention to carefully crafted language and economy of plot. "After Twenty Years" is set in New York and opens with a police officer, "looking strong and important," patrolling his beat very late in the evening, making sure his community is safe. Noticing an unfamiliar man standing in front "of a darkened shop," he stops and asks the man his business. The man tells the officer he is waiting for his childhood friend, Jimmy Wells, who he promised twenty years earlier to meet in front of this store at 10:00 p.m. on this date. The officer proceeds to ask him questions standard in community policing: has he heard from his friend during the intervening twenty years? What has he (the man) been doing? The man (and the narrator through descriptive detail) reveals information that only a seasoned police officer would consider important: that he has moved frequently and quickly; that he wears an expensive, bejeweled watch; that he seems to be a hustler. Moreover, the police officer asks the man how long he will wait for his friend in order to get more crucial detail. Twenty minutes after his encounter with the officer, the man is greeted by who he thinks is Jimmy Wells. In a surprising twist, the man (named Bob) soon realizes that this man is not Jimmy Wells. In fact, he is another police officer come to arrest Bob for crimes committed in Chicago. The real Jimmy Wells is the first officer he encountered. The story underscores the importance of police discretion and the challenges police officers encounter when they have to deal with friends and family who may be criminals.

————— ✀ —————

"After Twenty Years"

by O. Henry

The policeman on the beat moved up the avenue impressively. The impressiveness was habitual and not for show, for spectators were few. The time was barely 10 o'clock at night, but chilly gusts of wind with a taste of rain in them had well nigh depeopled the streets.

Trying doors as he went, twirling his club with many intricate and artful movements, turning now and then to cast his watchful eye adown the pacific thoroughfare, the officer, with his stalwart form and slight swagger, made a fine picture of a guardian of the peace. The vicinity was one that kept early hours. Now and then you might see the lights of a cigar store or of an all-night lunch counter; but the majority of the doors belonged to business places that had long since been closed.

When about midway of a certain block the policeman suddenly slowed his walk. In the doorway of a darkened hardware store a man leaned, with an unlighted cigar in his mouth. As the policeman walked up to him the man spoke up quickly.

"It's all right, officer," he said, reassuringly. "I'm just waiting for a friend. It's an appointment made twenty years ago. Sounds a little funny to you, doesn't it? Well, I'll explain if you'd like to make certain it's all straight. About that long ago there used to be a restaurant where this store stands—'Big Joe' Brady's restaurant."

"Until five years ago," said the policeman. "It was torn down then."

The man in the doorway struck a match and lit his cigar. The light showed a pale, square-jawed face with keen eyes, and a little white scar near his right eyebrow. His scarfpin was a large diamond, oddly set.

"Twenty years ago to-night," said the man, "I dined here at 'Big Joe' Brady's with Jimmy Wells, my best chum, and the finest chap in the world. He and I were raised here in New York, just like two brothers, together. I was eighteen and Jimmy was twenty. The next morning I was to start for the West to make my fortune. You couldn't have dragged Jimmy out of New York; he thought it was the only place on earth. Well, we agreed that night that we would meet here again exactly twenty years from that date and time, no matter what our conditions might be or from what distance we might have to come. We figured that in twenty years each of us ought to have our destiny worked out and our fortunes made, whatever they were going to be."

"It sounds pretty interesting," said the policeman. "Rather a long time between meets, though, it seems to me. Haven't you heard from your friend since you left?"

"Well, yes, for a time we corresponded," said the other. "But after a year or two we lost track of each other. You see, the West is a pretty big proposition, and I kept hustling around over it pretty lively. But I know Jimmy will meet me here if he's alive, for he always was the truest, stanchest old chap in the world. He'll never forget. I came a thousand miles to stand in this door tonight, and it's worth it if my old partner turns up."

Source: O. Henry, "After Twenty Years," *The Four Million*, 1906.

The waiting man pulled out a handsome watch, the lids of it set with small diamonds.

"Three minutes to ten," he announced. "It was exactly ten o'clock when we parted here at the restaurant door."

"Did pretty well out West, didn't you?" asked the policeman.

"You bet! I hope Jimmy has done half as well. He was a kind of plodder, though, good fellow as he was. I've had to compete with some of the sharpest wits going to get my pile. A man gets in a groove in New York. It takes the West to put a razor-edge on him."

The policeman twirled his club and took a step or two.

"I'll be on my way. Hope your friend comes around all right. Going to call time on him sharp?"

"I should say not!" said the other. "I'll give him half an hour at least. If Jimmy is alive on earth he'll be here by that time. So long, officer."

"Good-night, sir," said the policeman, passing on along his beat, trying doors as he went.

There was now a fine, cold drizzle falling, and the wind had risen from its uncertain puffs into a steady blow. The few foot passengers astir in that quarter hurried dismally and silently along with coat collars turned high and pocketed hands. And in the door of the hardware store the man who had come a thousand miles to fill an appointment, uncertain almost to absurdity, with the friend of his youth, smoked his cigar and waited.

About twenty minutes he waited, and then a tall man in a long overcoat, with collar turned up to his ears, hurried across from the opposite side of the street. He went directly to the waiting man.

"Is that you, Bob?" he asked, doubtfully.

"Is that you, Jimmy Wells?" cried the man in the door.

"Bless my heart!" exclaimed the new arrival, grasping both the other's hands with his own. "It's Bob, sure as fate. I was certain I'd find you here if you were still in existence. Well, well, well!—twenty years is a long time. The old gone, Bob; I wish it had lasted, so we could have had another dinner there. How has the West treated you, old man?"

"Bully; it has given me everything I asked it for. You've changed lots, Jimmy. I never thought you were so tall by two or three inches."

"Oh, I grew a bit after I was twenty."

"Doing well in New York, Jimmy?"

"Moderately. I have a position in one of the city departments. Come on, Bob; we'll go around to a place I know of, and have a good long talk about old times."

The two men started up the street, arm in arm. The man from the West, his egotism enlarged by success, was beginning to outline the history of his career. The other, submerged in his overcoat, listened with interest.

At the corner stood a drug store, brilliant with electric lights. When they came into this glare each of them turned simultaneously to gaze upon the other's face.

The man from the West stopped suddenly and released his arm.

"You're not Jimmy Wells," he snapped. "Twenty years is a long time, but not long enough to change a man's nose from a Roman to a pug."

"It sometimes changes a good man into a bad one," said the tall man. "You've been under arrest for ten minutes, 'Silky' Bob. Chicago thinks you may have dropped over our way and wires us she wants to have a chat with you. Going quietly, are you? That's sensible. Now, before we go on to the station here's a note I was asked to hand you. You may read it here at the window. It's from Patrolman Wells."

The man from the West unfolded the little piece of paper handed him. His hand was steady when he began to read, but it trembled a little by the time he had finished. The note was rather short.

"*Bob: I was at the appointed place on time. When you struck the match to light your cigar I saw it was the face of the man wanted in Chicago. Somehow I couldn't do it myself, so I went around and got a plain clothes man to do the job. JIMMY.*"

Critical Thinking

Re-read the opening of the story. How does O. Henry establish Officer Wells' authority and experience as a cop?

How does the real Jimmy Wells prompt so much information from Bob?

Was Officer Wells right not to arrest his own friend?

Should he have been more lenient on Bob because he is his friend?

What other challenges might police face when dealing with family and friends?

Section 3

The American Court System

Chapter 6

The Court System

Presumption of Innocence?

Alice's Adventures in Wonderland—an excerpt
by Lewis Carroll (Charles Lutwidge Dodgson)

Lewis Carroll (1832–1898) was the pen name of English writer Charles Lutwidge Dodgson. Known for both *Alice's Adventures in Wonderland* and its sequel *Through the Looking-Glass*, Dodgson was a mathematician at Oxford for much of his adult life. Dodgson's works are famous for their nonsensical and absurd stories that appealed to children while also offering a level of social satire for their parents.

For many the courtroom scene of the Knave of Hearts on trial for stealing the Queen's tarts is more than a satire of the Victorian courts; it can be seen as an analogy of the American court system. Like Alice, most have a view of the courts based upon their reading or, today, from television or cinema. Yet upon becoming an observer such as Alice, the absurdity of the trial quickly comes into question starting with the competence of the jury. In the United States it is accepted that almost all can become a juror responsible for, in some cases, life and death decisions. Where the courts hope someone of intelligence and common sense serves, it can just as easily be a prejudiced, low-intelligence individual easily manipulated by one of the attorneys arguing the case. In a civil trial one could have a borderline illiterate seamstress with a sixth grade education deciding if an oil refinery had the appropriate safety policies and procedures in place when determining the culpability for the death of an employee, or she may just as easily be making a judgment as to the scientific evidence being presented in a murder case that a defense attorney is relying on to prove the innocence of her defendant.

At times one may suspect that the decision of a trial has already been determined by a judge, just as the King was ready for the jury to read their verdict before any witness had even testified. With a judge in some localities having first served only as a prosecutor before being appointed or elected to the bench, a defendant or his attorney might question if the judge has an inappropriate relationship with the prosecutor. In Texas, for example, one judge was found to have been communicating with the prosecutor via text messages during the trial, attempting to assist her in asking appropriate questions of the witnesses while the trial was in progress. This brings into question if the judge had already determined the outcome, much as the Queen has when she comments, "Sentence first—verdict afterwards."

An example of a judge imitating the King in admitting or disallowing evidence on a whim and making up his rules as the trial progresses (Rule 42) was recently seen in a court case where the judge allowed a deputy sheriff to search a car because the driver was obeying all the traffic laws and from the deputy's perspective that was probable cause to suspect he was a criminal transporting drugs. The judge, of course, never acknowledged that his decision meant that whether one obeyed the law or disobeyed the law, by his legal reasoning the deputy could stop and search anyone's auto.

With the King constantly threatening witnesses (which a judge can actually do, for example, by holding someone in "contempt" who refuses to testify and placing the witness in jail until they do so), the individuals in the court acquiescing unquestionably to the judge's decisions, the Knave's trial never determining his guilt or innocence and with the court's focus on the trivial in lieu of justice, Dodgson lampoons the entire legal system.

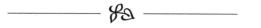

"CHAPTER XI. Who Stole the Tarts?"

Extracts from Alice's Adventures in Wonderland by Lewis Carroll

The King and Queen of Hearts were seated on their throne when they arrived, with a great crowd assembled about them—all sorts of little birds and beasts, as well as the whole pack of cards: the Knave was standing before them, in chains, with a soldier on each side to guard him; and near the King was the White Rabbit, with a trumpet in one hand, and a scroll of parchment in the other. In the very middle of the court was a table, with a large dish of tarts upon it: they looked so good, that it made Alice quite hungry to look at them—'I wish they'd get the trial done,' she thought, 'and hand round the refreshments!' But there seemed to be no chance of this, so she began looking at everything about her, to pass away the time.

Alice had never been in a court of justice before, but she had read about them in books, and she was quite pleased to find that she knew the name of nearly everything there. 'That's the judge,' she said to herself, 'because of his great wig.'

The judge, by the way, was the King; and as he wore his crown over the wig, (look at the frontispiece if you want to see how he did it,) he did not look at all comfortable, and it was certainly not becoming.

Source: Lewis Carroll, *Alice's Adventures in Wonderland,* 1865.

'And that's the jury-box,' thought Alice, 'and those twelve creatures,' (she was obliged to say 'creatures,' you see, because some of them were animals, and some were birds,) 'I suppose they are the jurors.' She said this last word two or three times over to herself, being rather proud of it: for she thought, and rightly too, that very few little girls of her age knew the meaning of it at all. However, 'jury-men' would have done just as well.

The twelve jurors were all writing very busily on slates. 'What are they doing?' Alice whispered to the Gryphon. 'They can't have anything to put down yet, before the trial's begun.'

'They're putting down their names,' the Gryphon whispered in reply, 'for fear they should forget them before the end of the trial.'

'Stupid things!' Alice began in a loud, indignant voice, but she stopped hastily, for the White Rabbit cried out, 'Silence in the court!' and the King put on his spectacles and looked anxiously round, to make out who was talking.

Alice could see, as well as if she were looking over their shoulders, that all the jurors were writing down 'stupid things!' on their slates, and she could even make out that one of them didn't know how to spell 'stupid,' and that he had to ask his neighbour to tell him. 'A nice muddle their slates'll be in before the trial's over!' thought Alice.

One of the jurors had a pencil that squeaked. This of course, Alice could not stand, and she went round the court and got behind him, and very soon found an opportunity of taking it away. She did it so quickly that the poor little juror (it was Bill, the Lizard) could not make out at all what had become of it; so, after hunting all about for it, he was obliged to write with one finger for the rest of the day; and this was of very little use, as it left no mark on the slate.

'Herald, read the accusation!' said the King.

On this the White Rabbit blew three blasts on the trumpet, and then unrolled the parchment scroll, and read as follows:—

'The Queen of Hearts, she made some tarts,
All on a summer day:
The Knave of Hearts, he stole those tarts,
And took them quite away!'

'Consider your verdict,' the King said to the jury.

'Not yet, not yet!' the Rabbit hastily interrupted. 'There's a great deal to come before that!'

'Call the first witness,' said the King; and the White Rabbit blew three blasts on the trumpet, and called out, 'First witness!'

The first witness was the Hatter. He came in with a teacup in one hand and a piece of bread-and-butter in the other. 'I beg pardon, your Majesty,' he began, 'for bringing these in: but I hadn't quite finished my tea when I was sent for.'

'You ought to have finished,' said the King. 'When did you begin?'

The Hatter looked at the March Hare, who had followed him into the court, arm-in-arm with the Dormouse. 'Fourteenth of March, I think it was,' he said.

'Fifteenth,' said the March Hare.

'Sixteenth,' added the Dormouse.

'Write that down,' the King said to the jury, and the jury eagerly wrote down all three dates on their slates, and then added them up, and reduced the answer to shillings and pence.

'Take off your hat,' the King said to the Hatter.

'It isn't mine,' said the Hatter.

'Stolen!' the King exclaimed, turning to the jury, who instantly made a memorandum of the fact.

'I keep them to sell,' the Hatter added as an explanation; 'I've none of my own. I'm a hatter.'

Here the Queen put on her spectacles, and began staring at the Hatter, who turned pale and fidgeted.

'Give your evidence,' said the King; 'and don't be nervous, or I'll have you executed on the spot.'

This did not seem to encourage the witness at all: he kept shifting from one foot to the other, looking uneasily at the Queen, and in his confusion he bit a large piece out of his teacup instead of the bread-and-butter.

Just at this moment Alice felt a very curious sensation, which puzzled her a good deal until she made out what it was: she was beginning to grow larger again, and she thought at first she would get up and leave the court; but on second thoughts she decided to remain where she was as long as there was room for her.

'I wish you wouldn't squeeze so.' said the Dormouse, who was sitting next to her. 'I can hardly breathe.'

'I can't help it,' said Alice very meekly: 'I'm growing.'

'You've no right to grow here,' said the Dormouse.

'Don't talk nonsense,' said Alice more boldly: 'you know you're growing too.'

'Yes, but I grow at a reasonable pace,' said the Dormouse: 'not in that ridiculous fashion.' And he got up very sulkily and crossed over to the other side of the court.

All this time the Queen had never left off staring at the Hatter, and, just as the Dormouse crossed the court, she said to one of the officers of the court, 'Bring me the list of the singers in the last concert!' on which the wretched Hatter trembled so, that he shook both his shoes off.

'Give your evidence,' the King repeated angrily, 'or I'll have you executed, whether you're nervous or not.'

'I'm a poor man, your Majesty,' the Hatter began, in a trembling voice, '—and I hadn't begun my tea—not above a week or so—and what with the bread-and-butter getting so thin—and the twinkling of the tea—'

'The twinkling of the what?' said the King.

'It began with the tea,' the Hatter replied.

'Of course twinkling begins with a T!' said the King sharply. 'Do you take me for a dunce? Go on!'

'I'm a poor man,' the Hatter went on, 'and most things twinkled after that—only the March Hare said—'

'I didn't!' the March Hare interrupted in a great hurry.

'You did!' said the Hatter.

'I deny it!' said the March Hare.

'He denies it,' said the King: 'leave out that part.'

'Well, at any rate, the Dormouse said—' the Hatter went on, looking anxiously round to see if he would deny it too: but the Dormouse denied nothing, being fast asleep.

'After that,' continued the Hatter, 'I cut some more bread-and-butter—'

'But what did the Dormouse say?' one of the jury asked.

'That I can't remember,' said the Hatter.

'You MUST remember,' remarked the King, 'or I'll have you executed.'

The miserable Hatter dropped his teacup and bread-and-butter, and went down on one knee. 'I'm a poor man, your Majesty,' he began.

'You're a very poor speaker,' said the King.

Here one of the guinea-pigs cheered, and was immediately suppressed by the officers of the court. (As that is rather a hard word, I will just explain to you how it was done. They had a large canvas bag, which tied up at the mouth with strings: into this they slipped the guinea-pig, head first, and then sat upon it.)

'I'm glad I've seen that done,' thought Alice. 'I've so often read in the newspapers, at the end of trials, "There was some attempts at applause, which was immediately suppressed by the officers of the court," and I never understood what it meant till now.'

'If that's all you know about it, you may stand down,' continued the King.

'I can't go no lower,' said the Hatter: 'I'm on the floor, as it is.'

'Then you may SIT down,' the King replied.

Here the other guinea-pig cheered, and was suppressed.

'Come, that finished the guinea-pigs!' thought Alice. 'Now we shall get on better.'

'I'd rather finish my tea,' said the Hatter, with an anxious look at the Queen, who was reading the list of singers.

'You may go,' said the King, and the Hatter hurriedly left the court, without even waiting to put his shoes on.

'—and just take his head off outside,' the Queen added to one of the officers: but the Hatter was out of sight before the officer could get to the door.

'Call the next witness!' said the King.

The next witness was the Duchess's cook. She carried the pepper-box in her hand, and Alice guessed who it was, even before she got into the court, by the way the people near the door began sneezing all at once.

'Give your evidence,' said the King.

'Shan't,' said the cook.

The King looked anxiously at the White Rabbit, who said in a low voice, 'Your Majesty must cross-examine THIS witness.'

'Well, if I must, I must,' the King said, with a melancholy air, and, after folding his arms and frowning at the cook till his eyes were nearly out of sight, he said in a deep voice, 'What are tarts made of?'

'Pepper, mostly,' said the cook.

'Treacle,' said a sleepy voice behind her.

'Collar that Dormouse,' the Queen shrieked out. 'Behead that Dormouse! Turn that Dormouse out of court! Suppress him! Pinch him! Off with his whiskers!'

For some minutes the whole court was in confusion, getting the Dormouse turned out, and, by the time they had settled down again, the cook had disappeared.

'Never mind!' said the King, with an air of great relief. 'Call the next witness.' And he added in an undertone to the Queen, 'Really, my dear, YOU must cross-examine the next witness. It quite makes my forehead ache!'

Alice watched the White Rabbit as he fumbled over the list, feeling very curious to see what the next witness would be like, '—for they haven't got much evidence YET,' she said to herself. Imagine her surprise, when the White Rabbit read out, at the top of his shrill little voice, the name 'Alice!'

CHAPTER XII. Alice's Evidence

'Here!' cried Alice, quite forgetting in the flurry of the moment how large she had grown in the last few minutes, and she jumped up in such a hurry that she tipped over the jury-box with the edge of her skirt, upsetting all the jurymen on to the heads of the crowd below, and there they lay sprawling about, reminding her very much of a globe of goldfish she had accidentally upset the week before.

'Oh, I BEG your pardon!' she exclaimed in a tone of great dismay, and began picking them up again as quickly as she could, for the accident of the goldfish kept running in her head, and she had a vague sort of idea that they must be collected at once and put back into the jury-box, or they would die.

'The trial cannot proceed,' said the King in a very grave voice, 'until all the jurymen are back in their proper places—ALL,' he repeated with great emphasis, looking hard at Alice as he said do.

Alice looked at the jury-box, and saw that, in her haste, she had put the Lizard in head downwards, and the poor little thing was waving its tail about in a melancholy way, being quite unable to move. She soon got it out again, and put it right; 'not that it signifies much,' she said to herself; 'I should think it would be QUITE as much use in the trial one way up as the other.'

As soon as the jury had a little recovered from the shock of being upset, and their slates and pencils had been found and handed back to them, they set to work very diligently to write out a history of the accident, all except the Lizard, who seemed too much overcome to do anything but sit with its mouth open, gazing up into the roof of the court.

'What do you know about this business?' the King said to Alice.

'Nothing,' said Alice.

'Nothing WHATEVER?' persisted the King.

'Nothing whatever,' said Alice.

'That's very important,' the King said, turning to the jury. They were just beginning to write this down on their slates, when the White Rabbit interrupted: 'UNimportant, your Majesty means, of course,' he said in a very respectful tone, but frowning and making faces at him as he spoke.

'UNimportant, of course, I meant,' the King hastily said, and went on to himself in an undertone,

'important—unimportant—unimportant—important—' as if he were trying which word sounded best.

Some of the jury wrote it down 'important,' and some 'unimportant.' Alice could see this, as she was near enough to look over their slates; 'but it doesn't matter a bit,' she thought to herself.

At this moment the King, who had been for some time busily writing in his note-book, cackled out 'Silence!' and read out from his book, 'Rule Forty-two. ALL PERSONS MORE THAN A MILE HIGH TO LEAVE THE COURT.'

Everybody looked at Alice.

'I'M not a mile high,' said Alice.

'You are,' said the King.

'Nearly two miles high,' added the Queen.

'Well, I shan't go, at any rate,' said Alice: 'besides, that's not a regular rule: you invented it just now.'

'It's the oldest rule in the book,' said the King.

'Then it ought to be Number One,' said Alice.

The King turned pale, and shut his note-book hastily. 'Consider your verdict,' he said to the jury, in a low, trembling voice.

'There's more evidence to come yet, please your Majesty,' said the White Rabbit, jumping up in a great hurry; 'this paper has just been picked up.'

'What's in it?' said the Queen.

'I haven't opened it yet,' said the White Rabbit, 'but it seems to be a letter, written by the prisoner to—to somebody.'

'It must have been that,' said the King, 'unless it was written to nobody, which isn't usual, you know.'

'Who is it directed to?' said one of the jurymen.

'It isn't directed at all,' said the White Rabbit; 'in fact, there's nothing written on the OUT-SIDE.' He unfolded the paper as he spoke, and added 'It isn't a letter, after all: it's a set of verses.'

'Are they in the prisoner's handwriting?' asked another of the jurymen.

'No, they're not,' said the White Rabbit, 'and that's the queerest thing about it.' (The jury all looked puzzled.)

'He must have imitated somebody else's hand,' said the King. (The jury all brightened up again.)

'Please your Majesty,' said the Knave, 'I didn't write it, and they can't prove I did: there's no name signed at the end.'

'If you didn't sign it,' said the King, 'that only makes the matter worse. You MUST have meant some mischief, or else you'd have signed your name like an honest man.'

There was a general clapping of hands at this: it was the first really clever thing the King had said that day.

'That PROVES his guilt,' said the Queen.

'It proves nothing of the sort!' said Alice. 'Why, you don't even know what they're about!'

'Read them,' said the King.

The White Rabbit put on his spectacles. 'Where shall I begin, please your Majesty?' he asked.

'Begin at the beginning,' the King said gravely, 'and go on till you come to the end: then stop.'

These were the verses the White Rabbit read:—

'They told me you had been to her,
And mentioned me to him:
She gave me a good character,
But said I could not swim.

He sent them word I had not gone
(We know it to be true):
If she should push the matter on,
What would become of you?

I gave her one, they gave him two,
You gave us three or more;
They all returned from him to you,
Though they were mine before.

If I or she should chance to be
Involved in this affair,
He trusts to you to set them free,
Exactly as we were.

My notion was that you had been
(Before she had this fit)
An obstacle that came between
Him, and ourselves, and it.

Don't let him know she liked them best,
For this must ever be
A secret, kept from all the rest,
Between yourself and me.'

'That's the most important piece of evidence we've heard yet,' said the King, rubbing his hands; 'so now let the jury—'

'If any one of them can explain it,' said Alice, (she had grown so large in the last few minutes that she wasn't a bit afraid of interrupting him,) 'I'll give him sixpence. *I* don't believe there's an atom of meaning in it.'

The jury all wrote down on their slates, 'SHE doesn't believe there's an atom of meaning in it,' but none of them attempted to explain the paper.

'If there's no meaning in it,' said the King, 'that saves a world of trouble, you know, as we needn't try to find any. And yet I don't know,' he went on, spreading out the verses on his knee, and looking at them with one eye; 'I seem to see some meaning in them, after all."— SAID I COULD NOT SWIM—" you can't swim, can you?' he added, turning to the Knave.

The Knave shook his head sadly. 'Do I look like it?' he said. (Which he certainly did NOT, being made entirely of cardboard.)

'All right, so far,' said the King, and he went on muttering over the verses to himself: '"WE KNOW IT TO BE TRUE—" that's the jury, of course—"I GAVE HER ONE, THEY GAVE HIM TWO—" why, that must be what he did with the tarts, you know—'

'But, it goes on "THEY ALL RETURNED FROM HIM TO YOU,"' said Alice.

'Why, there they are!' said the King triumphantly, pointing to the tarts on the table. 'Nothing can be clearer than THAT. Then again—"BEFORE SHE HAD THIS FIT—" you never had fits, my dear, I think?' he said to the Queen.

'Never!' said the Queen furiously, throwing an inkstand at the Lizard as she spoke. (The unfortunate little Bill had left off writing on his slate with one finger, as he found it made no mark; but he now hastily began again, using the ink, that was trickling down his face, as long as it lasted.)

'Then the words don't FIT you,' said the King, looking round the court with a smile. There was a dead silence.

'It's a pun!' the King added in an offended tone, and everybody laughed, 'Let the jury consider their verdict,' the King said, for about the twentieth time that day.

'No, no!' said the Queen. 'Sentence first—verdict afterwards.'

'Stuff and nonsense!' said Alice loudly. 'The idea of having the sentence first!'

'Hold your tongue!' said the Queen, turning purple.

'I won't!' said Alice.

'Off with her head!' the Queen shouted at the top of her voice. Nobody moved.

'Who cares for you?' said Alice, (she had grown to her full size by this time.) 'You're nothing but a pack of cards!'

At this the whole pack rose up into the air, and came flying down upon her: she gave a little scream, half of fright and half of anger, and tried to beat them off, and found herself lying on the bank, with her head in the lap of her sister, who was gently brushing away some dead leaves that had fluttered down from the trees upon her face.

'Wake up, Alice dear!' said her sister; 'Why, what a long sleep you've had!'

'Oh, I've had such a curious dream!' said Alice, and she told her sister, as well as she could remember them, all these strange Adventures of hers that you have just been reading about; and when she had finished, her sister kissed her, and said, 'It WAS a curious dream, dear, certainly: but now run in to your tea; it's getting late.' So Alice got up and ran off, thinking while she ran, as well she might, what a wonderful dream it had been.

But her sister sat still just as she left her, leaning her head on her hand, watching the setting sun, and thinking of little Alice and all her wonderful Adventures, till she too began dreaming after a fashion, and this was her dream:—

First, she dreamed of little Alice herself, and once again the tiny hands were clasped upon her knee, and the bright eager eyes were looking up into hers—she could hear the very tones of her voice, and see that queer little toss of her head to keep back the wandering hair that WOULD always get into her eyes—and still as she listened, or seemed to listen, the whole place around her became alive with the strange creatures of her little sister's dream.

The long grass rustled at her feet as the White Rabbit hurried by—the frightened Mouse splashed his way through the neighbouring pool—she could hear the rattle of the teacups as the

March Hare and his friends shared their never-ending meal, and the shrill voice of the Queen ordering off her unfortunate guests to execution—once more the pig-baby was sneezing on the Duchess's knee, while plates and dishes crashed around it—once more the shriek of the Gryphon, the squeaking of the Lizard's slate-pencil, and the choking of the suppressed guinea-pigs, filled the air, mixed up with the distant sobs of the miserable Mock Turtle.

So she sat on, with closed eyes, and half believed herself in Wonderland, though she knew she had but to open them again, and all would change to dull reality—the grass would be only rustling in the wind, and the pool rippling to the waving of the reeds—the rattling teacups would change to tinkling sheep-bells, and the Queen's shrill cries to the voice of the shepherd boy—and the sneeze of the baby, the shriek of the Gryphon, and all the other queer noises, would change (she knew) to the confused clamour of the busy farm-yard—while the lowing of the cattle in the distance would take the place of the Mock Turtle's heavy sobs.

Lastly, she pictured to herself how this same little sister of hers would, in the after-time, be herself a grown woman; and how she would keep, through all her riper years, the simple and loving heart of her childhood: and how she would gather about her other little children, and make THEIR eyes bright and eager with many a strange tale, perhaps even with the dream of Wonderland of long ago: and how she would feel with all their simple sorrows, and find a pleasure in all their simple joys, remembering her own child-life, and the happy summer days.

Critical Thinking

Why does the public accept judges or prosecutors violating the law or the court's own guidelines?

What punishment should a judge be given if she intentionally ignores the law?

Should evidence obtained illegally be admitted in court to be used against a defendant?

If no, what should be done? If yes, what if it were a serial murderer at issue?

Ethics and Professionalism: Vagrancies of Justice

"An Act of Prostitution"

by James Alan McPherson

NOTE: This short story in not included in this anthology but may be found on the Internet or at your university or college library.

James Alan McPherson (1943–2016) is an African American short story writer and essayist who was born in Savannah, Georgia, graduated from Harvard Law School, and attended the Iowa's Writers' Workshop, and Yale Law School. Though trained to be a lawyer, McPherson choose to pursue a literary career. He won the Pulitzer Prize for fiction in 1978. He has taught English at the University of California, Santa Cruz, Harvard University, and Yale University.

The story "An Act of Prostitution" (1969) is informed by McPherson's interest and education in the legal system. Injustice abounds within the courtroom in this story, along with plenty of race, gender, and class issues. Justice is not blind in this story. The two white public defenders, Jimmy and Ralph, judge which of their clients deserves a better defense on variables such as appearance, prior offenses, and marital partners. Neither man takes seriously the white prostitute, Philomena, because she is heavy, a repeat offender, and—most damning of all for them—married to a black man. Of the three defendants who come before the judge, only the one who has a hired lawyer is properly defended. Right up until the present day, the poor are forced to accept public defenders, who have heavy case-loads and little money to hire investigators. Like the public defenders in the story, the judge does not conduct himself professionally or impartially, as he is required to do. He insults and mocks both the first defendant who comes before him and Philomena. The second defendant, black Army veteran Irving Williams, is charged with assaulting a police officer, but Williams claims police brutality.

Critical Thinking

What cross examination techniques do you see Williams's lawyer use when questioning the police officer? Is he effective and how so?

Does the justice system portrayed in this story seem equitable for the poor? Why or why not?

The judge does not censure twenty-five black men in the back of courtroom when they scream insults at the court-appointed detective who acts as the prosecutor for Williams. Why does the judge behave so timidly, and why does he send the case to another court? Note that this story is set in the late 1960s, a period that was racially charged: Martin Luther King Jr. had been assassinated in 1968 and the revolutionary Black Panthers were monitoring and reacting to police brutality. How might those events have influenced the judge? Is that legitimate?

Can you think of current examples when a judge is swayed by public opinion or current events? Reflect on the title of this story. Might McPherson be referring to characters other than Philomena?

"The Lottery"
by Shirley Jackson

Shirley Jackson's (1916–1965) short story, "The Lottery", brought much consternation to the readers of the *New Yorker* magazine in 1948 when it was first published. Some saw it as a critique of the rural, small-town lifestyle many were a part of and still idealized while others were simply at a loss at understanding its meaning. She would later state that "Explaining just what I had hoped the story to say is very difficult. I suppose, I hoped, by setting a particularly brutal ancient rite in the present and in my own village to shock the story's readers with a graphic dramatization of the pointless violence and general inhumanity in their own lives."

It can also be seen as a metaphor for the criminal justice system, in its randomness in who and how it deals with those it is meant to serve and, at times, its "pointless violence and general inhumanity." The vagrancies of the system extend from minor traffic violations to the execution of convicted murderers. The law cannot be enforced against every person who commits a traffic violation so officers randomly select those the law will be enforced against, the decision based on a variety of factors. Some departments require officers to achieve a quota of traffic violation citations each shift while a neighboring community may not require any traffic stops so the issuance of a citation is at the whim of an officer who has no production demands hanging over his or her head. In criminal cases, police discretion in determining who is arrested leads, in many cases, to widely varying rates of arrest across the nation. Some counties have an arrest rate of only 11 per 10,000 people while the bordering county has a rate exceeding 2,500 per 10,000. The randomness of where one lives, works, or drives can become a major determining factor in receiving a traffic ticket or in spending the night in jail.

After an arrest the prosecutor has the authority to determine the progress of a criminal case, in some cases simply based on her own preconceptions, predisposition, or prejudices. Believing that a young, first-offender's indiscretion shouldn't brand him as a criminal the rest of his life, she may offer him the opportunity to enter a pretrial diversion program where he will have no criminal record after staying out of trouble for six months where a prosecutor in the next county may believe that "sparing the rod spoils the child" and demand jail time, and the consequent criminal record, as a deterrence to any future violation.

Possibly the most extreme example of the randomness of the justice system and its similarity to a lottery is in the use of the death penalty against convicted murders. A study recently found that of 3,100 counties within the United States only five prosecutors in five different counties from across the nation accounted for at least 440 prisoners being sent to death row, 1 out of every 20 condemned to death since the Supreme Court reaffirmed the death penalty in 1976. In Harris County, Texas, the site of the city of Houston, during a two-decade career District Attorney Johnny Holmes sent 201 people to death row before his retirement in 2000. Since his retirement Harris County death sentences have dropped over 90 percent, down to one a year. The arbitrariness and inconsistency from county to county and state to state (almost 20 states preclude a death sentence) led at least one Supreme Court judge to question the constitutionality of the death penalty.

—————————— ℘ ——————————

"The Lottery"
by Shirley Jackson

The morning of June 27th was clear and sunny, with the fresh warmth of a full-summer day; the flowers were blossoming profusely and the grass was richly green. The people of the village began to gather in the square; between the post office and the bank, around ten o'clock; in some towns there were so many people that the lottery took two days and had to be started on June 26th, but in this village, where there were only about three hundred people, the whole lottery took less than two hours, so it could begin at ten o'clock in the morning and still be through in time to allow the villagers to get home for noon dinner.

The children assembled first, of course. School was recently over for the summer, and the feeling of liberty sat uneasily on most of them; they tended to gather together quietly for a while before they broke into boisterous play, and their talk was still of the classroom and the teacher, of books and reprimands. Bobby Martin had already stuffed his pockets full of stones, and the other boys soon followed his example, selecting the smoothest and roundest stones; Bobby and Harry Jones and Dickie Delacroix—the villagers pronounced this name "Dellacroy"—eventually made a great pile of stones in one corner of the square and guarded it against the raids of the other boys. The girls stood aside, talking among themselves, looking over their shoulders at the boys, and the very small children rolled in the dust or clung to the hands of their older brothers or sisters.

Soon the men began to gather, surveying their own children, speaking, of planting and rain, tractors and taxes. They stood together, away from the pile of stones in the corner, and their jokes were quiet and they smiled rather than laughed. The women, wearing faded house dresses and sweaters, came shortly after their menfolk. They greeted one another and exchanged bits of gossip as they went to join their husbands. Soon the women, standing by their husbands, began to call to their children, and the children came reluctantly, having to be called four or five times. Bobby Martin ducked under his mother's grasping hand and ran, laughing, back to the pile of stones. His father spoke up sharply, and Bobby came quickly and took his place between his father and his oldest brother.

———————————

The lottery was conducted—as were the square dances, the teen-age club, the Halloween program—by Mr. Summers, who had time and energy to devote to civic activities. He was a round-faced, jovial man and he ran the coal business, and people were sorry for him, because he had no children and his wife was a scold. When he arrived in the square, carrying the black wooden box, there was a murmur of conversation among the villagers, and he waved and called, "Little late today, folks," The postmaster, Mr. Graves, followed him, carrying a three-legged stool, and the stool was put in the center of the square and Mr. Summers set the black box down on it. The villagers kept their distance, leaving a space between themselves and the stool, and when Mr. Summers said, "Some of you fellows want to give me a hand?" there was a hesitation before two men, Mr. Martin and his oldest son, Baxter, came forward to hold the box steady on the stool while Mr. Summers stirred up the papers inside it.

The original paraphernalia for the lottery had been lost long ago, and the black box now resting on the stool had been put into use even before Old Man Warner, the oldest man in town, was born. Mr. Summers spoke frequently to the villagers about making a new box, but no one liked to upset even as much tradition as was represented by the black box. There was a story that the present box had been made with some pieces of the box that had preceded it, the one that had been constructed when the first people settled down to make a village here. Every year, after the lottery, Mr. Summers began talking again about a new box, but every year the subject was allowed to fade off without anything's being done. The black box grew shabbier each year; by now it was no longer completely black but splintered badly along one side to show the original wood color, and in some places faded or stained.

Mr. Martin and his oldest son, Baxter, held the black box securely on the stool until Mr. Summers had stirred the papers thoroughly with his hand. Because so much of the ritual had been forgotten or discarded, Mr. Summers had been successful in having slips of paper substituted for the chips of wood that had been used for generations. Chips of wood, Mr. Summers had argued, had been all very well when the village was tiny, but now that the population was more than three hundred and likely to keep on growing, it was necessary to use something that would fit more easily into the black box. The night before the lottery, Mr. Summers and Mr. Graves made up the slips of paper and put them in the box, and it was then taken to the safe of Mr. Summers' coal company and locked up until Mr. Summers was ready to take it to the square next morning. The rest of the year, the box was put away, sometimes one place, sometimes another; it had spent one year in Mr. Graves's barn and another year underfoot in the post office, and sometimes it was set on a shelf in the Martin grocery and left there.

There was a great deal of fussing to be done before Mr. Summers declared the lottery open. There were the lists to make up—of heads of families, heads of households in each family, members of each household in each family. There was the proper swearing-in of Mr. Summers by the postmaster, as the official of the lottery; at one time, some people remembered, there had been a recital of some sort, performed by the official of the lottery, a perfunctory, tuneless chant that had been rattled off duly each year; some people believed that the official of the lottery used to stand just so when he said or sang it, others believed that he was supposed to walk among the people, but years and years ago this part of the ritual had been allowed to lapse. There had been, also, a ritual salute, which the official of the lottery had had to use in addressing each person who came up to draw from the box, but this also had changed with time, until now it was felt necessary only for the official to speak to each person approaching. Mr. Summers was very good at all this; in his clean white shirt and blue jeans, with one hand resting carelessly on the black box, he seemed very proper and important as he talked interminably to Mr. Graves and the Martins.

Just as Mr. Summers finally left off talking and turned to the assembled villagers, Mrs. Hutchinson came hurriedly along the path to the square, her sweater thrown over her shoulders, and slid into place in the back of the crowd. "Clean forgot what day it was," she said to Mrs. Delacroix, who stood next to her, and they both laughed softly. "Thought my old man was out back stacking wood," Mrs. Hutchinson went on, "and then I looked out the window and the kids were gone, and then I remembered it was the twenty-seventh and came a-running." She dried her hands on her apron, and Mrs. Delacroix said, "You're in time, though. They're still talking away up there."

Mrs. Hutchinson craned her neck to see through the crowd and found her husband and children standing near the front. She tapped Mrs. Delacroix on the arm as a farewell and began to make her way through the crowd. The people separated good-humoredly to let her through; two or three people said, in voices just loud enough to be heard across the crowd, "Here comes your Missus, Hutchinson," and "Bill, she made it after all." Mrs. Hutchinson reached her husband, and Mr. Summers, who had been waiting, said cheerfully, "Thought we were going to have to get on without you, Tessie." Mrs. Hutchinson said, grinning, "Wouldn't have me leave m'dishes in the sink, now, would you, Joe?" and soft laughter ran through the crowd as the people stirred back into position after Mrs. Hutchinson's arrival.

"Well, now," Mr. Summers said soberly, "guess we better get started, get this over with, so's we can go back to work. Anybody ain't here?"

"Dunbar," several people said. "Dunbar, Dunbar."

Mr. Summers consulted his list. "Clyde Dunbar," he said. "That's right. He's broke his leg, hasn't he? Who's drawing for him?"

"Me, I guess," a woman said, and Mr. Summers turned to look at her. "Wife draws for her husband," Mr. Summers said. "Don't you have a grown boy to do it for you, Janey?" Although Mr. Summers and everyone else in the village knew the answer perfectly well, it was the business of the official of the lottery to ask such questions formally. Mr. Summers waited with an expression of polite interest while Mrs. Dunbar answered.

"Horace's not but sixteen yet," Mrs. Dunbar said regretfully. "Guess I gotta fill in for the old man this year."

"Right," Mr. Summers said. He made a note on the list he was holding. Then he asked, "Watson boy drawing this year?"

A tall boy in the crowd raised his hand. "Here," he said. "I'm drawing for m'mother and me." He blinked his eyes nervously and ducked his head as several voices in the crowd said things like "Good fellow, Jack," and "Glad to see your mother's got a man to do it."

"Well," Mr. Summers said, "guess that's everyone. Old Man Warner make it?"

"Here," a voice said, and Mr. Summers nodded.

A sudden hush fell on the crowd as Mr. Summers cleared his throat and looked at the list. "All ready?" he called. "Now, I'll read the names—heads of families first—and the men come up and take a paper out of the box. Keep the paper folded in your hand without looking at it until everyone has had a turn. Everything clear?"

The people had done it so many times that they only half listened to the directions; most of them were quiet, wetting their lips, not looking around. Then Mr. Summers raised one hand high and said, "Adams." A man disengaged himself from the crowd and came forward. "Hi, Steve," Mr. Summers said, and Mr. Adams said, "Hi, Joe." They grinned at one another humorlessly and nervously. Then Mr. Adams reached into the black box and took out a folded paper. He held it firmly by one corner as he turned and went hastily back to his place in the crowd, where he stood a little apart from his family, not looking down at his hand.

"Allen," Mr. Summers said. "Andrews. . . . Bentham."

"Seems like there's no time at all between lotteries any more," Mrs. Delacroix said to Mrs. Graves in the back row. "Seems like we got through with the last one only last week."

"Time sure goes fast," Mrs. Graves said.

"Clark. . . . Delacroix."

"There goes my old man," Mrs. Delacroix said. She held her breath while her husband went forward.

"Dunbar," Mr. Summers said, and Mrs. Dunbar went steadily to the box while one of the women said, "Go on, Janey," and another said, "There she goes."

"We're next," Mrs. Graves said. She watched while Mr. Graves came around from the side of the box, greeted Mr. Summers gravely, and selected a slip of paper from the box. By now, all through the crowd there were men holding the small folded papers in their large hands, turning them over and over nervously. Mrs. Dunbar and her two sons stood together, Mrs. Dunbar holding the slip of paper.

"Harburt. . . . Hutchinson."

"Get up there, Bill," Mrs. Hutchinson said, and the people near her laughed.

"Jones."

"They do say," Mr. Adams said to Old Man Warner, who stood next to him, "that over in the north village they're talking of giving up the lottery."

Old Man Warner snorted. "Pack of crazy fools," he said. "Listening to the young folks, nothing's good enough for *them*. Next thing you know, they'll be wanting to go back to living in caves, nobody work any more, live *that* way for a while. Used to be a saying about 'Lottery in June, corn be heavy soon.' First thing you know, we'd all be eating stewed chickweed and acorns. There's *always* been a lottery," he added petulantly. "Bad enough to see young Joe Summers up there joking with everybody."

"Some places have already quit lotteries," Mrs. Adams said.

"Nothing but trouble in *that*," Old Man Warner said stoutly. "Pack of young fools."

"Martin." And Bobby Martin watched his father go forward. "Overdyke. . . . Percy."

"I wish they'd hurry," Mrs. Dunbar said to her older son. "I wish they'd hurry."

"They're almost through," her son said.

"You get ready to run tell Dad," Mrs. Dunbar said.

Mr. Summers called his own name and then stepped forward precisely and selected a slip from the box. Then he called, "Warner."

"Seventy-seventh year I been in the lottery," Old Man Warner said as he went through the crowd. "Seventy-seventh time."

"Watson." The tall boy came awkwardly through the crowd. Someone said, "Don't be nervous, Jack," and Mr. Summers said, "Take your time, son."

"Zanini."

After that, there was a long pause, a breathless pause, until Mr. Summers, holding his slip of paper in the air, said, "All right, fellows." For a minute, no one moved, and then all the slips of paper were opened. Suddenly, all women began to speak at once, saying, "Who is it?," "Who's got it?," "Is it the Dunbars?," "Is it the Watsons?" Then the voices began to say, "It's Hutchinson. It's Bill." "Bill Hutchinson got it."

"Go tell your father," Mrs. Dunbar said to her older son.

People began to look around to see the Hutchinsons. Bill Hutchinson was standing quiet, staring down at the paper in his hand. Suddenly, Tessie Hutchinson shouted to Mr. Summers, "You didn't give him time enough to take any paper he wanted. I saw you. It wasn't fair."

"Be a good sport, Tessie," Mrs. Delacroix called, and Mrs. Graves said, "All of us took the same chance."

"Shut up, Tessie," Bill Hutchinson said.

"Well, everyone," Mr. Summers said, "that was done pretty fast, and now we've got to be hurrying a little more to get done in time." He consulted his next list. "Bill," he said, "you draw for the Hutchinson family. You got any other households in the Hutchinsons?"

"There's Don and Eva," Mrs. Hutchinson yelled. "Make *them* take their chance!"

"Daughters draw with their husbands' families, Tessie," Mr. Summers said gently. "You know that as well as anyone else."

"It wasn't *fair*," Tessie said.

"I guess not, Joe," Bill Hutchinson said regretfully. "My daughter draws with her husband's family, that's only fair. And I've got no other family except the kids."

"Then, as far as drawing for families is concerned, it's you," Mr. Summers said in explanation, "and as far as drawing for households is concerned, that's you, too. Right?"

"Right," Bill Hutchinson said.

"How many kids, Bill?" Mr. Summers asked formally.

"Three," Bill Hutchinson said. "There's Bill, Jr., and Nancy, and little Dave. And Tessie and me."

"All right, then," Mr. Summers said. "Harry, you got their tickets back?"

Mr. Graves nodded and held up the slips of paper. "Put them in the box, then," Mr. Summers directed. "Take Bill's and put it in."

"I think we ought to start over," Mrs. Hutchinson said, as quietly as she could. "I tell you it wasn't *fair*. You didn't give him time enough to choose. *Every*body saw that."

Mr. Graves had selected the five slips and put them in the box, and he dropped all the papers but those onto the ground, where the breeze caught them and lifted them off.

"Listen, everybody," Mrs. Hutchinson was saying to the people around her.

"Ready, Bill?" Mr. Summers asked, and Bill Hutchinson, with one quick glance around at his wife and children, nodded.

"Remember," Mr. Summers said, "take the slips and keep them folded until each person has taken one. Harry, you help little Dave." Mr. Graves took the hand of the little boy, who came willingly with him up to the box. "Take a paper out of the box, Davy," Mr. Summers said. Davy put his hand into the box and laughed. "Take just *one* paper," Mr. Summers said. "Harry, you hold it for him." Mr. Graves took the child's hand and removed the folded paper from the tight fist and held it while little Dave stood next to him and looked up at him wonderingly.

"Nancy next," Mr. Summers said. Nancy was twelve, and her school friends breathed heavily as she went forward, switching her skirt, and took a slip daintily from the box. "Bill, Jr.," Mr. Summers said, and Billy, his face red and his feet overlarge, nearly knocked the box over as he got a paper out. "Tessie," Mr. Summers said. She hesitated for a minute, looking around defiantly, and then set her lips and went up to the box. She snatched a paper out and held it behind her.

"Bill," Mr. Summers said, and Bill Hutchinson reached into the box and felt around, bringing his hand out at last with the slip of paper in it.

The crowd was quiet. A girl whispered, "I hope it's not Nancy," and the sound of the whisper reached the edges of the crowd.

"It's not the way it used to be," Old Man Warner said clearly. "People ain't the way they used to be."

"All right," Mr. Summers said. "Open the papers. Harry, you open little Dave's."

Mr. Graves opened the slip of paper and there was a general sigh through the crowd as he held it up and everyone could see that it was blank. Nancy and Bill, Jr., opened theirs at the same time, and both beamed and laughed, turning around to the crowd and holding their slips of paper above their heads.

"Tessie," Mr. Summers said. There was a pause, and then Mr. Summers looked at Bill Hutchinson, and Bill unfolded his paper and showed it. It was blank.

"It's Tessie," Mr. Summers said, and his voice was hushed. "Show us her paper, Bill."

Bill Hutchinson went over to his wife and forced the slip of paper out of her hand. It had a black spot on it, the black spot Mr. Summers had made the night before with the heavy pencil in the coal-company office. Bill Hutchinson held it up, and there was a stir in the crowd.

"All right, folks," Mr. Summers said. "Let's finish quickly."

Although the villagers had forgotten the ritual and lost the original black box, they still remembered to use stones. The pile of stones the boys had made earlier was ready; there were stones on the ground with the blowing scraps of paper that had come out of the box. Mrs. Delacroix selected a stone so large she had to pick it up with both hands and turned to Mrs. Dunbar. "Come on," she said. "Hurry up."

Mrs. Dunbar had small stones in both hands, and she said, gasping for breath, "I can't run at all. You'll have to go ahead and I'll catch up with you."

The children had stones already, and someone gave little Davy Hutchinson a few pebbles.

Tessie Hutchinson was in the center of a cleared space by now, and she held her hands out desperately as the villagers moved in on her. "It isn't fair," she said. A stone hit her on the side of the head.

Old Man Warner was saying, "Come on, come on, everyone." Steve Adams was in the front of the crowd of villagers, with Mrs. Graves beside him.

"It isn't fair, it isn't right," Mrs. Hutchinson screamed, and then they were upon her.

Critical Thinking

For many involved in the criminal justice system, its arbitrariness has all the earmarks of a lottery. Arrested in one city versus another, assigned to one judge instead of an alternative choice, having the case handled by one prosecutor instead of a different one, hiring one attorney over another all have an impact on the case beyond the actual evidence of guilt or innocence. Sometimes, as in Mrs. Hutchinson's case, it feels as if it is simply the luck of the draw.

Can you give an example of the arbitrariness in the justice system that may have happened to you or a friend?

Can you think of anything that can be done to make the justice system more consistent?

Would consistency better achieve justice? For that matter, what is justice?

Chapter 7

Inside a Courtroom

Witness Testimony

"Witness for the Prosecution"
by Agatha Christie

NOTE: This short story is not included in this anthology but may be found on the Internet, both as a short story and as a play, or at your university or college library.

Agatha Christie (1890–1976) was a renowned British mystery author famous for her detectives Jane Marple and Hercule Poirot. She perfected the detective procedural that set the standard for mystery writers that came after her. "Witness for the Prosecution" was originally a short story published as "Traitor Hands" in *Flynn's Weekly* in 1925, and then under its current title in a short story collection that appeared in 1933. Christie later rewrote the story as a play, with a revised ending, that was the basis for a movie adaptation in 1957 that starred Tyrone Power and Marlene Dietrich.

The story opens with solicitor Mr. Mayherne interviewing his client Leonard Vole, who has been arrested for the murder of the elderly and wealthy Emily French. French was in love with Vole, believed him unmarried, and thus made him her heir. Believing his client guilty because of seemingly irrefutable evidence, Mayherne seeks nevertheless to build a defense for Vole, who manages to convince his solicitor that he did not commit murder by arguing that his wife Romaine can provide him with an alibi. When Mayherne visits Romaine, however, he discovers that not only are she and Vole not married, but also that she intends to be a witness for the prosecution to secure a guilty conviction for her common-law husband. After a disastrous preliminary hearing that ensures Vole's trial for murder, Mayherne receives a letter from a woman who claims she has evidence that will prove Vole's innocence. When he visits this woman, she hands over a stack of letters allegedly written by Romaine, one of which exposes her plot to get rid of Vole so that she can be with her lover. Armed with this damning evidence, Mayherne is confident that his client is innocent. The following day, Sir Wilfred Roberts, barrister for Vole's defense, cross-examines Romaine on the witness stand, exposing her perjury when he presents her letter as proof of her duplicity. Vole is found not guilty and set free. Although happy for his client, Mayherne is troubled by what he sees as a physical resemblance between Romaine and the woman who provided him with Romaine's letters. Confronting Romaine, he discovers that she concocted the entire story, from appearing to hate her husband to disguising herself as the other woman and writing fake letters. An actress, Romaine knew she could construct such a plot to free her husband from the hangman's noose. The real twist of the story, and Romaine's true motives, come at the very end. As you read Christie's courtroom narrative, consider how Mayherne gathers evidence to defend his client.

Critical Thinking

Is Mayherne too gullible to believe evidence that would clear his client? Should he have been more diligent?

How plausible is Christie's plot twist? Could it actually happen in our criminal justice system?

Do you think Vole knew what his wife had planned? Are there any clues in the narrative that point to Vole's guilt?

As a reader, were you convinced of Vole's guilt or innocence, and based on what evidence?

The Prosecution and the Defense

"The Lawyers Know Too Much"
by Carl Sandberg

Carl Sandberg (1878–1967) was a modern American writer, poet, and editor who won three Pulitzer prizes. He often used satire in his writing as a way to convey his message.

The humorous poem "The Lawyers Know Too Much" (1920) indicates that people had a low opinion of lawyers even a hundred years ago. Yet that view of attorneys actually extends at least back to the Roman Empire. Ammianus Marcellinus' history of the fourth century Roman Empire, known as *Res Gestae*, depicts some of those practicing law as "sowing the seeds of all sorts of quarrels" where "rashness tries to pass itself off as freedom of speech and reckless audacity as firmness of purpose." He also remarked that others, in an attempt to gain glory, "sharpen their venal tongues to attack the truth." He accused some of being "shameless, headstrong, and ignorant" of the law, unable to "remember that they ever possessed a law-book." Little has changed as a recent Pew Research Center survey found lawyers at the bottom of a list of ten occupations (which included the military, teachers, doctors, journalists, and business execs) when Americans were asked if lawyers contribute to society's well-being. Time seems not to have tempered Sandberg's poor view of American barristers.

"The Lawyers Know too Much"
by Carl Sandburg

The lawyers, Bob, know too much.
They are chums of the books of old John Marshall.
They know it all, what a dead hand wrote,
A stiff dead hand and its knuckles crumbling,
The bones of the fingers a thin white ash.
The lawyers know
a dead man's thought too well.

Source: Carl Sandburg, "The Lawyers Know too Much," *The Complete Poems of Carl Sandburg,* 1950.

In the heels of the higgling lawyers, Bob,
Too many slippery ifs and buts and howevers,
Too much hereinbefore provided whereas,
Too many doors to go in and out of.

When the lawyers are through
What is there left, Bob?
Can a mouse nibble at it
And find enough to fasten a tooth in?

Why is there always a secret singing
When a lawyer cashes in?
Why does a hearse horse snicker
Hauling a lawyer away?

The work of a bricklayer goes to the blue.
The knack of a mason outlasts a moon.
The hands of a plasterer hold a room together.
The land of a farmer wishes him back again.
Singers of songs and dreamers of plays
Build a house no wind blows over.
The lawyers—tell me why a hearse horse snickers
hauling a lawyer's bones.

Critical Thinking

What does John Marshall, the fourth Chief Justice of the Supreme Court, represent in this poem?

What does the persona in this poem tell the listener Bob that lawyers know too well?

What does the persona infer that lawyers don't know enough about?

Why does the second stanza of the poem give examples of legal language?

The questions that the persona asks in the third and fourth stanzas infer what about lawyers?

How does the final stanza of the poem compare the legacy of laymen and writers to that of lawyers?

Do lawyers still have a bad reputation? Why or why not?

"The Lawyer's Ways"
by Paul Laurence Dunbar

Paul Laurence Dunbar (1872–1906) was a prolific African American poet, novelist, and playwright who wrote during the post-Reconstruction era (beginning in 1873), a period of both great opportunity for free black people and crushing segregation ushered in by Jim Crow laws. He was most famous for the work he wrote in a Negro dialect reminiscent of the antebellum South, a dialect that made his writing seem more realistic to readers, especially white readers whose perceptions of African Americans were rooted in negative stereotypes of their intellectual and literary abilities. Racism in the North and Jim Crow laws in the South contributed to the construction of institutionalized racism in the criminal justice system, one that most often denied black defendants' due process. The poem "The Lawyers' Ways" is written in Negro dialect, from the point of view of a black observer in a local courthouse. The narrator describes his confusion over the sharply contrasting profiles of criminal defendants constructed by the prosecutor and the defense attorney. The prosecutor paints the "pris'ner/In a coat o' deep-dyed sin," prompting the speaker to wonder "How the Lord had come to fashion/Sich an awful man as him." In contrast, the defense attorney portrays the defendant as "a martyr/That was brought to sacrifice." The speaker is left to ponder how a defendant can be both an angel and a devil. Indeed, the poem exemplifies the roles of prosecution and defense attorneys: the former must, on behalf of the state, make a convincing case for the defendant's guilt, while the latter's job is to defend her client's rights and interests.

"The Lawyers' Ways"
by Paul Laurence Dunbar

I've been list'nin' to them lawyers
In the court house up the street,
An' I've come to the conclusion
That I'm most completely beat.
Fust one feller riz to argy,
An' he boldly waded in

Source: Paul Laurence Dunbar, from "Lyrics of a Lowly Life" 1896.

As he dressed the tremblin' pris'ner
In a coat o' deep-dyed sin.

Why, he painted him all over
In a hue o' blackest crime,
An' he smeared his reputation
With the thickest kind o' grime,
Tell I found myself a-wond'rin',
In a misty way and dim,
How the Lord had come to fashion
Sich an awful man as him.

Then the other lawyer started,
An' with brimmin', tearful eyes,
Said his client was a martyr
That was brought to sacrifice.
An' he give to that same pris'ner
Every blessed human grace,
Tell I saw the light o' virtue
Fairly shinin' from his face.

Then I own 'at I was puzzled
How sich things could rightly be;
An' this aggervatin' question
Seems to keep a-puzzlin' me.
So, will some one please inform me,
An' this mystery unroll—
How an angel an' a devil
Can persess the self-same soul?

Critical Thinking

What effect does Dunbar's use of dialect have on your perception of the narrator and his description of each lawyer?

Is the speaker's characterization of "the lawyers' ways" accurate or too simplistic?

If members of a jury have similar reactions as the speaker's, how can they arrive at a fair verdict?

The Defense

"The Corpus Delicti"
by Melville Post

Melville Post (1869–1930), an American author born in Harrison County, West Virginia, was at one time the highest-paid magazine writer in America. Ellery Queen called the attorney-turned-author's stories "an out-of-this-world target for future detective-story writers."

The detective story "The Corpus Delicti" (1896) has an unusual twist since the reader knows early in the story who the murderer is and how he commits the murder. The defense attorney in the story encourages his client to kill a woman who is blackmailing the man over her husband's murder, and then the attorney manipulates the law to free his client. In 1890s New York State a person could not be convicted of murdering someone unless there was direct, not just circumstantial, evidence. The story's title is a Latin term meaning "body of the crime."

---- ℘ℛ ----

"The Corpus Delicti"
by Melville Davisson Post

I

"That man Mason," said Samuel Walcott, "is the mysterious member of this club. He is more than that; he is the mysterious man of New York."

"I was much surprised to see him," answered his companion, Marshall St. Clair, of the great law firm of Seward, St. Clair & De Muth. "I had lost track of him since he went to Paris as counsel for the American stockholders of the Canal Company. When did he come back to the States?"

"He turned up suddenly in his ancient haunts about four months ago," said Walcott, "as grand, gloomy, and peculiar as Napoleon ever was in his palmiest days. The younger members of the club called him 'Zanona Redivivus.' He wanders through the house usually late at night, apparently without noticing anything or anybody. His mind seems to be deeply and busily at

Source: Melville Davisson Post from *The Strange Schemes of Randolph Mason*, 1896.

work, leaving his bodily self to wander as it may happen. Naturally, strange stories are told of him; indeed, his individuality and his habit of doing some unexpected thing, and doing it in such a marvelously original manner that men who are experts at it look on in wonder, cannot fail to make him an object of interest.

"He has never been known to play at any game whatever, and yet one night he sat down to the chess table with old Admiral Du Brey. You know the admiral is the great champion since he beat the French and English officers in the tournament last winter. Well, you also know that the conventional openings at chess are scientifically and accurately determined. To the utter disgust of Du Brey, Mason opened the game with an unheard-of attack from the extremes of the board. The old admiral stopped and, in a kindly patronizing way, pointed out the weak and absurd folly of his move and asked him to begin again with some one of the safe openings. Mason smiled and answered that if one had a head that he could trust he could use it; if not, then it was the part of wisdom to follow blindly the dead forms of some man who had a head. Du Brey was naturally angry and set himself to demolish Mason as quickly as possible. The game was rapid for a few moments. Mason lost piece after piece. His opening was broken and destroyed and its utter folly apparent to the lookers-on. The admiral smiled and the game seemed all one-sided, when, suddenly, to his utter horror, Du Brey found that his king was in a trap. The foolish opening had been only a piece of shrewd strategy. The old admiral fought and cursed and sacrificed his pieces, but it was of no use. He was gone. Mason checkmated him in two moves and arose wearily.

"'Where in Heaven's name, man,' said the old admiral, thunderstruck, 'did you learn that master-piece?'

"'Just here,' replied Mason. 'To play chess, one should know his opponent. How could the dead masters lay down rules by which you could be beaten, sir? They had never seen you'; and thereupon he turned and left the room. Of course, St. Clair, such a strange man would soon become an object of all kinds of mysterious rumors. Some are true and some are not. At any rate, I know that Mason is an unusual man with a gigantic intellect. Of late he seems to have taken a strange fancy to me. In fact, I seem to be the only member of the club that he will talk with, and I confess that he startles and fascinates me. He is an original genius, St. Clair, of an unusual order."

"I recall vividly," said the younger man, "that before Mason went to Paris he was considered one of the greatest lawyers of this city and he was feared and hated by the bar at large. He came here, I believe, from Virginia and began with the high-grade criminal practice. He soon became famous for his powerful and ingenious defenses. He found holes in the law through which his clients escaped, holes that by the profession at large were not suspected to exist, and that frequently astonished the judges. His ability caught the attention of the great corporations. They tested him and found in him learning and unlimited resources. He pointed out methods by which they could evade obnoxious statutes, by which they could comply with the apparent letter of the law and yet violate its spirit, and advised them well in that most important of all things, just how far they could bend the law without breaking it. At the time he left for Paris he had a vast clientage and he was in the midst of a brilliant career. The day he took passage from New York, the bar lost sight of him. No matter how great a man may be, the wave soon closes over him in a city like this. In a few years

Mason was forgotten. Now only the older practitioners would recall him, and they would do so with hatred and bitterness. He was a tireless, savage, uncompromising fighter, always a recluse."

"Well," said Walcott, "he reminds me of a great world-weary cynic, transplanted from some ancient mysterious empire. When I come into the man's presence I feel instinctively the grip of his intellect. I tell you, St. Clair, Randolph Mason is the mysterious man of New York."

At this moment a messenger boy came into the room and handed Mr. Walcott a telegram. "St. Clair," said the gentleman, rising, "the directors of the Elevated are in session, and we must hurry." The two men put on their coats and left the house.

Samuel Walcott was not a club man after the manner of the Smart Set, and yet he was in fact a club man. He was a bachelor in the latter thirties, and resided in a great silent house on the avenue. On the street he was a man of substance, shrewd and progressive, backed by great wealth. He had various corporate interests in the larger syndicates, but the basis and foundation of his fortune was real estate. His houses on the avenue were the best possible property, and his elevator row in the importers' quarter was indeed a literal gold mine. It was known that, many years before, his grandfather had died and left him the property, which, at that time, was of no great value. Young Walcott had gone out into the gold-fields and had been lost sight of and forgotten. Ten years afterward he had turned up suddenly in New York and taken possession of his property, then vastly increased in value. His speculations were almost phenomenally successful, and, backed by the now-enormous value of his real property, he was soon on a level with the merchant princes. His judgment was considered sound, and he had the full confidence of his business associates for safety and caution. Fortune heaped up riches around him with a lavish hand. He was unmarried and the halo of his wealth caught the keen eye of the matron with marriageable daughters. He was invited out, caught by the whirl of society, and tossed into its maelstrom. In a measure he reciprocated. He kept horses and a yacht. His dinners at Delmonico's and the club were above reproach. But with all he was a silent man with a shadow deep in his eyes, and seemed to court the society of his fellow, not because he loved them, but because he either hated or feared solitude. For years the strategy of the matchmaker had gone gracefully afield, but Fate is relentless. If she shields the victim from the traps of men, it is not because she wishes him to escape, but because she is pleased to reserve him for her own trap. So it happened that, when Virginia St. Clair assisted Mrs. Miriam Steuvisant at her midwinter reception, this same Samuel Walcott fell deeply and hopelessly and utterly in love, and it was so apparent to the beaten generals present that Mrs. Miriam Steuvisant applauded herself, so to speak, with encore after encore. It was good to see this courteous, silent man literally at the feet of the young debutante. He was there of right. Even the mothers of marriageable daughters admitted that. The young girl was brown-haired, browneyed, and tall enough, said the experts, and of the blue blood royal, with all the grace, courtesy, and inbred genius of such princely heritage.

Perhaps it was objected by the censors of the Smart Set that Miss St. Clair's frankness and honesty were a trifle old-fashioned, and that she was a shadowy bit of a puritan; and perhaps it was of these same qualities that Samuel Walcott received his hurt. At any rate the hurt was there and deep, and the new actor stepped up into the old, time-worn, semi-tragic drama, and began his role with a tireless, utter sincerity that was deadly dangerous if he lost.

II

Perhaps a week after the conversation between St. Clair and Walcott, Randolph Mason stood in the private writing-room of the club with his hands behind his back.

He was a man apparently in the middle forties; tall and reasonably broad across the shoulders; muscular without being either stout or lean. His hair was thin and of a brown color, with erratic streaks of gray. His forehead was broad and high and of a faint reddish color. His eyes were restless, inky black, and not over-large. The nose was big and muscular and bowed. The eyebrows were black and heavy, almost bushy. There were heavy furrows running from the nose downward and outward to the corners of the mouth. The mouth was straight and the jaw was heavy, and square.

Looking at the face of Randolph Mason from above, the expression in repose was crafty and cynical; viewed from below upward, it was savage and vindictive, almost brutal; while from the front, if looked squarely in the face, the stranger was fascinated by the animation of the man and at once concluded that his expression was fearless and sneering. He was evidently of Southern extraction and a man of unusual power.

A fire smoldered on the hearth. It was a crisp evening in the early fall, and with that far-off touch of melancholy which ever heralds the coming winter, even in the midst of a city. The man's face looked tired and ugly. His long white hands were clasped tight together. His entire figure and face wore every mark of weakness and physical exhaustion; but his eyes contradicted. They were red and restless.

In the private dining-room the dinner party was in the best of spirits. Samuel Walcott was happy. Across the table from him was Miss Virginia St. Clair, radiant, a tinge of color in her cheeks. On their side, Mrs. Miriam Steuvisant and Marshall St. Clair were brilliant and light-hearted. Walcott looked at the young girl and the measure of his worship was full. He wondered for the thousandth time how she could possibly love him and by what earthly miracle she had come to accept him, and how it would be always to have her across the table from him, his own table in his own house.

They were about to rise from the table when one of the waiters entered the room and handed Walcott an envelope. He thrust it quickly into his pocket. In the confusion of rising the others did not notice him, but his face was ash-white and his hands trembled violently as he placed the wraps around the bewitching shoulders of Miss St. Clair.

"Marshall," he said, and despite the powerful effort his voice was hollow, "you will see the ladies safely cared for, I am called to attend a grave matter."

"All right, Walcott," answered the young man, with cheery good-nature, "you are too serious, old man; trot along."

"The poor dear," murmured Mrs. Steuvisant, after Walcott had helped them to the carriage and turned to go up the steps of the club, "the poor dear is hard hit, and men are such funny creatures when they are hard hit."

Samuel Walcott, as his fate would, went direct to the private writing-room and opened the door. The lights were not turned on and in the dark he did not see Mason motionless by the mantel-shelf. He went quickly across the room to the writing-table, turned on one of the lights, and, taking the envelope from his pocket, tore it open. Then he bent down by the light to read the contents. As his eyes ran over the paper, his jaw fell. The skin drew away from his cheek-bones and his face seemed literally to sink in. His knees gave way under him and he would have gone down in a heap had it not been for Mason's long arms that closed around him and held him up. The human economy is ever mysterious. The moment the new danger threatened, the latent power of the man as an animal, hidden away in the centers of intelligence, asserted itself. His hand clutched the paper and, with a half slide, he turned in Mason's arms. For a moment he stared up at the ugly man whose thin arms felt like wire ropes.

"You are under the dead-fall, aye," said Mason. "The cunning of my enemy is sublime."

"Your enemy?" gasped Walcott. "When did you come into it? How in God's name did you know it? How your enemy?"

Mason looked down at the wide, bulging eyes of the man.

"Who should know better than I?" he said. "Haven't I broken through all the traps and plots that she could set?"

"She? She trap you?" The man's voice was full of horror.

"The old schemer," muttered Mason. "The cowardly old schemer, to strike in the back; but we can beat her. She did not count on my helping you—I, who know her so well."

Mason's face was red, and his eyes burned. In the midst of it all he dropped his hands and went over to the fire. Samuel Walcott arose, panting, and stood looking at Mason, with his hands behind him on the table. The naturally strong nature and the rigid school in which the man had been trained presently began to tell. His composure in part returned and he thought rapidly. What did this strange man know? Was he simply making shrewd guesses, or had he some mysterious knowledge of this matter? Walcott could not know that Mason meant only Fate, that he believed her to be his great enemy. Walcott had never before doubted his own ability to meet any emergency. This mighty jerk had carried him off his feet. He was unstrung and panic-stricken. At any rate this man had promised help. He would take it. He put the paper and envelope carefully into his pocket, smoothed out his rumpled coat, and going over to Mason touched him on the shoulder.

"Come," he said, "if you are to help me we must go."

The man turned and followed him without a word. In the hall Mason put on his hat and overcoat, and the two went out into the street. Walcott hailed a cab, and the two were driven to his house on the avenue. Walcott took out his latch-key, opened the door, and led the way into the library. He turned on the light and motioned Mason to seat himself at the table. Then he went into another room and presently returned with a bundle of papers and a decanter of brandy. He poured out a glass of the liquor and offered it to Mason. The man shook his head. Walcott poured the contents of the glass down his own throat. Then he set the decanter down and drew up a chair on the side of the table opposite Mason.

"Sir," said Walcott, in a voice deliberate, indeed, but as hollow as a sepulcher, "I am done for. God has finally gathered up the ends of the net, and it is knotted tight."

"Am I not here to help you?" said Mason, turning savagely. "I can beat Fate. Give me the details of her trap."

He bent forward and rested his arms on the table. His streaked gray hair was rumpled and on end, and his face was ugly. For a moment Walcott did not answer. He moved a little into the shadow; then he spread the bundle of old yellow papers out before him.

"To begin with," he said, "I am a living lie, a gilded, crime-made sham, every bit of me. There is not an honest piece anywhere. It is all lie. I am a liar and a thief before men. The property which I possess is not mine, but stolen from a dead man. The very name which I bear is not my own, but is the bastard child of a crime. I am more than all that—I am a murderer; a murderer before the law; a murderer before God; and worse than a murderer before the pure woman whom I love more than anything that God could make."

He paused for a moment and wiped the perspiration from his face.

"Sir," said Mason, "this is all drivel, infantile drivel. What you are is of no importance. How to get out is the problem, how to get out."

Samuel Walcott leaned forward, poured out a glass of brandy, and swallowed it.

"Well," he said, speaking slowly, "my right name is Richard Warren. In the spring of 1879 I came to New York and fell in with the real Samuel Walcott, a young man with a little money and some property which his grandfather had left him. We became friends, and concluded to go to the far west together. Accordingly we scraped together what money we could lay our hands on, and landed in the gold-mining regions of California. We were young and inexperienced, and our money went rapidly. One April morning we drifted into a little shack camp, away up in the Sierra Nevadas, called Hell's Elbow. Here we struggled and starved for perhaps a year. Finally, in utter desperation, Walcott married the daughter of a Mexican gambler, who ran an eating-house and a poker joint. With them we lived from hand to mouth in a wild, God-forsaken way for several years. After a time the woman began to take a strange fancy to me. Walcott finally noticed it, and grew jealous.

"One night, in a drunken brawl, we quarreled, and I killed him. It was late at night, and, beside the woman, there were four of us in the poker room—the Mexican gambler, a half-breed devil called Cherubim Pete, Walcott, and myself. When Walcott fell, the half-breed whipped out his weapon and fired at me across the table; but the woman, Nina San Croix, struck his arm, and, instead of killing me, as he intended, the bullet mortally wounded her father, the Mexican gambler. I shot the half-breed through the forehead and turned around, expecting the woman to attack me. On the contrary, she pointed to the window and bade me wait for her on the cross-trail below.

"It was fully three hours later before the woman joined me at the place indicated. She had a bag of gold dust, a few jewels that belonged to her father, and a package of papers. I asked her why she had stayed behind so long, and she replied that the men were not killed outright and that she had brought a priest to them and waited until they had died. This was the truth, but not all the truth. Moved by superstition or foresight, the woman had induced the priest to take down the sworn statements of the two dying men, seal it, and give it to her. This paper she brought with her. All this I learned afterward. At the time I knew nothing of this damning evidence.

"We struck out together for the Pacific coast. The country was lawless. The privations we endured were almost past belief. At times the woman exhibited cunning and ability that were almost genius; and through it all, often in the very fingers of death, her devotion to me never wavered. It was dog-like and seemed to be her only object on earth. When we reached San Francisco, the woman put these papers into my hands." Walcott took up the yellow package, and pushed it across the table to Mason.

"She proposed that I assume Walcott's name, and that we come boldly to New York and claim the property. I examined the papers, found a copy of a will by which Walcott inherited the property, a bundle of correspondence, and sufficient documentary evidence to establish his identity beyond the shadow of a doubt. Desperate gambler as I now was, I quailed before the daring plan of Nina San Croix. I urged that I, Richard Warren, would be known, that the attempted fraud would be detected and would result in investigation, and perhaps unearth the whole horrible matter.

"The woman pointed out how much I resembled Walcott, what vast changes ten years of such life as we had led would naturally be expected to make in men, how utterly impossible it would be to trace back the fraud to Walcott's murder at Hell's Elbow, in the wild passes of the Sierra Nevadas. She bade me remember that we were both outcasts, both crime-branded, both enemies of man's law and God's; that we had nothing to lose; we were both sunk to the bottom. Then she laughed, and said that she had not found me a coward until now, but that if I had turned chicken-hearted, that was the end of it, of course. The result was, we sold the gold dust and jewels in San Francisco, took on such evidences of civilization as possible, and purchased passage to New York on the best steamer we could find.

"I was growing to depend on the bold gambler spirit of this woman, Nina San Croix; I felt the need of her strong, profligate nature. She was of a queer breed and a queerer school. Her mother was the daughter of a Spanish engineer, and had been stolen by the Mexican, her father. She herself had been raised and educated as best as might be in one of the monasteries along the Rio Grande, and had there grown to womanhood before her father, fleeing into the mountains of California, carried her with him.

"When we landed in New York I offered to announce her as my wife, but she refused, saying that her presence would excite comment and perhaps attract the attention of Walcott's relatives. We therefore arranged that I should go alone into the city, claim the property, and announce myself as Samuel Walcott, and that she should remain undercover until such time as we could feel the ground safe under us.

"Every detail of the plan was fatally successful. I established my identity without difficulty and secured the property. It had increased vastly in value, and I, as Samuel Walcott, soon found myself a rich man. I went to Nina San Croix in hiding and gave her a large sum of money, with which she purchased a residence in a retired part of the city, far up in a northern suburb. Here she lived secluded and unknown while I remained in the city, living here as a wealthy bachelor.

"I did not attempt to abandon the woman, but went to her from time to time in disguise and under cover of the greatest secrecy. For a time everything ran smooth, the woman was still devoted to me above everything else, and thought always of my welfare first and seemed content to wait so long as I thought best. My business expanded. I was sought after and consulted and drawn into the higher life of New York, and more and more felt that the woman was an albatross on my neck. I put her off with one excuse after another. Finally she began to suspect me and demanded that I should recognize her as my wife. I attempted to point out the difficulties. She met them all by saying that we should both go to Spain, there I could marry her, and we could return to America and drop into my place in society without causing more than a passing comment.

"I concluded to meet the matter squarely once for all. I said that I would convert half of the property into money and give it to her, but that I would not marry her. She did not fly into a storming rage as I had expected, but went quietly out of the room and presently returned with two papers, which she read. One was the certificate of her marriage to Walcott duly authenticated; the other was the dying statement of her father, the Mexican gambler, and of Samuel Walcott, charging me with murder. It was in proper form and certified by the Jesuit priest.

"'Now,' she said, sweetly, when she had finished, 'which do you prefer, to recognize your wife or to turn all the property over to Samuel Walcott's widow and hang for his murder?'

"I was dumbfounded and horrified. I saw the trap that I was in and I consented to do anything she should say if she would only destroy the papers. This she refused to do. I pleaded with her and implored her to destroy them. Finally she gave them to me with a great show of returning confidence, and I tore them into bits and threw them into the fire.

"That was three months ago. We arranged to go to Spain and do as she said. She was to sail this morning and I was to follow. Of course I never intended to go. I congratulated myself on the fact that all trace of evidence against me was destroyed and that her grip was now broken. My plan was to induce her to sail, believing that I would follow. When she was gone I would marry Miss St. Clair, and if Nina San Croix should return I would defy her and lock her up as a lunatic. But I was reckoning like an infernal ass, to imagine for a moment that I could thus hoodwink such a woman as Nina San Croix.

"Tonight I received this." Walcott took the envelope from his pocket and gave it to Mason. "You saw the effect of it; read it and you will understand why. I felt the death hand when I saw her writing on the envelope."

Mason took the paper from the envelope. It was written in Spanish and ran:

"Greeting to RICHARD WARREN.

"The great Señor does his Little Nina injustice to think she would go away to Spain and leave him to the beautiful America. She is not so thoughtless. Before she goes, she shall be, oh so very rich! and the dear Señor shall be, oh so very safe! The archbishop and the kind church hate murderers.

"*Nina San Croix.*

"Of course, fool, the papers you destroyed were copies.

"*N. San C.*"

To this was pinned a line in a delicate, aristocratic hand, saying that the archbishop would willingly listen to Madam San Croix's statement if she would come to him on Friday morning at eleven.

"You see," said Walcott, desperately, "there is no possible way out. I know the woman—when she decides to do a thing that is the end of it. She has decided to do this."

Mason turned around from the table, stretched out his long legs, and thrust his hands deep into his pockets. Walcott sat with his head down, watching Mason hopelessly, almost indifferently, his face blank and sunken. The ticking of the bronze clock on the mantel shelf was loud, painfully loud. Suddenly Mason drew his knees in and bent over, put both his bony hands on the table, and looked at Walcott.

"Sir," he said, "this matter is in much shape that there is only one thing to do. This growth must be cut out at the roots, and cut out quickly. This is the first fact to be determined, and a fool would know it. The second fact is that you must do it yourself. Hired killers are like the grave and the daughters of the horse,—leech—they cry always, 'Give, Give.' They are only palliatives, not cures. By using them you swap perils. You simply take a stay of execution at best. The common criminal would know this. These are the facts of your problem. The master plotters of crime would see here but two difficulties to meet:

"A practical method for accomplishing the body of the crime.

"A cover for the criminal agent.

"They would see no farther, and attempt to guard no farther. After they had provided a plan for the killing and a means by which the killer could cover his trail and escape from the theater of the homicide, they would believe all the requirements of the problems met, and would stop. The greatest, the very giants among them, have stopped here and have been in great error.

"In every crime, especially in the great ones, there exists a third element, preeminently vital. This third element the master plotters have either overlooked or else have not had the genius to construct. They plan with rare cunning to baffle the victim. They plan with vast wisdom, almost genius, to baffle the trailer. But they fail utterly to provide any plan for baffling the punisher. Ergo, their plots are fatally defective and often result in ruin. Hence the vital necessity for providing the third element—the escape *ipso jure*."

Mason arose, walked around the table, and put his hand firmly on Samuel Walcott's shoulder. "This must be done tomorrow night," he continued; "you must arrange your business matters tomorrow and announce that you are going on a yacht cruise, by order of your physician, and may not return for some weeks. You must prepare your yacht for a voyage, instruct your men to touch at a certain point on Staten Island, and wait until six o'clock day after tomorrow morning. If you do not come aboard by that time, they are to go to one of the South American ports and remain until further orders. By this means your absence for an indefinite period will be explained. You will go to Nina San Croix in the disguise which you have always used, and from her to the yacht, and by this means step out of your real status and back into it without leaving traces. I will come here tomorrow evening and furnish you with everything that you shall need and give you full and exact instructions in every particular. These details you must execute with the greatest care, as they will be vitally essential to the success of my plan."

Through it all Walcott had been silent and motionless. Now he arose, and in his face there must have been some premonition of protest, for Mason stepped back and put out his hand. "Sir," he said, with brutal emphasis, "not a word. Remember that you are only the hand, and the hand does not think." Then he turned around abruptly and went out of the house.

III

The place which Samuel Walcott had selected for the residence of Nina San Croix was far up in a northern suburb of New York. The place was very old. The lawn was large and ill-kept; the house, a square old-fashioned brick, was set far back from the street and partly hidden by trees. Around it all was a rusty iron fence. The place had the air of genteel ruin, such as one finds in the Virginias.

On a Thursday of November, about three o'clock in the afternoon, a little man, driving a dray, stopped in the alley at the rear of the house. As he opened the back gate an old Negro woman came down the steps from the kitchen and demanded to know what he wanted. The drayman asked if the lady of the house was in. The old Negro answered that she was asleep at this hour and could not be seen.

"That is good," said the little man; "now there won't be any row. I brought up some cases of wine which she ordered from our house last week and which the boss told me to deliver at once, but I forgot it until today. Just let me put it in the cellar now, Auntie, and don't say a word to the lady about it and she won't ever know that it was not brought up on time."

The drayman stopped, fished a silver dollar out of his pocket, and gave it to the old Negro. "There now, Auntie," he said, "my job depends upon the lady not knowing about this wine; keep it mum."

"Dat's all right, honey," said the old servant, beaming like a May morning. "De cellar door is open, carry it all in and put it in de back part and nobody ain't never going to know how long it has been in dar."

The old Negro went back into the kitchen and the little man began to unload the dray. He carried in five wine cases and stowed them away in the back part of the cellar as the old woman had directed. Then, after having satisfied himself that no one was watching, he took from the dray two heavy paper sacks, presumably filled with flour, and a little bundle wrapped in an old newspaper; these he carefully hid behind the wine cases in the cellar. After a while he closed the door, climbed on his dray, and drove off down the alley.

About eight o'clock in the evening of the same day a Mexican sailor dodged in the front gate and slipped down to the side of the house. He stopped by the window and tapped on it with his finger. In a moment a woman opened the door. She was tall, lithe, and splendidly proportioned, with a dark Spanish face and straight hair. The man stepped inside. The woman bolted the door and turned round.

"Ah," she said, smiling, "it is you, Señor? How good of you."

The man started. "Whom else did you expect?" he said quickly.

"Oh!" laughed the woman, "perhaps the archbishop."

"Nina!" said the man, in a broken voice that expressed love, humility, and reproach. His face was white under the black sunburn.

For a moment the woman wavered. A shadow flitted over her eyes, then she stepped back. "No," she said, "not yet."

The man walked across to the fire, sank down in a chair, and covered his face with his hands. The woman stepped up noiselessly behind him and leaned over the chair. The man was either in great agony or else he was a superb actor, for the muscles of his neck twitched violently and his shoulders trembled.

"Oh," he muttered, as though echoing his thoughts, "I can't do it, I can't!"

The woman caught the words and leaped up as though some one had struck her in the face. She threw back her head. Her nostrils dilated and her eyes flashed.

"You can't do it!" she cried. "Then you do love her! You shall do it! Do you hear me? You shall do it! You killed him! You got rid of him! But you shall not get rid of me. I have the evidence, all of it. The archbishop will have it tomorrow. They shall hang you! Do you hear me? They shall hang you!"

The woman's voice rose, it was loud and shrill. The man turned slowly round without looking up, and stretched out his arms toward the woman. She stopped and looked down at him. The fire glittered for a moment and then died out of her eyes, her bosom heaved and her lips began to tremble. With a cry she flung herself into his arms, caught him around the neck, and pressed his face up against her cheek.

"Oh! Dick, Dick," she sobbed, "I do love you so! I can't live without you! Not another hour, Dick! I do want you so much, so much, Dick!"

The man shifted his right arm quickly, slipped a great Mexican knife out of his sleeve, and passed his fingers slowly up the woman's side until he felt the heart beat under his hand, then he raised the knife, gripped the handle tight, and drove the keen blade into the woman's bosom. The hot blood gushed out over his arm and down on his leg. The body, warm and limp, slipped down in his arms. The man got up, pulled out the knife, and thrust it into a sheath at his belt, unbuttoned the dress, and slipped it off of the body. As he did this a bundle of papers dropped upon the floor; these he glanced at hastily and put into his pocket. Then he took the dead woman up in his arms, went out into the hall, and started to go up the stairway. The body was relaxed and heavy, and for that reason difficult to carry. He doubled it up into an awful heap, with the knees against the chin, and walked slowly and heavily up the stairs and out into the bath-room. There he laid the corpse down on the tiled floor. Then he opened the window, closed the shutters, and lighted the gas. The bath-room was small and contained an ordinary steel tub, porcelain-lined, standing near the window and raised about six inches above the floor. The sailor went over to the tub, pried up the metal rim of the outlet with his knife, removed it, and fitted into it place a porcelain disk which he took from his pocket; to this disk was attached a long platinum wire, the end of which he fastened on the outside of the tub. After he had done this he went back to the body, stripped off its clothing, put it down in the tub, and began to dismember it with the great Mexican knife. The knife was strong and sharp as a razor. The man worked rapidly and with the greatest care.

When he had finally cut the body into as small pieces as possible, he replaced the knife in its sheath, washed his hands, and went out of the bathroom and downstairs to the lower hall. The sailor seemed perfectly familiar with the house. By a side door he passed into the cellar. There he lighted the gas, opened one of the wine cases, and taking up all the bottles that he could conveniently carry, returned to the bath-room. There he poured the contents into the tub on the dismembered body and then returned to the cellar with the empty bottles, which he replaced in the wine cases. This he continued to do until all the cases but one were emptied and the bathtub was more than half full of liquid. The liquid was sulfuric acid.

When the sailor returned to the cellar with the last empty wine bottles, he opened the fifth case, which really contained wine, took some of it out, and poured a little into each of the empty bottles in order to remove any possible odor of the sulfuric acid. Then he turned out the gas and brought up to the bath-room with him the two paper flour sacks and the little heavy bundle. These sacks were filled with nitrate of soda. He set them down by the door, opened the little bundle, and took out two long rubber tubes, each attached to a heavy gas burner, not unlike the ordinary burners of a small gas-stove. He fastened the tubes to two of the gas jets, put the burners under the tub, turned the gas on full, and lighted it. Then he threw into the tub the woman's clothing and the papers which he had found on her body, after which he took up the two heavy sacks of nitrate of soda and dropped them carefully into the sulfuric acid. When he had done this he went quickly out of the bath-room and closed the door.

The deadly acids at once attacked the body and began to destroy it; as the heat increased, the acids boiled and the destructive process was rapid and awful. From time to time the sailor opened the door of the bath-room cautiously and, holding a wet towel over his mouth and nose, looked in at his horrible work. At the end of a few hours there was only a swimming mass in the tub. When the man looked at four o'clock, it was all a thick, murky liquid. He turned off the gas quickly and stepped back out of the room. For perhaps half an hour he waited in the hall; finally, when the acids had cooled so that they no longer gave off fumes, he opened the door and went in, took hold of the platinum wire and, pulling the porcelain disk from the stop-cock, allowed the awful contents of the tub to run out. Then he turned on the hot water, rinsed the tub clean, and replaced the metal outlet. Removing the rubber tubes, he cut them into pieces, broke the porcelain disk, and rolling up the platinum wire, washed it all down the sewer pipe.

The fumes had escaped through the open window; this he now closed and set himself to putting the bath-room in order, and effectually removing every trace of his night's work. The sailor moved around with the very greatest degree of care. Finally, when he had arranged everything to his complete satisfaction, he picked up the two burners, turned out the gas, and left the bath-room, closing the door after him. From the bath-room he went directly to the attic, concealed the two rusty burners under a heap of rubbish, and then walked carefully and noiselessly down the stairs and the lower hall. As he opened the door and stepped into the room where he had killed the woman, two police officers sprang out and seized him. The man screamed like a wild beast taken in a trap, and sank down.

"Oh! oh!" he cried, "it was no use! It was no use to do it!" Then he recovered himself in a manner and was silent. The officers handcuffed him, summoned the patrol, and took him at once to the station-house. There he said he was a Mexican sailor and that his name was Victor Ancona; but he would say nothing further. The following morning he sent for Randolph Mason and the two were long together.

IV

The obscure defendant charged with murder has little reason to complain of the law's delays. The morning following the arrest of Victor Ancona, the newspapers published long sensational articles, denounced him as a fiend, and convicted him. The grand jury, as it happened, was in session. The preliminaries were soon arranged and the case was railroaded into trial. The indictment contained a great many counts and charged the prisoner with the murder of Nina San Croix by striking, stabbing, choking, poisoning, and so forth.

The trial had continued for three days and had appeared so overwhelmingly one-sided that the spectators who were crowded into the courtroom had grown to be violent and bitter partisans, to such an extent that the police watched them closely. The attorneys for the People were dramatic and denunciatory and forced their case with arrogant confidence. Mason, as counsel for the prisoner, was indifferent and listless. Throughout the entire trial he had sat almost motionless at the table, his gaunt form bent over, his long legs drawn up under his chair, and his weary, heavy-muscled face, with its restless eyes, fixed and staring out over the heads of the jury, was like a tragic mask. The bar, and even the judge, believed that the prisoner's counsel had abandoned his case.

The evidence was all in and the People rested. It had been shown that Nina San Croix had resided for many years in the house in which the prisoner was arrested; that she had lived by herself, with no other companion than an old Negro servant; that her past was unknown, and that she received no visitors, save the Mexican sailor, who came to her house at long intervals. Nothing whatever was shown tending to explain who the prisoner was or whence he had come. It was shown that on Tuesday preceding the killing the archbishop had received a communication from Nina San Croix, in which she said she desired to make a statement of the greatest import, and asking for an audience. To this the archbishop replied that he would willingly grant her a hearing if she would come to him at eleven o'clock on Friday morning. Two policemen testified that about eight o'clock on the night of Thursday they had noticed the prisoner slip into the gate of Nina San Croix's residence and go down to the side of the house, where he was admitted; that his appearance and seeming haste had attracted their attention; that they had concluded that it was some clandestine amour, and out of curiosity had both slipped down to the house and endeavored to find a position from which they could see into the room, but were unable to do so and were about to go back to the street when they heard a woman's voice cry out in great anger: "I know that you love her and that you want to get rid of me, but you shall not do it! You murdered him, but you shall not murder me! I have all the evidence to convict you of murdering him! The archbishop will have it tomorrow! They shall hang you! Do you hear me? They shall hang you for this murder!" That thereupon one of the policeman proposed that they should break into the house and see what was wrong, but the other had urged that it was only the usual lovers' quarrel and if they should interfere they would find nothing upon which a charge could be based and would only be laughed at by the chief; that they had waited and listened for a time, but hearing nothing further had gone back to the street and contented themselves with keeping a strict watch on the house.

The People proved further, that on Thursday evening Nina San Croix had given the old Negro domestic a sum of money and dismissed her, with the instruction that she was not to return until sent for. The old woman testified that she had gone directly to the house of her son, and later had discovered that she had forgotten some articles of clothing which she needed; that thereupon she had returned to the house and had gone up the back way to her room—this was about eight o'clock; that while there she had heard Nina San Croix's voice in great passion and remembered that she had used the words stated by the policeman; that these sudden, violent cries had frightened her greatly and she had bolted the door and been afraid to leave the room; shortly thereafter, she had heard heavy footsteps ascending the stairs, slowly and with great difficulty, as though someone were carrying a heavy burden; that therefore her fear had increased and that she had put out the light and hidden under the bed. She remembered hearing the footsteps moving about upstairs for many hours, how long she could not tell. Finally, about half-past four in the morning she crept out, opened the door, slipped downstairs, and ran out into the street. There she had found the policemen and requested them to search the house.

The two officers had gone to the house with the woman. She had opened the door and they had just had time to step back into the shadow when the prisoner entered. When arrested, Victor Ancona had screamed with terror and cried out, "It was no use! It was no use to do it!"

The chief of police had come to the house and instituted a careful search. In the room below, from which the cries had come, he found a dress which was identified as belonging to

Nina San Croix and which she was wearing when last seen by the domestic, about six o'clock that evening. This dress was covered with blood, and had a slit about two inches long in the left side of the bosom, into which the Mexican knife, found on the prisoner, fitted perfectly. These articles were introduced in evidence, and it was shown that the slit would be exactly over the heart of the wearer, and that such a wound would certainly result in death. There was much blood on one of the chairs and on the floor. There was also blood on the prisoner's coat and the leg of his trousers, and the heavy Mexican knife was also bloody. The blood was shown by the experts to be human blood.

The body of the woman was not found, and the most rigid and tireless search failed to develop the slightest trace of the corpse, or the manner of its disposal. The body of the woman had disappeared as completely as though it had vanished into the air.

When counsel announced that he had closed for the People, the judge turned and looked gravely down at Mason. "Sir," he said, "the evidence for the defense may now be introduced."

Randolph Mason arose slowly and faced the judge.

"If your Honor please," he said, speaking slowly and distinctly, "the defendant has no evidence to offer." He paused while a murmur of astonishment ran over the court-room. "But, if your Honor please," he continued, "I move that the jury be directed to find the prisoner not guilty."

The crowd stirred. The counsel for the People smiled. The judge looked sharply at the speaker over his glasses. "On what ground?" he said curtly.

"On the ground," replied Mason, "that the *corpus delicti* has not been proven."

"Ah!" said the judge, for once losing his judicial gravity.

Mason sat down abruptly. The senior counsel for the prosecution was on his feet in a moment.

"What!" he said. "The gentleman bases his motion on a failure to establish the *corpus delicti*? Does he jest or has he forgotten the evidence? The term '*corpus delicti*' is technical, and means the body of the crime, or the substantial fact that a crime has been committed. Does anyone doubt it in this case? It is true that no one actually saw the prisoner kill the decedent, and that he has so successfully hidden the body that it has not been found, but the powerful chain of circumstances, clear and close-linked, proving motive, the criminal agency, and the criminal act, is overwhelming.

"The victim in this case is on the eve of making a statement that would prove fatal to the prisoner. The night before the statement is to be made he goes to her residence. They quarrel. Her voice is heard, raised high in the greatest passion, denouncing him, and charging that he is a murderer, that she has the evidence and will reveal it, that he shall be hanged and that he shall not be rid of her. Here is the motive for the crime, clear as light. Are not the bloody knife, the bloody dress, the bloody clothes of the prisoner, unimpeachable witnesses to the criminal act? The criminal agency of the prisoner has not the shadow of a possibility to obscure it. His motive is gigantic. The blood on him, and his despair when arrested, cry, 'Murder! murder!' with a thousand tongues.

"Men may lie, but circumstances cannot. The thousand hopes and fears and passions of men may delude, or bias the witness. Yet it is beyond the human mind to conceive that a clear, complete chain of concatenated circumstances can be in error. Hence it is that the greatest jurists have declared that such evidence, being rarely liable to delusion or fraud, is safest and most powerful. The machinery of human justice cannot guard against the remote and improbable doubt. The inference is persistent in the affairs of men. It is the only means by which the human mind reaches the truth. If you forbid the jury to exercise it, you bid them work after first striking off their hands. Rule out the irresistible inference, and the need of justice is come in this land; and you may as well leave the spider to weave his web through the abandoned court-room."

The attorney stopped, looked down at Mason with a pompous sneer, and retired to his place at the table. The judge sat thoughtful and motionless. The jurymen leaned forward in their seats.

"If your Honor please," said Mason, rising, "this is a matter of law, plain, clear, and so well settled in the State of New York that even counsel for the People should know it. The question before your Honor is simple. If the *corpus delicti,* the body of the crime, has been proven, as required by the laws of the commonwealth, then this case should go to the jury. If not, then it is the duty of this court to direct the jury to find the prisoner not guilty. There is here no room for judicial discretion. Your Honor has but to recall and apply the rigid rule announced by our courts prescribing distinctly how the *corpus delicti* in murder must be proven.

"The prisoner here stands charged with the highest crime. The law demands, first, that the crime, as a fact, be established. The fact that the victim is indeed dead must first be made certain before anyone can be convicted of her killing, because, so long as there remains the remotest doubt as to the death, there can be no certainty as to the criminal agent, although the circumstantial evidence indicating the guilt of the accused may be positive, complete, and utterly irresistible. In murder, the *corpus delicti,* or body of the crime, is composed of two elements:

"Death, as a result.

"The criminal agency of another as the means.

"It is the fixed and immutable law of this state, laid down in the leading case of Ruloff *v.* The People, and binding upon this court, that both components of the *corpus delicti* shall not be established by circumstantial evidence. There must be direct proof of one or the other of the these two component elements of the *corpus delicti.* If one is proven by direct evidence, the other may be presumed; but both shall not be presumed from circumstances, no matter how powerful, how cogent, or how completely overwhelming the circumstances may be. In other words no man can be convicted of murder in the State of New York, unless the body of the victim be found and identified, or there be direct proof that the prisoner did some act adequate to produce death, and did it in such a manner as to account for the disappearance of the body."

The face of the judge cleared and grew hard. The members of the bar were attentive and alert; they were beginning to see the legal escape open up. The audience were puzzled; they did not yet understand. Mason turned to the counsel for the People. His ugly face was bitter with contempt.

"For three days," he said, "I have been tortured by this useless and expensive farce. If counsel for the People had been other than play-actors, they would have known in the beginning that Victor Ancona could not be convicted for murder, unless he were confronted in this courtroom with a living witness, who had looked into the dead face of Nina San Croix; or, if not that, a living witness who had seen him drive the dagger into her bosom.

"I care not if the circumstantial evidence in this case were so strong and irresistible as to be overpowering; if the judge on the bench, if the jury, if every man within sound of my voice, were convinced of the guilt of the prisoner to the degree of certainty that is absolute; if the circumstantial evidence left in the mind no shadow of the remotest improbable doubt; yet, in the absence of the eyewitnesses, this prisoner cannot be punished, and this court must compel the jury to acquit him."

The audience now understood, and they were dumfounded. Surely this was not the law. They had been taught that the law was common sense, and this—this was anything else.

Mason saw it all, and grinned. "In its tenderness," he sneered, "the law shields the innocent. The good law of New York reaches out its hand and lifts the prisoner out of the clutches of the fierce jury that would hang him."

Mason sat down. The room was silent. The jurymen looked at each other in amazement. The counsel for the People arose. His face was white with anger, and incredulous.

"Your Honor," he said, "this doctrine is monstrous. Can it be said that, in order to evade punishment, the murderer has only to hide or destroy the body of the victim or sink it into the sea? Then, if he is not seen to kill, the law is powerless and the murderer can snap his finger in the face of retributive justice. If this is the law, then the law for the highest crime is a dead letter. The great commonwealth winks at murder and invites every man to kill his enemy, provided he kill him in secret and hide him. I repeat, your Honor"—the man's voice was now loud and angry and rang through the court-room—"that this doctrine is monstrous!"

"So said Best, and Story, and many another," muttered Mason, "and the law remained."

"The court," said the judge, abruptly, "desires no further argument."

The counsel for the People resumed his seat. His face lighted up with triumph. The court was going to sustain him.

The judge turned and looked down at the jury. He was grave, and spoke with deliberate emphasis.

"Gentlemen of the jury," he said, "the rule of Lord Hale obtains in this state and is binding upon me. It is the law as stated by counsel for the prisoner: that to warrant conviction of murder there must be direct proof either of the death, as of the finding and identification of the corpse, or of criminal violence adequate to produce death, and exerted in such a manner as to account for the disappearance of the body; and it is only when there is direct proof of the one that the other can be established by circumstantial evidence. This is law, and cannot now be departed from. I do not presume to explain its wisdom. Chief-Justice Johnson has observed, in the leading case, that it may have its probable foundation in the idea that where direct proof is absent as to both the fact of the death and of criminal violence capable of producing death, no evidence can rise to the degree of moral certainty that the individual is dead by criminal intervention, or even lead by direct inference to this result; and that, where the fact of death is not certainly ascertained, all inculpatory circumstantial evidence wants the key necessary for its satisfactory interpretation, and cannot be depended on to furnish more than probable results. It may be, also, that such a rule has some reference to the dangerous possibility that a general preconception of guilt, or a general excitement of popular feeling, may creep in to supply the place of evidence, if, upon other than direct proof of death or a cause of death, a jury are permitted to pronounce a prisoner guilty.

"In this case the body has not been found and there is no direct proof of criminal agency on the part of the prisoner, although the chain of circumstantial evidence is complete and irresistible in the highest degree. Nevertheless, it is all circumstantial evidence, and under the laws of New York the prisoner cannot be punished. I have no right of discretion. The law does not permit a conviction in this case, although every one of us may be morally certain of the prisoner's guilt. I am, therefore, gentlemen of the jury, compelled to direct you to find the prisoner not guilty."

"Judge," interrupted the foreman, jumping up in the box, "we cannot find the verdict under our oath; we know that this man is guilty."

"Sir," said the judge, "this is matter of law in which the wishes of the jury cannot be considered. The clerk will write a verdict of not guilty, which you, as foreman, will sign."

The spectators broke out into a threatening murmur that began to grow and gather volume. The judge rapped on his desk and ordered the bailiffs promptly to suppress any demonstration on the part of the audience. Then he directed the foreman to sign the verdict prepared by the clerk. When this was done he turned to Victor Ancona; his face was hard and there was a cold glitter in his eyes.

"Prisoner at the bar," he said, "you have been put to trail before this tribunal on a charge of cold-blooded and atrocious murder. The evidence produced against you was of such powerful and overwhelming character that it seems to have left no doubt in the minds of the jury, nor indeed in the mind of any person present in this court-room.

"Had the question of your guilt been submitted to these twelve arbiters, a conviction would certainly have resulted and the death penalty would have been imposed. But the law, rigid, passionless, even-eyed, has thrust in between you and the wrath of your fellows and saved you from it. I do not cry out against the impotency of the law; it is perhaps as wise as imperfect humanity could make it. I deplore, rather, the genius of evil men who, by cunning design, are enabled to slip through the fingers of this law. I have no word of censure or admonition for you, Victor Ancona. The law of New York compels me to acquit you. I am only its mouthpiece, with my individual wishes throttled. I speak only those things which the law directs I shall speak.

"You are now at liberty to leave this court-room, not guiltless of the crime of murder, perhaps, but at least rid of its punishment. The eyes of men may see Cains' mark on your brow, but the eyes of the law are blind to it."

When the audience fully realized what the judge had said they were amazed and silent. They know as well as men could know that Victor Ancona was guilty of murder, and yet he was now going out of the courtroom free. Could it happen that the law protected only against the blundering rogue? They had heard always of the boasted completeness of the law which magistrates from time immemorial had labored to perfect, and now when the skillful villain sought to evade it, they saw how weak a thing it was.

V

The wedding march of Lohengrin floated out from the Episcopal Church of St. Mark, clear and sweet, and perhaps heavy with its paradox of warning. The theater of this coming contract before high heaven was a wilderness of roses worth the taxes of a country. The high caste of Manhattan, by the grace of the check-book, were present, clothed in Parisian purple and fine linen, cunningly and marvelously wrought.

Over in her private pew, ablaze with jewels and decked with fabrics from the deft hand of many a weaver, sat Mrs. Miriam Steuvisant as imperious and self-complacent as a queen. To her it was all a kind of triumphal procession, proclaiming her ability as a general. With her were a choice few of the *genus homo,* which obtains at the five-o'clock teas, instituted, say the sages, for the purpose of sprinkling the holy water of Lethe.

"Czarina," whispered Reggie Du Puyster, leaning forward, "I salute you. The ceremony *sub jugum* is superb."

"Walcott is an excellent fellow," answered Mrs. Steuvisant, "not a vice, you know, Reggie."

"Aye, Empress," put in the other, "a purist taken in the net. The clean-skirted one has come to the altar. *Vive la vertu!*"

Samuel Walcott, still sunburned from his cruise, stood before the chancel with the only daughter of the blue-blooded St. Clairs. His face was clear and honest and his voice firm. This was life and not romance. The lid of the sepulcher had closed and he had slipped from under it. And now, and ever after, the hand red with murder was clean as any.

The minister raised his voice, proclaiming the holy union before God, and this twain, half pure, half foul, now by divine ordinance one flesh, bowed down before it. No blood cried from the ground. The sunlight of high noon streamed down through the windowpanes like a benediction.

Back in the pew of Mrs. Miriam Steuvisant, Reggie Du Puyster turned down his thumb. "Habet!" he said.

Critical Thinking

Since in this story the murderer destroyed all traces of the body, he could not be found guilty. Is this the standard of proof today?

Did you find the prosecution convincing? The defense? Why or why not?

Is the judge's reticence about establishing a precedent a valid objection to convicting the defendant?

Why does Post include the wedding scene at the story's end?

Does Post appear to be shining a light on a weakness in the criminal justice system at the time, and if so, what is he revealing?

How could this be a warning for today's criminal justice system as well?

Ethics and Professionalism: Defense Attorneys

"The Letter"
by W. Somerset Maugham

NOTE: This short story in not included in this anthology but may be found on the Internet or at your university or college library.

W. Somerset Maugham (1874–1965) was a British playwright, novelist, and short story writer. His semibiographical novel *Of Human Bondage* is his most celebrated work. His family—father, grandfather, and three brothers—consisted of lawyers; however, Maugham broke with this tradition and received a medical degree in London in 1897. Maugham traveled widely and used those travel destinations as settings in his fiction. While visiting Singapore in 1924, Maugham heard the story of the trial of Eurasian Ethel Mabel Proudlock, who was married to a headmaster of a prestigious secondary school for boys. In her home in Kuala Lumpur, Malaysia, Proudlock had shot a man whom she claimed tried to rape her. Though Proudlock was convicted of murder and sentenced to death, the European community in Malaysia appealed and won a pardon for her (after she had been detained in jail for five months). Proudlock moved to England with her young daughter and later to America, where she died in 1977. Maugham fashioned his short story "The Letter" (1924) after this real-life case. The story was made into a play, which was performed in London and on Broadway, and then into a 1940 film, starring Bette Davis.

"The Letter" is told in the third person from the perspective of a defense attorney, Mr. Joyce, in Singapore. Joyce zealously defends his client, Leslie Crosbie, after she murders a neighbor, Hammond, by shooting him six times. At first, Leslie claims that she acted in self-defense when Hammond attempted to rape her. After building his strategy on self-defense, Joyce is presented with the opportunity of having Leslie's husband buy a letter from Louise to Hammond that would incriminate her.

In the 1920s, when this story was written, Singapore was under British rule, so the criminal courts would be subject to law similar to the U.S. Fifth Amendment, which protects a defendant from self-incrimination. The prosecution would have been required to disclose evidence that might show the defendant is not guilty, but is the defense obligated to present evidence that might lead to finding his client guilty? Initially, Joyce appears to think he has that obligation because when Leslie asks him about the possibility of obtaining the letter, he says, "'Do you think it's so simple as all that to secure possession of an unwelcome piece of evidence? It's no different from suborning a witness. You have no right to make any such suggestion to me.'" By suborning a witness, he means bribing a witness to lie or commit perjury. Yet despite Joyce's protestations, he does something he declares "unjustifiable": he arranges for Mr. Crosbie to buy the letter because otherwise the letter holder will take it to the prosecution.

Critical Thinking

Do you find Leslie's first version of her murder of Hammond believable? Why or why not?

What about that version concerned her lawyer?

How does Joyce plan to use the bigotry of the jury regarding Hammond's living with a Chinese woman to his client's advantage? Why do you think Joyce takes such a chance?

How believable is Leslie's second version of the murder (once the letter comes to light)? What if Leslie had told Joyce the truth at this point—rather than after the trial—what would have been his responsibility if any? Would Joyce be obligated to put his client on the stand?

How would our criminal justice system be different if defense attorneys were allowed to withhold evidence that might shed light on the case, as Joyce did?

The Jury: Deliberations and Beyond

"Beyond Any Doubt"
by Robert O'Neil Bristow

NOTE: This short story in not included in this anthology but may be found on the Internet or at your university or college library.

Robert O'Neil Bristow (1926-), an American writer and educator born in St. Louis, earned his B.A. and M.A. in Journalism from the University of Oklahoma. He served in the United States Naval Reserve from 1944 to 1945, worked as a journalist for several years in the 1950s, and then for 27 years was an English professor at Winthrop College in North Carolina, where he has been professor emeritus since 1987.

"Beyond Any Doubt" (1962) is a story about Tom Howell, a man on a death penalty jury who agonizes over his "reasonable doubt" as he decides how to vote. For much of the story, Tom is the only hold out—the other eleven juror members, all male, are certain of the defendant's guilt. Group dynamics are readily apparent in this story, and individual jurors' prejudices challenge the idea of an impartial jury.

Critical Thinking

What influence might the foreman have on the jury? What misconceptions about a juror's duty do some of these characters display?

Should the defendant's prior record be a persuasion point for them? Why or why not?

Can jury members separate themselves from their past experiences in regard to verdicts?

Tom repeats the phrase "reasonable doubt" several times—why is this concept a sticking point for him?

Is Carl's attempted blackmail of Tom a crime? How could such behavior in the jury room thwart justice?

Do you consider Tom's refusal to be bullied or pressured brave? Why or why not?

Do you think that the vote will go the way Tom hopes? What do you think changes the jurors' minds?

Jury deliberations are, of course, closed for obvious reasons of confidentiality and fairness. Does this fictional account of what might go on in a jury room seem realistic? Why or why not?

Chapter 8

Sentencing and Judgment

Goals of Sentencing

Merchant of Venice—"Quality of Mercy" Speech
by William Shakespeare

Born during the Elizabethan era of English history, Shakespeare (1564–1616) is considered the world's foremost dramatist. An actor, poet, and playwright, he was also a skilled businessman, having partnered in the London acting company know as the Lord Chamberlain's Men, later renamed the King's Men after the coronation of James I. Over a dozen of his 38 plays were in print by 1600 including *Romeo and Juliet* and *The Merchant of Venice*.

Many of his plays weave crime and justice into the narrative, with *Hamlet* and *Macbeth* addressing treason, a character in *The Winter's Tale* being a pickpocket, sex outside of marriage leading to an arrest and possible execution in *Measure for Measure*, and an accusation of adultery in *The Winter's Tale*. Many of his works also include a comedic constable playing the fool including Elbow in *Measure for Measure*, Dull in *Love's Labor Lost* and, the most infamous of all, Dogberry of *Much Ado About Nothing*.

Shakespeare's work has such a resonance in jurisprudence that his writings have been quoted in court decisions on innumerable occasions. After the conviction of the surviving Boston Marathon murderer, the federal judge quoted a line from the play *Julius Caesar* in his final remarks: "One of Shakespeare's characters observes: 'The evil that men do lives after them. The good oft interred with their bones.' So it will be for Dzhokhar Tsarnaev." He was following a long tradition, both in Europe and in the United States, of jurists using the words of the Bard to express their legal argument, opinion, or decision.

In *The Merchant of Venice* the concept of mercy comes to the forefront through the requirements of contract law when Shylock demands that if a loan goes unpaid his long disliked antagonist must forfeit his bond, a pound of his own flesh, that Shylock required to guarantee a loan he had given to the antagonist's friend. The "judge" in the case, the lover of the original borrower in disguise, asks Shylock to show mercy and not require the flesh bond to be forfeited.

———————— ℬ ————————

"The Merchant of Venice, Act IV, Scene I"
[The quality of mercy is not strained]
by William Shakespeare

The quality of mercy is not strained;
It droppeth as the gentle rain from heaven
Upon the place beneath. It is twice blest;
It blesseth him that gives and him that takes:
'Tis mightiest in the mightiest; it becomes
The throned monarch better than his crown:
His sceptre shows the force of temporal power,
The attribute to awe and majesty,
Wherein doth sit the dread and fear of kings;
But mercy is above this sceptred sway;
It is enthronèd in the hearts of kings,
It is an attribute to God himself;
And earthly power doth then show likest God's
When mercy seasons justice. Therefore, Jew,
Though justice be thy plea, consider this,
That, in the course of justice, none of us
Should see salvation: we do pray for mercy;
And that same prayer doth teach us all to render
The deeds of mercy. I have spoke thus much
To mitigate the justice of thy plea;
Which if thou follow, this strict court of Venice
Must needs give sentence 'gainst the merchant there.

———————

Source: William Shakespeare, *The Merchant of Venice*, 1598.

Critical Thinking

Mercy is not a matter of right but is rather a gift, a matter of grace. The offender cannot earn mercy but may have it granted out of compassion, though his remorse, repentance, and reparations may give inspiration for doing so. Within the justice system, a pardon, whether presidential or gubernatorial, is the most recognized form of mercy. For the president, it may be in the form of a full pardon or simply a commutation of an overly harsh sentence given by a federal court. The pardon or commutation is a way to temper the law, bestowing the mercy of the government upon the offender. Though the president has no authority to pardon an offender convicted under state law, most governors have similar authority for state violations.

Mercy can also extend to the criminal court by minimizing a penalty, again not because the offender has earned the right to a lower sentence or that the demands of fairness require one (such as when a juvenile first-offender is minimally sanctioned with the expectation that she will not get into trouble again) but, instead, because the court has for some reason chosen to do so. It may be because the victim himself has forgiven the perpetrator and requests the court to show compassion and mercy or, possibly, that the offender may have already suffered to the extent that further retributive action may be seen as unseemly and inappropriate by the public.

On the other hand, when mercy leads to sentences that do not comply with the legislatures' intent and the normal dictates of the justice system, questions arise. Does the lack of consistency when granting mercy in sentencing undermine the trust and credibility of the court in the public's eye?

Does the consistent use of mercy lead to its potential codification in the sentencing procedure with the courts coming to eventually consider its use a matter of right instead of a matter of grace and undercutting the very definition of mercy?

How does one oversee the use of mercy to avoid its misuse or abuse?

Without it, how does one prevent the harshness of the law from demanding more than is fair and just for a given offense?

Shakespeare continues to be read 400 years later not only for his compelling characters and use of language but also for creating stories that delineate the human condition while transcending time and place. Shakespeare's "Quality of Mercy" speech is no less applicable today than it was four centuries ago.

Types of Sentences

"A Wasted Day"
by Richard Harding Davis

Richard Harding Davis (1864–1916) was a journalist, fiction writer, and dramatist who gained notoriety as the first American war correspondent to report on the Spanish American War and World War I. He wrote for the *New York Herald, The Times, and Scribner's Magazine*, and eventually became a managing editor of *Harper's Weekly*. He was also the son of American author Rebecca Harding Davis (whose major works included *Life in the Iron Mills*).

"A Wasted Day" (1903; 1916) is a short story that gently savages the privileged, wealthy class of New York's Wall Street elite and their willful ignorance of the lives of the working class and the poor. One morning, Arnold Thorndike, reputedly the wealthiest banker in the city, is interrupted by his private secretary informing him that a former employee for his firm, Henry Spear, has been convicted of theft. Spear's probation officer has sent a request for a character reference on his behalf, hoping to get his sentence reduced. Thorndike is annoyed by the interruption, focused on more important matters such as purchasing a painting for $40,000 dollars and coordinating expensive landscaping on his private property. Moreover, Thorndike doubts Spear's moral fortitude after hearing that Spear was drunk when he was arrested. Nevertheless, Thorndike decides to help Spear by going to the courthouse the following morning to speak to the judge before Spear's sentencing. Thorndike's motives are self-serving rather than altruistic: he will wield his wealth and privileged status to save his former stenographer from prison and thus be recognized as not only the Wisest Man (a sarcastic moniker given to him by his enemies), but also as a generous philanthropist willing to deviate from his daily routine that includes a railroad purchase and "the new wing to his art gallery." Indeed, "he could not help but appreciate the dramatic qualities of the situation; that the richest man in Wall Street should appear in person to plead for a humble and weaker brother."

Thorndike's self-interested altruism, however, means little once he arrives at the courthouse and is forced to wait in the assistant district attorney's office instead of being taken straight to the judge. He is annoyed that "he had wasted his own time" and must sit with people with whom he never associates and whose lives he knows nothing about: the poor, immigrants, and petty criminals. He decides not to complain when he finds out the judge is running late "because these people were not apparently aware of the sacrifice he was making." When he is led to the courtroom where Spears will be sentenced, he is shocked, feeling a loss of identity, because he cannot gain entrance on his own merit but rather as a guest of the assistant district attorney. His humiliation continues when the judge scolds him in open court for laughing during a lawyer's prepared speech. Again and again, Thorndike's time is not valued any more or less than anyone else's at the courthouse.

Forced to listen to several sentencing cases and to Spear's probation officer, Mrs. Austin, plead on behalf of her clients, Thorndike notices a change in himself, "something that had been long untouched, long in disuse": in short, empathy and compassion. He asks the assistant district attorney Andrews if he can give money to Mrs. Austin to help her probationers get back on their feet. Feeling "a genial glow of personal pleasure," Thorndike tells Andrews he cannot see his senior clerk (who has tried to get into the courtroom to deliver a message). As the day continues, he grows increasingly interested in the cases he hears. Finally, when Spear's case is before the judge, Thorndike is denied the opportunity for personal glory after Spear's current employer asks for leniency, thus gaining Spear probation. Thorndike must come to terms with the fact that he wasn't needed. Still, his presence is noted by the judge, who asks to speak to Thorndike after the hearing. Explaining that while the law cannot and should not be influenced by wealth, privilege, or status, Spear's "unselfish and public-spirited" behavior is worth noting. Thorndike takes the rest of the day off and rewards his clerk and the assistant district attorney with lunch, telling both that he doesn't care how much his "wasted day" cost him financially: "it was worth it."

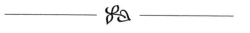

"A Wasted Day"
by Richard Harding Davis

When its turn came, the private secretary, somewhat apologetically, laid the letter in front of the Wisest Man in Wall Street.

"From Mrs. Austin, probation officer, Court of General Sessions," he explained. "Wants a letter about Spear. He's been convicted of theft. Comes up for sentence Tuesday."

"Spear?" repeated Arnold Thorndike.

"Young fellow, stenographer, used to do your letters last summer going in and out on the train."

The great man nodded. "I remember. What about him?"

The habitual gloom of the private secretary was lightened by a grin.

"Went on the loose; had with him about five hundred dollars belonging to the firm; he's with Isaacs & Sons now, shoe people on Sixth Avenue. Met a woman and woke up without the money. The next morning he offered to make good, but Isaacs called in the policeman. When they looked into it, they found the boy had been drunk. They tried to withdraw the charge, but he'd been committed. Now, the probation officer is trying to get the judge to suspend sentence. A letter from you, sir, would—"

Source: Richard Harding Davis, 1864–1916.

It was evident the mind of the great man was elsewhere. Young men who, drunk or sober, spent the firm's money on women who disappeared before sunrise did not appeal to him. Another letter submitted that morning had come from his art agent in Europe. In Florence he had discovered the Correggio he had been sent to find. It was undoubtedly genuine, and he asked to be instructed by cable. The price was forty thousand dollars. With one eye closed, and the other keenly regarding the inkstand, Mr. Thorndike decided to pay the price; and with the facility of long practice dismissed the Correggio, and snapped his mind back to the present.

"Spear had a letter from us when he left, didn't he?" he asked. "What he has developed into, *since* he left us—" he shrugged his shoulders. The secretary withdrew the letter and slipped another in its place.

"Homer Firth, the landscape man," he chanted, "wants permission to use blue flint on the new road, with turf gutters, and to plant silver firs each side. Says it will run to about five thousand dollars a mile."

"No!" protested the great man firmly, "blue flint makes a country place look like a cemetery. Mine looks too much like a cemetery now. Landscape gardeners!" he exclaimed impatiently. "Their only idea is to insult nature. The place was better the day I bought it, when it was running wild; you could pick flowers all the way to the gates." Pleased that it should have recurred to him, the great man smiled. "Why, Spear," he exclaimed, "always took in a bunch of them for his mother. Don't you remember, we used to see him before breakfast wandering around the grounds picking flowers?" Mr. Thorndike nodded briskly. "I liked his taking flowers to his mother."

"He *said* it was to his mother," suggested the secretary gloomily.

"Well, he picked the flowers, anyway," laughed Mr. Thorndike. "He didn't pick our pockets. And he had the run of the house in those days. As far as we know," he dictated, "he was satisfactory. Don't say more than that."

The secretary scribbled a mark with his pencil. "And the landscape man?"

"Tell him," commanded Thorndike, "I want a wood road, suitable to a farm; and to let the trees grow where God planted them."

As his car slid downtown on Tuesday morning the mind of Arnold Thorndike was occupied with such details of daily routine as the purchase of a railroad, the Japanese loan, the new wing to his art gallery, and an attack that morning, in his own newspaper, upon his pet trust. But his busy mind was not too occupied to return the salutes of the traffic policemen who cleared the way for him. Or, by some genius of memory, to recall the fact that it was on this morning young Spear was to be sentenced for theft. It was a charming morning. The spring was at full tide, and the air was sweet and clean. Mr. Thorndike considered whimsically that to send a man to jail with the memory of such a morning clinging to him was adding a year to his sentence. He regretted he had not given the probation officer a stronger letter. He remembered the young man now, and favorably. A shy, silent youth, deft in work, and at other times conscious and embarrassed. But that, on the part of a stenographer, in the presence of the Wisest Man in Wall Street, was not unnatural. On occasions Mr. Thorndike had put even royalty—frayed, impecunious royalty, on the lookout for a loan—at its ease.

The hood of the car was down, and the taste of the air, warmed by the sun, was grateful. It was at this time, a year before, that young Spear picked the spring flowers to take to his mother. A year from now where would young Spear be?

It was characteristic of the great man to act quickly, so quickly that his friends declared he was a slave to impulse. It was these same impulses, leading so invariably to success, that made his enemies call him the Wisest Man. He leaned forward and touched the chauffeur's shoulder. "Stop at the Court of General Sessions," he commanded. What he proposed to do would take but a few minutes. A word, a personal word from him to the district attorney, or the judge, would be enough. He recalled that a Sunday Special had once calculated that the working time of Arnold Thorndike brought him in two hundred dollars a minute. At that rate, keeping Spear out of prison would cost a thousand dollars.

Out of the sunshine Mr. Thorndike stepped into the gloom of an echoing rotunda, shut in on every side, hung by balconies, lit, many stories over-head, by a dirty skylight. The place was damp, the air acrid with the smell of stale tobacco juice, and foul with the presence of many unwashed humans. A policeman, chewing stolidly, nodded toward an elevator shaft, and other policemen nodded him further on to the office of the district attorney. There Arnold Thorndike breathed more freely. He was again among his own people. He could not help but appreciate the dramatic qualities of the situation; that the richest man in Wall Street should appear in person to plead for a humble and weaker brother. He knew he could not escape recognition, his face was too well known, but, he trusted, for the sake of Spear, the reporters would make no display of his visit. With a deprecatory laugh, he explained why he had come. But the outburst of approbation he had anticipated did not follow.

The district attorney ran his finger briskly down a printed card. "Henry Spear," he exclaimed, "that's your man. Part Three, Judge Fallon. Andrews is in that court." He walked to the door of his private office. "Andrews!" he called.

He introduced an alert, broad-shouldered young man of years of much indiscretion and with a charming and inconsequent manner.

"Mr. Thorndike is interested in Henry Spear, coming up for sentence in Part Three this morning. Wants to speak for him. Take him over with you."

The district attorney shook hands quickly, and retreated to his private office. Mr. Andrews took out a cigarette and, as he crossed the floor, lit it.

"Come with me," he commanded. Somewhat puzzled, slightly annoyed, but enjoying withal the novelty of the environment and the curtness of his reception, Mr. Thorndike followed. He decided that, in his ignorance, he had wasted his own time and that of the prosecuting attorney. He should at once have sent in his card to the judge. As he understood it, Mr. Andrews was now conducting him to that dignitary, and, in a moment, he would be free to return to his own affairs, which were the affairs of two continents. But Mr. Andrews led him to an office, bare and small, and offered him a chair, and handed him a morning newspaper. There were people waiting in the room; strange people, only like those Mr. Thorndike had seen on ferry boats. They leaned forward toward young Mr. Andrews, fawning, their eyes wide with apprehension.

Mr. Thorndike refused the newspaper. "I thought I was going to see the judge," he suggested.

"Court doesn't open for a few minutes yet," said the assistant district attorney. "Judge is always late, anyway."

Mr. Thorndike suppressed an exclamation. He wanted to protest, but his clear mind showed him that there was nothing against which, with reason, he could protest. He could not complain because these people were not apparently aware of the sacrifice he was making. He had come among them to perform a kindly act. He recognized that he must not stultify it by a show of irritation. He had precipitated himself into a game of which he did not know the rules. That was all. Next time he would know better. Next time he would send a clerk. But he was not without a sense of humor, and the situation as it now was forced upon him struck him as amusing. He laughed good-naturedly and reached for the desk telephone.

"May I use this?" he asked. He spoke to the Wall Street office. He explained he would be a few minutes late. He directed what should be done if the market opened in a certain way. He gave rapid orders on many different matters, asked to have read to him a cablegram he expected from Petersburg, and one from Vienna.

"They answer each other," was his final instruction. "It looks like peace."

Mr. Andrews with genial patience had remained silent. Now he turned upon his visitors. A Levantine, burly, unshaven, and soiled, towered truculently above him. Young Mr. Andrews with his swivel chair tilted back, his hands clasped behind his head, his cigarette hanging from his lips, regarded the man dispassionately.

"You gotta hell of a nerve to come to see me," he commented cheerfully. To Mr. Thorndike, the form of greeting was novel. So greatly did it differ from the procedure of his own office that he listened with interest.

"Was it you," demanded young Andrews, in a puzzled tone, "or your brother who tried to knife me?" Mr. Thorndike, unaccustomed to cross the pavement to his office unless escorted by bank messengers and plain-clothesmen, felt the room growing rapidly smaller; the figure of the truculent Greek loomed to heroic proportions. The hand of the banker went vaguely to his chin, and from there fell to his pearl pin, which he hastily covered.

"Get out!" said young Andrews, "and don't show your face here—"

The door slammed upon the flying Greek. Young Andrews swung his swivel chair so that, over his shoulder, he could see Mr. Thorndike, "I don't like his face," he explained.

A kindly eyed, sad woman with a basket on her knee smiled upon. Andrews with the familiarity of an old acquaintance.

"Is that woman going to get a divorce from my son," she asked, "now that he's in trouble?"

"Now that he's in Sing Sing?" corrected Mr. Andrews. "I *hope* so! She deserves it. That son of yours, Mrs. Bernard," he declared emphatically, "is no good."

The brutality shocked Mr. Thorndike. For the woman he felt a thrill of sympathy, but at once saw that it was superfluous. From the secure and lofty heights of motherhood, Mrs. Bernard smiled down upon the assistant district attorney as upon a naughty child. She did not even deign a protest. She continued merely to smile. The smile reminded Thorndike of the smile on the face of a mother in a painting by Murillo he had lately presented to the chapel in the college he had given to his native town.

"That son of yours," repeated young Andrews, "is a leech. He's robbed you, robbed his wife. Best thing I ever did for *you* was to send him up the river."

The mother smiled upon him beseechingly.

"Could you give me a pass?" she said.

Young Andrews flung up his hands and appealed to Thorndike.

"Isn't that just like a mother?" he protested. "That son of hers has broken her heart, tramped on her, cheated her, hasn't left her a cent; and she comes to me for a pass, so she can kiss him through the bars! And I'll bet she's got a cake for him in that basket!"

The mother laughed happily; she knew now she would get the pass.

"Mothers," explained Mr. Andrews, from the depth of his wisdom, "are all like that; your mother, my mother. If you went to jail, your mother would be just like that."

Mr. Thorndike bowed his head politely. He had never considered going to jail, or whether, if he did, his mother would bring him cake in a basket. Apparently there were many aspects and accidents of life not included in his experience.

Young Andrews sprang to his feet, and, with the force of a hose flushing a gutter, swept his soiled visitors into the hall.

"Come on," he called to the Wisest Man, "the court is open."

In the corridors were many people, and with his eyes on the broad shoulders of the assistant district attorney, Thorndike pushed his way through them. The people who blocked his progress were of the class unknown to him. Their looks were anxious, furtive, miserable. They stood in little groups, listening eagerly to a sharp-faced lawyer, or, in sullen despair, eying each other. At a door a tipstaff laid his hand roughly on the arm of Mr. Thorndike.

"That's all right, Joe," called young Mr. Andrews, "he's with *me*." They entered the court and passed down an aisle to a railed enclosure in which were high oak chairs. Again, in his effort to follow, Mr. Thorndike was halted, but the first tipstaff came to his rescue. "All right," he signaled, "he's with Mr. Andrews."

Mr. Andrews pointed to one of the oak chairs. "You sit there," he commanded, "it's reserved for members of the bar, but it's all right. You're with *me*."

Distinctly annoyed, slightly bewildered, the banker sank between the arms of a chair. He felt he had lost his individuality. Andrews had become his sponsor. Because of Andrews he was tolerated. Because Andrews had a pull he was permitted to sit as an equal among police-court lawyers. No longer was he Arnold Thorndike. He was merely the man "with Mr. Andrews."

Then even Andrews abandoned him. "The judge'll be here in a minute, now," said the assistant district attorney, and went inside a railed enclosure in front of the judge's bench. There he greeted another assistant district attorney whose years were those of even greater indiscretion than the years of Mr. Andrews. Seated on the rail, with their hands in their pockets and their backs turned to Mr. Thorndike, they laughed and talked together. The subject of their discourse was one Mike Donlin, as he appeared in vaudeville.

To Mr. Thorndike it was evident that young Andrews had entirely forgotten him. He arose and touched his sleeve. With infinite sarcasm Mr. Thorndike began: "My engagements are not pressing, but—"

A court attendant beat with his palm upon the rail.

"Sit down!" whispered Andrews. "The judge is coming."

Mr. Thorndike sat down.

The court attendant droned loudly words Mr. Thorndike could not distinguish. There was a rustle of silk, and from a door behind him the judge stalked past. He was a young man, the type of the Tammany politician. On his shrewd, alert, Irish-American features was an expression of unnatural gloom. With a smile Mr. Thorndike observed that it was as little suited to the countenance of the young judge as was the robe to his shoulders, Mr. Thorndike was still smiling when young Andrews leaned over the rail.

"Stand up!" he hissed. Mr. Thorndike stood up.

After the court attendant had uttered more unintelligible words, every one sat down; and the financier again moved hurriedly to the rail.

"I would like to speak to him now before he begins," he whispered. "I can't wait."

Mr. Andrews stared in amazement. The banker had not believed the young man could look so serious.

"Speak to him *now*!" exclaimed the district attorney. "You've got to wait till your man comes up. If you speak to the judge, *now*—" The voice of Andrews faded away in horror.

Not knowing in what way he had offended, but convinced that it was only by the grace of Andrews he had escaped a dungeon, Mr. Thorndike retreated to his armchair.

The clock on the wall showed him that, already, he had given to young Spear one hour and a quarter. The idea was preposterous. No one better than himself knew what his time was really worth. In half an hour there was a board meeting; later he was to hold a post-mortem on a railroad; at every moment questions were being asked by telegraph, by cable, questions that involved the credit of individuals, of firms, of even the country. And the one man who could answer them was risking untold sums only that he might say a good word for an idle apprentice. Inside the railed enclosure a lawyer was reading a typewritten speech. He assured his honor that he must have more time to prepare his case. It was one of immense importance. The name of a most respectable business house was involved, and a sum of no less than nine hundred dollars. Nine hundred dollars! The contrast struck Mr. Thorndike's sense of humor full in the center. Unknowingly, he laughed and found himself as conspicuous as though he had appeared suddenly in his nightclothes. The tipstaffs beat upon the rail, the lawyer he had interrupted uttered an indignant exclamation, Andrews came hurriedly toward him, and the young judge slowly turned his head.

"Those persons," he said, "who cannot respect the dignity of this court will leave it." As he spoke, with his eyes fixed on those of Mr. Thorndike, the latter saw that the young judge had suddenly recognized him. But the fact of his identity did not cause the frown to relax or the rebuke to halt unuttered. In even, icy tones the judge continued: "And it is well they should remember that the law is no respecter of persons and that the dignity of this court will be enforced, no matter who the offender may happen to be."

Andrews slipped into the chair beside Mr. Thorndike and grinned sympathetically.

"Sorry!" he whispered, "Should have warned you. We won't be long now," he added encouragingly. "As soon as this fellow finishes his argument, the judge'll take up the sentences. Your man seems to have other friends; Isaacs & Sons are here, and the typewriter firm who taught him; but what *you* say will help most. It won't be more than a couple of hours now."

"A couple of hours!" Mr. Thorndike raged inwardly. A couple of hours in this place where he had been publicly humiliated. He smiled, a thin, sharklike smile. Those who made it their business to study his expression, on seeing it, would have fled. Young Andrews, not being acquainted with the moods of the great man, added cheerfully: "By one o'clock, anyway."

Mr. Thorndike began grimly to pull on his gloves. For all he cared now young Spear could go hang. Andrews nudged his elbow.

"See that old lady in the front row?" he whispered. "That's Mrs. Spear. What did I tell you; mothers are all alike. She's not taken her eyes off you since court opened. She knows you're her one best bet."

Impatiently Mr. Thorndike raised his head. He saw a little white-haired woman who stared at him. In her eyes was the same look he had seen in the eyes of men who, at times of panic, fled to him, beseeching, entreating, forcing upon him what was left of the wreck of their fortunes, if only he would save their honor.

"And here come the prisoners," Andrews whispered. "See Spear? Third man from the last." A long line, guarded in front and rear, shuffled into the courtroom, and, as ordered, ranged themselves against the wall. Among them were old men and young boys, well dressed, clever-looking rascals, collarless tramps, fierce-eyed aliens, smooth-shaven, thin-lipped Broadwayards—and Spear.

Spear, his head hanging, with lips white and cheeks ashen, and his eyes heavy with shame.

Mr. Thorndike had risen, and, in farewell, was holding out his hand to Andrews. He turned, and across the courtroom the eyes of the financier and the stenographer met. At the sight of the great man Spear flushed crimson, and then his look of despair slowly disappeared; and into his eyes there came incredulously hope and gratitude. He turned his head suddenly to the wall.

Mr. Thorndike stood irresolute and then sank back into his chair.

The first man in the line was already at the railing, and the questions put to him by the judge were being repeated to him by the other assistant district attorney and a court attendant. His muttered answers were in turn repeated to the judge.

"Says he's married, naturalized citizen, Lutheran Church, diecutter by profession."

The probation officer, her hands filled with papers, bustled forward and whispered.

"Mrs. Austin says," continued the district attorney, "she's looked into this case and asks to have the man turned over to her. He has a wife and three children; has supported them for five years."

"Is the wife in court?" the judge said.

A thin, washed-out, pretty woman stood up and clasped her hands in front of her.

"Has this man been a good husband to you, madam?" asked the young judge.

The woman broke into vehement assurances. No man could have been a better husband. Would she take him back? Indeed she would take him back. She held out her hands as though she would physically drag her husband from the pillory.

The judge bowed toward the probation officer, and she beckoned the prisoner to her.

Other men followed, and in the fortune of each Mr. Thorndike found himself, to his surprise, taking a personal interest. It was as good as a play. It reminded him of the Sicilians he had seen in London in their little sordid tragedies. Only these actors were appearing in their proper persons in real dramas of a life he did not know, but which appealed to something that had been long untouched, long in disuse. It was an uncomfortable sensation that left him restless because, as he appreciated, it needed expression, an outlet. He found this, partially, in praising, through Andrews, the young judge who had publicly rebuked him. Mr. Thorndike found him astute, sane; his queries intelligent, his comments just. And this probation officer, she, too, was capable, was she not? Smiling at his interest in what to him was an old story, the younger man nodded.

"I like her looks," whispered the great man. "Like her clear eyes and clean skin. She strikes me as able, full of energy, and yet womanly. These men when they come under her charge," he insisted, eagerly, "need money to start again, don't they?" He spoke anxiously. He believed he had found the clue to his restlessness. It was a desire to help; to be of use to these failures who had fallen and who were being lifted to their feet. Andrews looked at him curiously. "Anything you give her," he answered, "would be well invested."

"If you tell me her name and address?" whispered the banker. He was much given to charity, but it had been perfunctory, it was extended on the advice of his secretary. In helping here he felt a genial glow of personal pleasure. It was much more satisfactory than giving an Old Master to his private chapel.

In the rear of the courtroom there was a scuffle that caused every one to turn and look. A man, who had tried to force his way past the tipstaffs, was being violently ejected, and, as he disappeared, he waved a paper toward Mr. Thorndike. The banker recognized him as his chief clerk. Andrews rose anxiously. "That man wanted to get to you. I'll see what it is. Maybe it's important."

Mr. Thorndike pulled him back.

"Maybe it is," he said dryly. "but I can't see him now, I'm busy."

Slowly the long line of derelicts, of birds of prey, of sorry, weak failures, passed before the seat of judgment. Mr. Thorndike had moved into a chair nearer to the rail, and from time to time made a note upon the back of an envelope. He had forgotten the time or had chosen to disregard it. So great was his interest that he had forgotten the particular derelict he had come to serve, until Spear stood almost at his elbow.

Thorndike turned eagerly to the judge and saw that he was listening to a rotund, gray little man with beady, birdlike eyes who, as he talked, bowed and gesticulated. Behind him stood a younger man, a more modern edition of the other. He also bowed and, behind gold eyeglasses, smiled ingratiatingly.

The judge nodded and, leaning forward, for a few moments fixed his eyes upon the prisoner.

"You are a very fortunate young man," he said. He laid his hand upon a pile of letters. "When you were your own worst enemy, your friends came to help you. These letters speak for you; your employers, whom you robbed, have pleaded with me in your favor. It is urged, in your behalf, that at the time you committed the crime of which you are found guilty, you were intoxicated. In the eyes of the law, that is no excuse. Some men can drink and keep their senses. It appears you cannot. When you drink you are a menace to yourself—and, as is shown by this crime, to the community. Therefore, you must not drink. In view of the good character to which your friends have testified, and on the condition that you do not touch liquor, I will not sentence you to jail, but will place you in charge of the probation officer."

The judge leaned back in his chair and beckoned to Mr. Andrews. It was finished. Spear was free, and from different parts of the courtroom people were moving toward the door. Their numbers showed that the friends of the young man had been many. Mr. Thorndike felt a certain twinge of disappointment. Even though the result relieved and pleased him, he wished, in bringing it about, he had had some part.

He begrudged to Isaacs & Sons the credit of having given Spear his liberty. His morning had been wasted. He had neglected his own interests, and in no way assisted those of Spear. He was moving out of the railed enclosure when Andrews called him by name.

"His Honor," he said impressively, "wishes to speak to you."

The judge leaned over his desk and shook Mr. Thorndike by the hand. Then he made a speech. The speech was about public-spirited citizens who, to the neglect of their own interest, came to assist the ends of justice and fellow creatures in misfortune. He purposely spoke in a loud voice, and everyone stopped to listen.

"The law, Mr. Thorndike, is not vindictive," he said. "It wishes only to be just. Nor can it be swayed by wealth or political or social influences. But when there is good in a man, I, personally, want to know it, and when gentlemen like yourself, of your standing in this city, come here to speak a good word for a man, we would stultify the purpose of justice if we did not listen. I thank you for coming, and I wish more of our citizens were as unselfish and public-spirited."

It was all quite absurd and most embarrassing, but inwardly Mr. Thorndike glowed with pleasure. It was a long time since any one had had the audacity to tell him he had done well. From the friends of Spear there was a ripple of applause, which no tipstaff took it upon himself to suppress, and to the accompaniment of this, Mr. Thorndike walked to the corridor.

He was pleased with himself and his fellow man. He shook hands with Isaacs & Sons and congratulated them upon their public spirit, and the typewriter firm upon their public spirit. And then he saw Spear standing apart regarding him doubtfully.

Spear did not offer his hand, but Mr. Thorndike took it and shook it and said, "I want to meet your mother."

And when Mrs. Spear tried to stop sobbing long enough to tell him how happy she was, and how grateful, he instead told her what a fine son she had, and that he remembered when Spear used to carry flowers to town for her. And she remembered it, too, and thanked him for the flowers. And he told Spear, when Isaacs & Sons went bankrupt, which at the rate they were giving away their money to the Hebrew Hospital would be very soon, Spear must come back to him. And Isaacs & Sons were delighted at the great man's pleasantry and afterward repeated it many times, calling upon each other to bear witness, and Spear felt as though some one had given him a new backbone, and Andrews, who was guiding Thorndike out of the building, was thinking to himself what a great confidence man had been lost when Thorndike became a banker.

The chief clerk and two bank messengers were waiting by the automobile with written calls for help from the office. They pounced upon the banker and almost lifted him into the car.

"There's still time!" panted the chief clerk.

"There is not!" answered Mr. Thorndike. His tone was rebellious, defiant. It carried all the authority of a spoiled child of fortune. "I've wasted most of this day," he declared, "and I intend to waste the rest of it. Andrews," he called, "jump in, and I'll give you a lunch at Sherry's."

The vigilant protector of the public dashed back into the building.

"Wait till I get my hat!" he called.

As the two truants rolled up the avenue the spring sunshine warmed them, the sense of duties neglected added zest to their holiday, and young Mr. Andrews laughed aloud.

Mr. Thorndike raised his eyebrows inquiringly.

"I was wondering," said Andrews, "how much it cost you to keep Spear out of jail?"

"I don't care," said the great man guiltily; "it was worth it."

Critical Thinking

As you re-read the story, pay attention to those moments when Thorndike's class privilege is challenged. How does he react to these challenges?

Do his revelations in the last half of the story seem genuine?

Davis offers a hopeful view that the justice system pays no regard to wealth and status. To what extent is this actually the case?

Are poor people and privileged people treated equally by the justice system, especially with regard to legal representation and sentencing?

To Execute or Not to Execute

"Too Dear!"
by Leo Tolstóy

Leo Tolstoy (1828–1910) was a nineteenth century Russian writer best known for the novels *War and Peace* (1869) and *Anna Karenina* (1877). In 1857, Tolstoy witnessed a public execution in Paris that affected him deeply. Tolstoy was a devout Christian who advocated nonviolence; he influenced Gandhi's beliefs in nonresistance to violence.

"Too Dear!"(1897) is a humorous account of how the tiny Kingdom of Monaco is baffled by how to deal with a convicted murderer.

"Too Dear!"
by Leo Tolstóy

Near the borders of France and Italy, on the shore of the Mediterranean Sea, lies a tiny little kingdom called Monaco. Many a small country town can boast more inhabitants than this kingdom, for there are only about seven thousand of them all told, and if all the land in the kingdom were divided there would not be an acre for each inhabitant. But in this toy kingdom there is a real kinglet; and he has a palace, and courtiers, and ministers, and a bishop, and generals, and an army.

It is not a large army, only sixty men in all, but still it is an army. There are also taxes in this kingdom, as elsewhere: a tax on tobacco, and on wine and spirits, and a poll-tax. But though the people there drink and smoke as people do in other countries, there are so few of them that the Prince would have been hard put to it to feed his courtiers and officials and to keep himself, if he had not found a new and special source of revenue. This special revenue comes from a gaming house, where people play roulette. People play, and whether they win or lose the keeper always gets a percentage of the turnover, and out of his profits he pays a large sum to the Prince. The reason he pays so much is that it is the only such gambling establishment left in Europe. Some of the little German sovereigns used to keep gaming houses of the same kind, but some years ago they were forbidden to do so. The reason they were stopped was because these gaming houses did so much harm. A man would come and try his luck, then he would

Source: Leo Tolstóy, *Adaptation of a Story by Guy De Maupassant*, 1897.

risk all he had and lose it, then he would even risk money that did not belong to him and lose that, too, and then, in despair, he would drown or shoot himself. So the Germans forbade their rulers to make money in this way; but there was no one to stop the Prince of Monaco, and he remained with a monopoly of the business.

So now every one who wants to gamble goes to Monaco. Whether they win or lose, the Prince gains by it. 'You can't earn stone palaces by honest labour,' as the proverb says; and the Princelet of Monaco knows it is a dirty business, but what is he to do? He has to live; and to draw a revenue from drink and from tobacco is also not a nice thing. So he lives and reigns, and rakes in the money and holds his court with all the ceremony of a real king.

He has his coronation, his levees; he rewards, sentences, and pardons; and he also has his reviews, councils, laws and courts of justice: just like other kings, only all on a smaller scale.

Now it happened a few years ago that a murder was committed in this toy Prince's domains. The people of that kingdom are peaceable, and such a thing had not happened before. The judges assembled with much ceremony and tried the case in the most judicial manner. There were judges, and prosecutors, and jurymen and barristers. They argued and judged, and at last they condemned the criminal to have his head cut off as the law directs. So far so good. Next they submitted the sentence to the Prince. The Prince read the sentence and confirmed it. 'If the fellow must be executed, execute him.'

There was only one hitch in the matter; and that was that they had neither a guillotine for cutting heads off, nor the executioner. The Ministers considered the matter, and decided to address an inquiry to the French government, asking whether the French could not lend them a machine and an expert to cut off the criminal's head; and if so, would the French kindly inform them what it would cost. The letter was sent. A week later the reply came: a machine and an expert could be supplied, and the cost would be 16,000 francs. This was laid before the Prince. He thought it over. Sixteen thousand francs! 'The wretch is not worth the money,' said he. 'Can't it be done, somehow, cheaper? Why, 16,000 francs is more than two francs a head on the whole population. The people won't stand it, and it may cause a riot!'

So a Council was called to consider what could be done; and it was decided to send a similar inquiry to the Prince of Italy. The French government is republican, and has no proper respect for kings; but the Prince of Italy was a brother monarch, and might be induced to do the thing cheaper. So the letter was written, and a prompt reply was received.

The Italian government wrote that they would have pleasure in supplying both a machine and an expert; and the whole cost would be 12,000 francs, including travelling expenses. This was cheaper, but still it seemed too much. The rascal was really not worth the money. It would still mean nearly two francs more per head on the taxes. Another Council was called. They discussed and considered how it could be done with less expense. Could not one of the soldiers, perhaps, be got to do it in a rough and homely fashion? The General was called and was asked: 'Can't you find us a soldier who would cut the man's head off? In war they don't mind killing people. In fact, that is what they are trained for.' So the General talked it over with the soldiers to see whether one of them would not undertake the job. But none of the soldiers would do it. 'No,' they said, 'we don't know how to do it; it is not a thing we have been taught.'

What was to be done? Again Ministers considered and reconsidered. They assembled a Commission, and a Committee, and a Sub-Committee and at last they decided that the best thing would be to alter the death sentence to one of imprisonment for life. This would enable the Prince to show his mercy, and it would come cheaper.

The Prince agreed to this, and so the matter was arranged. The only hitch now was that there was no suitable prison for a man sentenced for life. There was a small lock-up where people were sometimes kept temporarily, but there was no strong prison fit for permanent use. However, they managed to find a place that would do, and they put the young fellow there and placed a guard over him. The guard had to watch the criminal, and had also to fetch his food from the palace kitchen.

The prisoner remained there month after month until a year had passed. But when a year had passed, the Princelet, looking over the account of his income and expenditure one day, noticed a new item of expenditure. This was for the keep of the criminal; nor was it a small item either. There was a special guard, and there was also the mans' food. It came to more than 600 francs a year. And the worst of it was that the fellow was still young and healthy, and might live for fifty years. When one came to reckon it up, the matter was serious. It would never do. So the Prince summoned his Ministers and said to them:

'You must find some cheaper way of dealing with this rascal. The present plan is too expensive.' And the Ministers met and considered and reconsidered, till one of them said, 'Gentlemen, in my opinion we must dismiss the guard.' 'But then,' rejoined another Minister, 'the fellow will run away.' 'Well,' said the first speaker, 'let him run away, and be hanged to him!' So they reported the result of their deliberations to the Princelet, and he agreed with them. The guard was dismissed, and they waited to see what would happen. All that happened was that at dinner-time the criminal came out, and, not finding his guard, he went to the Prince's kitchen to fetch his own dinner. He took what was given him, returned to the prison, shut the door on himself, and stayed inside. Next day the same thing occured. He went for his food at the proper time; but as for running away, he did not show the least sign of it! What was to be done? They considered the matter again.

'We shall have to tell him straight out,' said they, 'that we do not want to keep him.' So the Minister of Justice had him brought before him.

'Why do you not run away?' said the Minister. 'There is no guard to keep you. You can go where you like, and the Prince will not mind.'

'I dare say the Prince would not mind,' replied the man, 'but I have nowhere to go. What can I do? You have ruined my character by your sentence, and people will turn their backs on me. Besides, I have got out of the way of working. You have treated me badly. It is not fair. In the first place, when once you sentenced me to death you ought to have executed me; but you did not do it. That's one thing. I did not complain about that. Then you sentenced me to imprisonment for life and put a guard to bring me my food; but after a time you took him away again and I had to fetch my own food. Again I did not complain. But now you actually want me to go away! I can't agree to that. You may do as you like, but I won't go away!'

What was to be done? Once more the Council was summoned. What course could they adopt? The man would not go. They reflected and considered. The only way to get rid of him was to offer him a pension. And so they reported to the Prince. 'There is nothing else for it,' said they; 'we must get rid of him somehow.' The sum fixed was 600 francs, and this was announced to the prisoner.

'Well,' said he, 'I don't mind, so long as you undertake to pay it regularly. On that condition I am willing to go.

So the matter was settled. He received one-third of his annuity in advance, and left the king's dominions. It was only a quarter of an hour by rail; and he emigrated, and settled just across the frontier, where he bought a bit of land, started market-gardening, and now lives comfortably. He always goes at the proper time to draw his pension. Having received it he goes to the gaming tables, stakes two or three francs, sometimes wins and sometimes loses, and the returns home. He lives peaceably and well.

It is a good thing that he did not commit his crime in a country where they do not grudge expense to cut a man's head off, or to keep him in prison for life.

Critical Thinking

What considerations go into the kingdom's decision not to execute this criminal? Do you consider these legitimate reasons?

Have there been difficulties recently in the United States when it comes to the means of execution?

Like Soapy in Porter's (O. Henry) story, the criminal in Tolstoy's story prefers his cell to his freedom. What is his reasoning for this? What does this infer about the effect of prison on a person?

Why is the decision made to release the prisoner?

What is the kingdom's main concern as it makes decisions concerning the prisoner?

What is the significance of the title of this short story; keep in mind that "dear" can have the meaning of "high cost"?

What statement does Tolstoy appear to be making about the criminal justice system?

Race and Gender: Class

"Happy Event"
by Nadine Gordimer

NOTE: This short story in not included in this anthology but may be found on the Internet or at your university or college library.

Nadine Gordimer (1923–2014) was a South African short-story writer and novelist of international repute born in a Johannesburg suburb, winning the Nobel Prize in Literature in 1991. She was also a committed political and social activist in the anti-apartheid movement who advised Nelson Mandela on his defense speech in 1964, and became a member of the African National Congress when it was deemed illegal by the South African government. Moral and racial themes, especially the effects and consequences of oppressive, institutionalized racism enforced by South Africa's apartheid regime, figure prominently in her work, including "Happy Event" and "Crimes of Conscience," both included in this anthology.

 "Happy Event" (1956) is set in a well-to-do suburb of Johannesburg, where Ella and Allan Plainstow live in comfort with their two children and their black African servants, Thomasi and Lena. Apartheid, South Africa's racial segregation system, has been in place since 1948, but continues the racialized, segregationist policies of colonialism already long-established in the country. Against this background, Gordimer tells the similar stories, but with radically different outcomes, of Ella and Lena. The story opens with Ella returning from a nursing home after a short stay. Although not explicitly stated, Ella has likely had her pregnancy terminated. She and her husband already have two children and an upcoming six-month stay in Europe planned. Ella depends on Thomasi and Lena to run her household, and so when Thomasi complains that Lena is lazy and then unable to work on her scheduled laundry day (which will upset the entire week's routine, according to Ella), Ella visits Lena in her room, realizes that she is sick, and sends medicine to help her feel better. A week later, the police visit Ella to arrest Lena for killing her newborn infant. (Ella did not know Lena was pregnant.) As the trial nears, Ella and her friends commiserate, sharing their shock and horror that Lena, a black servant who looks after children and lives in their home is a baby killer. In the ensuing courtroom drama, Lena's moral fitness as a woman is determined along strictly racial (and racist) lines. She receives six months hard labor, while Ella and Allan spend those six months in Europe.

 As you read the story, consider how race and gender impact the outcomes for the female protagonists.

Critical Thinking

To what extent does race figure into Ella's privilege and Lena's lack of it?

Where do you see evidence of systemic racism not only in social relationships, but, more important, in the administration of justice and determination of guilt?

How would Ella's friends react if they knew she had had a termination?

What makes the title of Gordimer's story—"Happy Event"—ironic?

Section 4

The Consequences of Crime: Corrections

Chapter 9

Prisons and Jails

Corrections

"The Cop and the Anthem"
by O. Henry (William Sydney Porter)

William Sydney Porter (1862–1910) was an American short story writer known by his pen name: O. Henry. Porter assumed this name while in prison serving three years for embezzlement from the Austin, Texas, bank where he worked as a draftsman and bank teller. As a licensed pharmacist, Porter was allowed to work as the penitentiary hospital's druggist with a room not in a cellblock but in the hospital wing. In his writing Porter uses his experiences with the criminal justice system and incarceration, together with stories he obtained from fellow prisoners. His stories are well known for their word play and surprise endings.

"The Cop and the Anthem" (1904) features a protagonist that is one of Porter's stock characters: the tramp. Soapy, who is homeless in New York City during the winter, desires what most people avoid: a prison cell.

"The Cop and the Anthem"

by O. Henry

On his bench in Madison Square Soapy moved uneasily. When wild geese honk high of nights, and when women without sealskin coats grow kind to their husbands, and when Soapy moves uneasily on his bench in the park, you may know that winter is near at hand.

A dead leaf fell in Soapy's lap. That was Jack Frost's card. Jack is kind to the regular denizens of Madison Square, and gives fair warning of his annual call. At the corners of four streets he hands his pasteboard to the North Wind, footman of the mansion of All Outdoors, so that the inhabitants thereof may make ready.

Soapy's mind became cognizant of the fact that the time had come for him to resolve himself into a singular Committee of Ways and Means to provide against the coming rigor. And therefore he moved uneasily on his bench.

The hibernatorial ambitions of Soapy were not of the highest. In them were no considerations of Mediterranean cruises, of soporific Southern skies or drifting in the Vesuvian Bay. Three months on the Island was what his soul craved. Three months of assured board and bed and congenial company, safe from Boreas and blue-coats, seemed to Soapy the essence of things desirable.

For years the hospitable Blackwell's had been his winter quarters. Just as his more fortunate fellow New Yorkers had bought their tickets to Palm Beach and the Riviera each winter, so Soapy had made his humble arrangements for his annual hegira to the Island. And now the time was come. On the previous night three Sabbath newspapers, distributed beneath his coat, about his ankles and over his lap, had failed to repulse the cold as he slept on his bench near the spurting fountain in the ancient square. So the Island loomed big and timely in Soapy's mind. He scorned the provisions made in the name of charity for the city's dependents. In Soapy's opinion the Law was more benign than Philanthropy. There was an endless round of institutions, municipal and eleemosynary, on which he might set out and receive lodging and food accordant with the simple life. But to one of Soapy's proud spirit the gifts of charity are encumbered. It not in coin you must pay in humiliation of spirit for every benefit received at the hands of philanthropy. As Cæsar had his Brutus, every bed of charity must have its toll of a bath, every loaf of bread its compensation of a private and personal inquisition. Wherefore it is better to be a guest of the law, which, though conducted by rules, does not meddle unduly with a gentleman's private affairs.

Soapy, having decided to go to the Island, at once set about accomplishing his desire. There were many easy ways of doing this. The pleasantest was to dine luxuriously at some expensive restaurant; and then, after declaring insolvency, he handed over quietly and without uproar to a policeman. An accommodating magistrate would do the rest.

Source: O. Henry, "The Cop and the Anthem," 1904.

Soapy left his bench and strolled out of the square and across the level sea of asphalt, where Broadway and Fifth Avenue flow together. Up Broadway he turned, and halted at a glittering café, where are gathered together nightly the choicest products of the grape, the silkworm, and the protoplasm.

Soapy had confidence in himself from the lowest button of his vest upward. He was shaven, and his coat was decent and his neat black, readytied four-in-hand had been presented to him by a lady missionary on Thanksgiving Day. If he could reach a table in the restaurant unsuspected success would be his. The portion of him that would show above the table would raise no doubt in the waiter's mind. A roasted mallard duck, thought Soapy, would be about the thing—with a bottle of Chablis, and then Camembert, a demi-tasse and a cigar. One dollar for the cigar would be enough. The total would not be so high as to call forth any supreme manifestation of revenge from the café management; and yet the meat would leave him filled and happy for the journey to his winter refuge.

But as Soapy set foot inside the restaurant door the head waiter's eye fell upon his frayed trousers and decadent shoes. Strong and ready hands turned him about and conveyed him in silence and haste to the sidewalk and averted the ignoble fate of the menaced mallard.

Soapy turned off Broadway. It seemed that his route to the coveted Island was not to be an epicurean one. Some other way of entering limbo must be thought of.

At a corner of Sixth Avenue electric lights and cunningly displayed wares behind plate-glass made a shop window conspicuous. Soapy took a cobblestone and dashed it through the glass. People came running around the corner, a policeman in the lead. Soapy stood still, with his hands in his pockets, and smiled at the sight of brass buttons.

"Where's the man that done that?" inquired the officer, excitedly.

"Don't you figure out that I might have had something to do with it?" said Soapy, not without sarcasm, but friendly, as one greets good fortune.

The policeman's mind refused to accept Soapy even as a clue. Men who smash windows do not remain to parley with the law's minions. They take to their heels. The policeman saw a man halfway down the block running to catch a car. With drawn club he joined in the pursuit. Soapy, with disgust in his heart, loafed along, twice unsuccessful.

On the opposite side of the street was a restaurant of no great pretensions. It catered to large appetites and modest purses. Its crockery and atmosphere were thick; its soup and napery thin. Into this place Soapy took his accusive shoes and telltale trousers without challenge. At a table he sat and consumed beefsteak, flapjacks, doughnuts and pie. And then to the waiter he betrayed the fact that the minutest coin and himself were strangers.

"Now, get busy and call a cop," said Soapy. "And don't keep a gentleman waiting."

"No cop for youse," said the waiter, with a voice like butter cakes and an eye like the cherry in a Manhattan cocktail. "Hey, Con!"

Neatly upon his left ear on the callous pavement two waiters pitched Soapy. He arose joint by joint, as a carpenter's rule opens, and beat the dust from his clothes. Arrest seemed but a rosy dream. The Island seemed very far away. A policeman who stood before a drug store two doors away laughed and walked down the street.

Five blocks Soapy travelled before his courage permitted him to woo capture again. This time the opportunity presented what he fatuously termed to himself a "cinch." A young woman of a modest and pleasing guise was standing before a show window gazing with sprightly interest at its display of shaving mugs and ink-stands, and two yards from the window a large policeman of severe demeanor leaned against a water plug.

It was Soapy's design to assume the rôle of the despicable and execrated "masher." The refined and elegant appearance of his victim and the contiguity of the conscientious cop encouraged him to believe that he would soon feel the pleasant official clutch upon his arm that would insure his winter quarters on the right little, tight little isle.

Soapy straightened the lady missionary's ready-made tie, dragged his shrinking cuffs into the open, set his hat at a killing cant and sidled toward the young woman. He made eyes at her, was taken with sudden coughs and "hems," smiled, smirked and went brazenly through the impudent and contemptible litany, of the "masher." With half an eye Soapy saw that the policeman was watching him fixedly. The young woman moved away a few steps, and again bestowed her absorbed attention upon the shaving mugs. Soapy followed, boldly stepping to her side, raised his hat and said:

"Ah there, Bedelia! Don't you want to come and play in my yard?"

The policeman was still looking. The persecuted young woman had but to beckon a finger and Soapy would be practically en route for his insular haven. Already he imagined he could feel the cozy warmth of the stationhouse. The young woman faced him and, stretching out a hand, caught Soapy's coat sleeve.

"Sure, Mike," she said, joyfully, "if you'll blow me to a pail of suds. I'd have spoke to you sooner, but the cop was watching."

With the young woman playing the clinging ivy to his oak Soapy walked past the policeman overcome with gloom. He seemed doomed to liberty.

At the next corner he shook off his companion and ran. He halted in the district where by night are found the lightest streets, hearts, vows and librettos. Women in furs and men in greatcoats moved gaily in the wintry air. A sudden fear seized Soapy that some dreadful enchantment had rendered him immune to arrest. The thought brought a little of panic upon it, and when he came upon another policeman lounging grandly in front of a transplendent theatre he caught at the immediate straw of "disorderly conduct."

On the sidewalk Soapy began to yell drunken gibberish at the top of his harsh voice. He danced, howled, raved, and otherwise disturbed the welkin.

The policeman twirled his club, turned his back to Soapy and remarked to a citizen.

"'Tis one of them Yale lads celebratin' the goose egg they give to the Hartford College. Noisy; but no harm. We've instructions to lave them be."

Disconsolate, Soapy ceased his unavailing racket. Would never a policeman lay hands on him? In his fancy the Island seemed an unattainable Arcadia. He buttoned his thin coat against the chilling wind.

In a cigar store he saw a well-dressed man lighting a cigar at a swinging light. His silk umbrella he had set by the door on entering. Soapy stepped inside, secured the umbrella and sauntered off with it slowly. The man at the cigar light followed hastily.

"My umbrella," he said, sternly.

"Oh, is it?" sneered Soapy, adding insult to petit larceny. "Well, why don't you call a policeman? I took it. Your umbrella! Why don't you call a cop? There stands one on the corner."

The umbrella owner slowed his steps. Soapy did likewise, with a presentiment that luck would again run against him. The policeman looked at the two curiously.

"Of course," said the umbrella man—"that is—well, you know how these mistakes occur—I—if it's your umbrella I hope you'll excuse me—I picked it up this morning in a restaurant—If you recognize it as yours, why—I hope you'll—"

"Of course it's mine," said Soapy, viciously.

The ex-umbrella man retreated. The policeman hurried to assist a tall blonde in an opera cloak across the street in front of a street car that was approaching two blocks away.

Soapy walked eastward through a street damaged by improvements. He hurled the umbrella wrathfully into an excavation. He muttered against the men who wear helmets and carry clubs. Because he wanted to fall into their clutches, they seemed to regard him as a king who could do no wrong.

At length Soapy reached one of the avenues to the east where the glitter and turmoil was but faint. He set his face down this toward Madison Square, for the homing instinct survives even when the home is a park bench.

But on an unusually quiet corner Soapy came to a standstill. Here was an old church, quaint and rambling and gabled. Through one violet-stained window a soft light glowed, where, no doubt, the organist loitered over the keys, making sure of his mastery of the coming Sabbath anthem. For there drifted out to Soapy's ears sweet music that caught and held him transfixed against the convolutions of the iron fence.

The moon was above, lustrous and serene; vehicles and pedestrians were few; sparrows twittered sleepily in the eaves—for a little while the scene might have been a country churchyard. And the anthem that the organist played cemented Soapy to the iron fence, for he had known it well in the days when his life contained such things as mothers and roses and ambitions and friends and immaculate thoughts and collars.

The conjunction of Soapy's receptive state of mind and the influences about the old church wrought a sudden and wonderful change in his soul. He viewed with swift horror the pit into which he had tumbled, the degraded days, unworthy desires, dead hopes, wrecked faculties and base motives that made up his existence.

And also in a moment his heart responded thrillingly to this novel mood. An instantaneous and strong impulse moved him to battle with his desperate fate. He would pull himself out of the mire; he would make a man of himself again; he would conquer the evil that had taken possession of him. There was time; he was comparatively young yet: he would resurrect his old eager ambitions and pursue them without faltering. Those solemn but sweet organ notes had set up a revolution in him. To-morrow he would go into the roaring downtown district and find work. A fur importer had once offered him a place as driver. He would find him to-morrow and ask for the position. He would be somebody in the world. He would—

Soapy felt a hand laid on his arm. He looked quickly around into the broad face of a policeman.

"What are you doin' here?" asked the officer.

"Nothin'," said Soapy.

"Then come along," said the policeman.

"Three months on the Island," said the Magistrate in the Police Court the next morning.

Critical Thinking

Why does Soapy prefer being "the guest of the law" to staying in the "bed of charity"?

What are the alternatives for Soapy? What crimes does Soapy attempt so as to be arrested and housed at Ricker's Island?

What faulty assumptions by the police officers keep them from arresting Soapy?

What is ironic about the place where Soapy is finally arrested and about Soapy's state of mind at that point?

How is this a surprise ending?

Can you imagine a present-day scenario in which a person would prefer to be in prison rather than free?

Do former inmates sometimes have a difficult time making it in the world outside of prison? If so, why?

Chapter 10

Prison Life

Adjusting to Prison Life

"The Beast"

by Victor Hassine

Victor Hassine (1956–2008), an author and law school graduate (1981), spent over 25 years in a Pennsylvania prison. He was born in Egypt and raised in New Jersey. The case against Hassine involved a 1982 conspiracy involving him and two co-conspirators that resulted in the murder of one man and the shooting of two others. Hassine was sentenced to life imprisonment, in addition to several consecutive prison terms extending from two to twenty years. At the age of 52, Hassine appears to have hung himself while in prison. In his book *Life without Parole: Living in Prison Today* (which had four editions), he includes stories of prison life, interviews with other prisoners, and some short essays about his personal views of the U.S. criminal justice system. "The Beast" is one of those stories.

"The Beast" (2009) is a story told in the third person but through the point of view of a prison inmate, Buck. Note that the first five paragraphs personify the Beast, who represents the fear and evil that exist within the prison. The Beast is said to alter everyone it encounters and is interpreted differently by different people: some try to avoid it by remaining solitary, others by never being alone, and others by superstitiously changing their diet. Hassine alludes to how inmates cope with their lack of autonomy and security and the constant threat of violence from other inmates. Buck seems determined to face the Beast head on.

"The Beast"

by Victor Hassine

Danger stalked the prison forcing its inhabitants to live in a state of fear. Fear was so pervasive it became more than just a feeling—it became the Beast that ruled the compound, the Beast all men dreaded but never saw, the Beast that was always just a moment away, lurking in shadows.

What the Beast let live, it altered, leaving its mark on every man, woman, and child who dared enter its domain. Everyone tried to avoid this predator, despite the hopelessness of trying to avoid something they could not see. Then there were those who believed the Beast possessed the power to change its form and become anything or anyone at any time. Those who thought the Beast had human form, disassociated themselves from all of humanity, suspecting anyone and hence everyone of being the Beast. Like lone wolves, these frightened men walked the prison compound, cowering in anticipation of impending attack.

Some men suspected the Beast in the food they ate. They changed their diet, eating only fruits, vegetables, and garlic, hoping this would keep the animal away. Finally, there were those who felt that their safety depended on being constantly in the company of a large group of people. Thinking their antagonist would not attack the many, these men were never alone. Instead, they chose to abandon their individuality for the useless shelter of unquestioned conformity under the rule of others.

Then, of course, there was the physical evidence of the Beast that stood as a constant reminder of this creature's awesome might. The multiple layers of slimy fungus lining the walls and ceilings of the shower rooms had the footprints of the Beast. The uninterrupted chatter of loud voices that echoed throughout the prison carried the victory cry of the Beast. Wounds and scars bore the mark of the Beast. And blood everywhere, on the floor, on the walls and on clothing, was scabbed testimony of the Beast's savagery.

The Beast was everywhere in prison, ready to attack the suspecting and unsuspecting alike. It was this pervasive, pernicious foe that gave the prison its deadly character. It was the Beast who made the killers kill and the rapists rape because all men fear each other less than they fear the Beast.

Like everyone else in the prison, Buck knew of the Beast and was frightened by it. Unlike the others, he held an unhealthy curiosity that wanted to see the Beast; to know the face of the creature that threatened his life. He wanted to see the Beast and thereby be less afraid for having seen it or maybe to see it and to die.

Buck was certain Old Head had seen the Beast. He could see it in the old man's tired eyes, in the way the old man would always be looking around. The constant strain of seeking had caused large balloons of flesh to form beneath sunken eyes, which forced him to squint. Buck believed those vigilant eyes were looking for something they had seen before.

Buck never talked about the Beast to Old Head. Buck was worried that Old Head would sense his fear. Showing your fear in prison was the same as showing your ass; if you did, you could count on someone trying to exploit it. So Buck never spoke to his old friend about his fears even though he often wished he had the courage to do so.

Buck decided to walk the long corridor to the yard. Unavoidably, he ran into Silky the 'swag man,' who was trying to sell his nasty but popular bootlegged sandwiches.

"Hi, Buck, I got a real toe-tapper here for ya. I mean this sandwich is hollering and screaming—jumping up and down. Fried eggs, fish, and cheese hot out o' the kitchen. That's what I'm talking about!" pandered the merchant.

Though amused by Silky's salesmanship, Buck knew from painful experience the consequences of eating a "Silky Swag." Nevertheless, listening to the man's hustle made Buck's mouth water and hunger nip at his empty stomach. Buck was certain Silky could sell a hungry lion to a helpless lamb.

"Nah, Silky, I think I'll pass on this one. The last 'toe-tapper' you sold me gave me the runs," responded Buck while rubbing his belly.

"Hey, that wasn't one of my swags. I was selling that stuff for some dude on 'D' block as a favor. I swear I'll never do that again! I'll tell you what I'll do, Buck," persisted Silky. "I'll give you 'two for one on the eye' and if this sandwich ain't a smoker, well, you ain't got to pay me."

Buck began to smile, impressed by this man's drive and determination, yet remembering the churning pain of his stomach when digesting a Silky sandwich. This proved too great an obstacle for Silky's tempting offer to overcome. Then just before Buck could verbally reject the bargain, he heard a commotion behind him. Bumps ran up the back of his neck as blood rushed to every muscle in his body leaving his face pale and cold. The Beast was near.

Silky must have expected the Beast, too, because swags and all, he was gone. Obviously, Silky did not share Buck's need to see the face of the Beast and so it was that only Buck was there to turn around and face the animal.

A crowd of faceless men bubbled around directly in front of Buck in the boiling commotion of a prison dispute. The din of angry voices swelled while the putrid stink of the Beast filled Buck's nostrils. Despite the fear, Buck could not run away like Silky. Buck's curiosity and stupidity kept his feet from moving, and left him standing terrified before the crowd, reluctantly prepared for the attack of the Beast.

As the crowd grew and the noise increased, Buck expected to hear the savage cry of the Beast, but there was no howling. As Buck watched, what resembled a bolt of lightning came thundering down, hitting a man in the center of his chest. Unlike lightning, the silver flash did not just vanish into thin air. The silver streak just rested, lodged in the man's chest until blood turned the silver red. That's when the shank was pulled out of the man's chest and then plunged into his stomach where it was left, horizontal against the force of gravity.

The crowd soon disappeared and the voices were silenced as the corridor emptied more quickly than it had filled. Soon there was no one left in the corridor except one dying man against a wall, who was slowly sliding down to the floor, and Slim, who just stood there watching him die.

The man had his back against a wall, as his hands gripped the bloodied shank still protruding from his stomach. His life oozed out in a rhythmic pulse that marked a path downward to the cold concrete floor. As a gruesome puddle of blood welled up on the lonely walkway, morbid thoughts came over Buck who noted that blood was much darker than he had assumed and smelled as bad as a Silky swag.

The dying man, who was now on the floor, looked up at Buck and feebly tried to say something. While either begging, cursing or praying, the man then reached out his hand to Buck, who was still trying to break free from the grip of immobilizing fear. Spittle and more blood began to trickle down from the man's mouth. Buck became aware that the man was staring at him with glazed lifeless eyes. Buck had seen that look many times before on men who were high on drugs. The familiarity of the expression strengthened Buck's resolve to face the Beast once and for all, to force the thing from his nightmares.

Suddenly the dying man lurched forward with his hands still outstretched. Buck could hear the sound of air escaping from an open throat as the scent of death assaulted him. The man now lay dead at Buck's feet, which finally were able to move and take Buck away from the murder scene.

As Buck hurried down the corridor to the yard, he wondered if anyone could ever get any closer to seeing the Beast he'd seen reflected in the eyes of the dying man. Soon, guards were rushing past him in the direction of the killing. The foul stench of death, which lingered in his nose, was pushed deeper into him in the wake of their passing.

It was a sunny day in the yard and Buck could feel the warmth of the sun upon him. Nervously he lit a cigarette and began to walk the yard, more aware than ever that he could escape nothing in prison.

"Hey, Buck, what about that swag," asked Silky who had spotted him and managed to catch up with him. Silky was more eager than ever to sell his goods, as if the man's death somehow made his putrid sandwiches more palatable and less obscene.

Silky knew a man had died pitilessly a few moments ago. This realization made Buck hate the persistence of the merchant that a short while ago had humored him. Buck did not respond but instead began to walk faster. Silky followed and continued his efforts. Buck stopped and listened to the savage cry of a wild beast that he was certain everyone heard, but if anyone did hear it, they did not act like it. Buck was scared and confused. There was so much he had just seen, yet didn't understand.

"Well how about it, Slim?" asked Silky.

"Look, Silky, I don't want none of your lousy sandwiches. Now leave me alone," demanded an angry Buck.

Silky walked away, looking for another potential customer. Buck continued walking, preferring to be alone with his thoughts. The more Buck reflected on what he had just witnessed, the more he convinced himself the dead man never asked him for help. Halfway round the yard he convinced himself there was nothing more he could have done. On the second lap around the yard, he was sure it was none of his business. By the third lap, Buck had accepted the possibility that he was never there and he began to feel comfort in this denial. The Beast had gone away, and Buck forgot about the reflection he had never seen in the eyes of a man who had never lived to die.

Critical Thinking

In the course of the story, Buck interacts with two individuals: Silky, the inmate who tries to sell him sandwiches and an unnamed man who is murdered in the story. Can you see in Buck's interactions with Silky a glimpse of who Buck might have been before incarceration? Why do you think that is?

When a prison commotion takes place, Silky disappears, but Buck stands his ground as a man who is knifed falls at Buck's feet and reaches out to him as he dies. Does Buck's encounter with the murdered inmate demonstrate how Buck has been changed by the Beast?

Buck runs into the prison yard where Silky again tries to pawn his sandwiches off on Buck and addresses him as Slim. Look back at the narrator's use of the name Slim when he describes the murder. Could it be that Buck was the murderer? How would that explain Buck's convincing himself (in the last paragraph) that he was not even present for the murder?

How might Buck's sublimation of his emotions affect him once he is released?

What informal codes of conduct do Silky and Buck display that would not be tolerated outside the prison?

What lack of supervision in the prison does Hassine reveal? Can you find current examples of such inattentiveness within the prison system?

"The Prisoner"

by Elizabeth Browning

Elizabeth Browning (1806–1861) was a nineteenth century English poet who during her lifetime enjoyed more notoriety than her poet husband Robert Browning. American poet Emily Dickinson, who would have had few female literary role models, revered E. Browning and kept a portrait of the English poet in her bedroom. As a young woman, Browning was an invalid and often confined to her room, unable to perform domestic duties for her widowed father. This seclusion, which her father encouraged as he did not want his children to marry or leave him, allowed Browning to pursue her writing. Though raised in a prosperous family, Browning railed against social injustice in the case of slavery in America and child labor in England. Her major poem *Aurora Leigh* (1856) defends the right of women for education and meaningful work. At the time that she wrote "The Prisoner" (1853), Browning was living in Florence, Italy, with her husband, and writing about the Italian struggle for unification.

In this poem, Browning writes in the persona (dramatized character) of the marginalized, a prisoner, who opines about the effect that imprisonment has upon a person. This prisoner describes the sights, sounds, and feelings of the outside world in his/her memory. In the last few lines, these memories—like that of the river Rhine in Switzerland—are transformed into a heavenly vision. Browning might be making a political statement about the pitiful mental condition of someone confined by the state, or—given her strong belief in women's rights—she may have reflecting on the position of women in the nineteenth century, confined by lack of rights to partake in a meaningful way in the outside world.

"The Prisoner"

by Elizabeth Barrett Browning

I count the dismal time by months and years
Since last I felt the green sward under foot,
And the great breath of all things summer-
Met mine upon my lips. Now earth appears
As strange to me as dreams of distant spheres
Or thoughts of Heaven we weep at. Nature's lute

Source: Elizabeth Barrett Browning, 1806–1861.

Sounds on, behind this door so closely shut,
A strange wild music to the prisoner's ears,
Dilated by the distance, till the brain
Grows dim with fancies which it feels too
While ever, with a visionary pain,
Past the precluded senses, sweep and Rhine
Streams, forests, glades, and many a golden train
Of sunlit hills transfigured to Divine.

Critical Thinking

This poem is over 150 years old; do you think that it succeeds in representing the state of mind of some present day inmates?

Does this poem elicit sympathy for the prisoner in your opinion?

Female Inmates

"The Prisoner: A Fragment"
by Emily Bronte

Emily Bronte (1818–1848) was a nineteenth century English poet and novelist best known for her novel *Wuthering Heights* (1847). Like Elizabeth Browning, Bronte, too, influenced Emily Dickinson, who had a poem by Bronte read at her funeral. Bronte was born in Northern England, one of six children, to Marie Branwell and Irishman Patrick Bronte, a parish priest. Bronte was only three years old when her mother died, and her sisters became her closest friends. Though Bronte lived a reclusive life, she and her older sister Anne created poetry concentrated on the fictional island of Gondal; one of Bronte's surviving poems from that collection is "The Prisoner: A Fragment" (1845).

"The Prisoner: A Fragment" uses a male persona, a visitor to a prison, who is admitted by the jailer and who recalls the words spoken to him by the jailer and a female inmate. The young man, at first "Reckless of the lives wasting there away" and surprised by the darkness of the cells, spends much of the poem listening to the woman whom he describes as "sculptured marble saint," the prisoner. This woman reveals being struck and suffering, and yet she appears to have risen above her earthly conditions by accepting a "Messenger of hope"—her religious faith. The "torture" and "anguish" that she has endured have gained her a place in heaven and freed her. The last two lines of the poem—"Her cheek, her gleaming eye, declared that man had given/A sentence, unapproved, and overruled by Heaven"—indicate that only God has the right to judge this woman.

In Victorian times, women were considered to be the ones who kept their families, including their husbands, on the straight and narrow religiously. In Bronte's poem, the woman, though convicted by law and imprisoned, is the one who results victorious.

———————— ❧ ————————

"The Prisoner"

by Emily Bronte

A fragment.

In the dungeon-crypts idly did I stray,
Reckless of the lives wasting there away;
"Draw the ponderous bars! open, Warder stern!"
He dared not say me nay—the hinges harshly turn.

"Our guests are darkly lodged," I whisper'd, gazing through
The vault, whose grated eye showed heaven more gray than blue;
(This was when glad Spring laughed in awaking pride;)
"Ay, darkly lodged enough!" returned my sullen guide.

Then, God forgive my youth; forgive my careless tongue;
I scoffed, as the chill chains on the damp flagstones rung:
"Confined in triple walls, art thou so much to fear,
That we must bind thee down and clench thy fetters here?"

The captive raised her face; it was as soft and mild
As sculptured marble saint, or slumbering unwean'd child;
It was so soft and mild, it was so sweet and fair,
Pain could not trace a line, nor grief a shadow there!

The captive raised her hand and pressed it to her brow;
"I have been struck," she said, "and I am suffering now;
Yet these are little worth, your bolts and irons strong;
And, were they forged in steel, they could not hold me long."

Hoarse laughed the jailor grim: "Shall I be won to hear;
Dost think, fond, dreaming wretch, that I shall grant thy prayer?
Or, better still, wilt melt my master's heart with groans?
Ah! sooner might the sun thaw down these granite stones.

"My master's voice is low, his aspect bland and kind,
But hard as hardest flint the soul that lurks behind;

Source: Emily Bronte, "The Prisoner" published in 1846 collection *Poems by Currer, Ellis and Action Bell* under Emily's *nom de plume* 'Ellis Bell'.

And I am rough and rude, yet not more rough to see
Than is the hidden ghost that has its home in me."

About her lips there played a smile of almost scorn,
"My friend," she gently said, "you have not heard me mourn;
When you my kindred's lives, MY lost life, can restore,
Then may I weep and sue,—but never, friend, before!

"Still, let my tyrants know, I am not doomed to wear
Year after year in gloom, and desolate despair;
A messenger of Hope comes every night to me,
And offers for short life, eternal liberty.

"He comes with western winds, with evening's wandering airs,
With that clear dusk of heaven that brings the thickest stars.
Winds take a pensive tone, and stars a tender fire,
And visions rise, and change, that kill me with desire.

"Desire for nothing known in my maturer years,
When Joy grew mad with awe, at counting future tears.
When, if my spirit's sky was full of flashes warm,
I knew not whence they came, from sun or thunder-storm.

"But, first, a hush of peace—a soundless calm descends;
The struggle of distress, and fierce impatience ends;
Mute music soothes my breast—unuttered harmony,
That I could never dream, till Earth was lost to me.

"Then dawns the Invisible; the Unseen its truth reveals;
My outward sense is gone, my inward essence feels:
Its wings are almost free—its home, its harbour found,
Measuring the gulph, it stoops and dares the final bound,

"Oh I dreadful is the check—intense the agony—
When the ear begins to hear, and the eye begins to see;
When the pulse begins to throb, the brain to think again;
The soul to feel the flesh, and the flesh to feel the chain.

"Yet I would lose no sting, would wish no torture less;
The more that anguish racks, the earlier it will bless;
And robed in fires of hell, or bright with heavenly shine,
If it but herald death, the vision is divine!"

She ceased to speak, and we, unanswering, turned to go—
We had no further power to work the captive woe:
Her cheek, her gleaming eye, declared that man had given
A sentence, unapproved, and overruled by Heaven.

Critical Thinking

Do you think women are sent to jail or prison for committing the same types of offenses as men? If not, then what types of crimes do you think women are incarcerated for?

Currently, do you think that women prisoners are treated differently than male prisoners? Can you find examples where women have suffered abuse in prison?

Do you think that religious faith can play a part in incarceration? How so?

Chapter 11

Special Issues in Corrections

Return to Society

"The Prison Librarian"

by Sonia Tabriz and Victor Hassine

After Victor Hassine's death, Sonia Tabriz co-edited *Life without Parole: Living and Dying in Prison Today* (note the addition of the word "Dying") with Robert Johnson. Included in that book is the story "The Prison Librarian," which Tabriz edited and co-authored with Hassine. This story speaks to the power of hope in a place where hope appears to have been extinguished. Tabriz graduated *summa cum laude* and with University Honors from American University with a B.A. in Law & Society and a B.A. in Psychology. She earned a law degree from The George Washington University Law School in 2013 and is now a law firm associate, where she handles all areas of government contracting.

"The Prison Librarian" is essentially a story within a story. The narrator, a new inmate in prison, recalls a story told to him by "old convict" about Jack Jones, nicknamed Murder and Mayhem Jones or M & M Jones. The old convict escapes mentally by telling stories as does Jones by reading them.

———— ✿ ————

"The Prison Librarian"

by Sonia Tabriz and Victor Hassine

You shoulda seen me when I first came into this joint. I was scared and soft, and all I could see was "Sink or Swim" written on every tattoo, uniform, and wall. I decided I had to swim. I didn't want to end up like one of them floaters: weak cons treated like prison debris to be pushed, pulled, and used by anybody for any reason. A lot of fish—newbies—come up floaters.

I ain't proud of what I ended up doing in here to stay right. But like an old convict taught me, I had to do whatever it took to keep cons, guards, and insanity from creeping up behind me and taking away my pride. No sir, prison ain't no place for the weak. A man's got to stay vicious and heartless to swim with the sharks in these treacherous and hungry waters.

I'm not sure why, but that old convict schooled me well. Now I don't worry about anything 'cause I learned how to lurk silently, like a shadow, leaving cons anxious, wondering when I'll strike. The old con could have just as easily drowned me in the black depths of this angry sea, where no one would listen or care about my cries for help. But he didn't. Instead, he took me in and told me this story that I keep remembering; the one I've been telling some newbies, and wanna share with you.

I guess he decided to make me the keeper of his story so that I could pass it along when he moved on, like he did. I ain't ever before been the keeper of anything but trouble and bad luck. But I guess he just took a chance, hoping that there was still something more human than criminal inside of me. God, I hope that old bastard was right.

The story he told me was about a man, born Jack Jones, who was the meanest and most vicious street thug around; a man whose hard life had turned his heart stone cold. Those who knew him said he was a "hell-raiser," a demon who cared little about himself and even less about others. And this joint didn't make him any better. He became even angrier, with nothing to live for. He told everyone that he wanted to maim and kill as many people as he could, so their souls could be as empty, miserable, and dead as his own. So in time, Jack earned a more appropriate title, "Murder and Mayhem," or M&M.

A swift and solid hulk of a man, M&M started his bit with only a five-year sentence for savagely beating some folks whose only offense was to be happier than he was. But, within a few years, his sentence was increased to thirty years—for stabbing fellow convicts who he felt were not as strong, angry, or hateful as they should have been.

Eventually, M&M did stop stabbing people, but not because he had a change of heart or worried about getting more time behind bars. Not at all. It was just that, after years of being terrorized by M&M, cons and prison guards alike had learned to stay as far out of his reach as possible. And that was fine with M&M, because he was eager to do his time and leave prison.

Then he could take his mission to the unsuspecting people of the free world who he blamed for his cruel and heartless ways.

It eventually became a custom for passing convicts to shout out questions to M&M—from a safe distance, of course. It was always the same kinds of questions which received the same kinds of answers. But the cons didn't mind, and apparently neither did M&M, because he spared the fearful convicts their lives.

"What's happening, M&M?" cons would ask.

"Murder and mayhem when I get out; that's what's happening," would come a stern response.

"What you so mad about?" would come another question from behind.

"'Cause I ain't killed nobody today," an angry M&M would reply.

"What you gonna do when you get out?" someone would always ask.

"Make 'em pay," would be the answer, in a deep and deadly growl. And then the questions would start all over again, in an endless cycle of provocation and response.

Now, to the free world, this endless daily routine would seem unbelievable and considered the product of exaggeration. But, as any convict knows, prison is nothing but repetition and redundancy. Everything that a con says or does is something he's said or done a thousand times before. Only way you'll last is to give in to the routine and act cold and tough. Eventually that's all you become, but at least you're still alive. That's what the old con taught me before God answered his prayers and carried him out of this hole: "You gotta find somethin' to keep you from losin' your brains." He escaped this place by telling stories to new fish like me. And M&M? Well, he escaped by reading stories; one in particular, as it happens.

That's right, reading. In a world where most people communicated with their fists, enjoying a good read isn't how you'd expect a guy like M&M to handle his rage. But cracking open a good book was the only thing that didn't incite or provoke Murder & Mayhem to act on his name and crack open a few heads.

Once a week, for exactly two hours—which is all the prison rules allowed—M&M could be found in the small and shelf-bare prison library, sitting alone at a weathered wooden table, quietly turning the pages of a tattered book that he gripped awkwardly with his mighty, oversized hands. At first, other cons in the library would attempt to provoke M&M—like always, from a distance.

"Look who's got a soft side!" Or, "Hey! Is that a tear I see?" But no matter how much they tried, as long as M&M was in that pathetic prison library, he would not respond to any of their questions. It was as if the book he read possessed him, carrying him to a world so distant from his own that the massive, tattooed frame of his body could do nothing more than sit, awaiting the return of the M&M the cons all knew and feared.

The shabby prison library was run by a librarian, Sophia, a petite woman with fine strands of misty brown hair that cascaded down her back and fluttered with every step she took. She would have drawn no special notice if she'd worked in a library on the outs, besides maybe the snickers of young teens. But amidst the windowless gray walls of the prison library and surrounded by large men with faces set hard to make them look tough, such a small and delicate creature seemed as out of place as a warm smile.

It was truly a sight to see, when the kind and innocent librarian would stand near the menacing men as she made her rounds through the library. "Still working on that one? Let me know when you're ready for the next. The county cleared out their duplicates again this month so I have some new books in the back," Sophia would whisper gently, so as not to disturb the others. "I put aside a few mysteries, Nancy Drew I think. You may like them."

And the cons treated her right for the most part, knowing the guards would make their lives hell if they gave her any problems. But even with two guards standing at the library doors counting down Jack now knew it was a sin to kill a mockingbird, and he knew there lived a mockingbird in the heart of every person. But most importantly, Jack knew that prisoners, even the so-called hardened cons, were people too—with hearts housing mockingbirds that longed to break their silence and sing freely.

"Well, that's what happened for real," the old con told me. But as you might imagine, there are many variations to this story, each recalling a different version of the words spoken between the two and what book was given. Some even swore seeing M&M grin humbly, an act of humanity the monster had never before displayed. But, whatever was said or given that day, everyone agrees that when M&M continued down the hallway, there was a new air about him; like something heavy and unwanted had suddenly been lifted from his shoulders. The grudge he held against those he blamed for his misfortunes seemed to fade as his stern march turned into a proud walk. And the glare in his eyes began to reveal a broken soul, anxious to start anew rather than hold on angrily to the past. But despite this noticeable change in the man they had feared for so long, the cons resumed their cheering, spurred on perhaps by hope for themselves, clapping and hollering long after M&M had left the prison.

For weeks, months, and even years, those who remembered M&M eagerly searched newspapers, expecting to read that he had in fact carried out all the murder and mayhem he had spoken of. Never happened. Instead, a decade later, an article appeared in the local paper naming him "Citizen of the Year." It explained that upon leaving prison, Jack Jones had gotten a job, gone to school, and gotten married. With his wife, he had opened a bookstore, Burnt Offerings, which had become a very successful enterprise. The reason for the award, the article revealed, was that Jack Jones had donated money to build a free public library in his old neighborhood. And at the end of every month, when he would clean out his shelves to stock newly released books, Jack would bring by any easy or interesting reads to the prison where Sophia, the librarian, would offer them to the cons—as she had done with him years ago.

His life was changed, Jack explained to the columnist, not by thirty years of incarceration, but by a book he had received and the kind librarian who had given it to him. He wouldn't name the book, but simply stated what it taught him: inside a tough man beats a tender heart.

So this is the story I've been telling the newbies, who walk in here acting all tough but quickly realize they are just as lost as the rest of us. Having become an old con myself over the years, I am finally preparing to take my walk down the long corridor to freedom; but instead of excitement, I feel lonely and scared. You see, like Murder & Mayhem, I too spent most of my time here trying to act hard; waiting for my chance to get back at the happy-go-lucky people on the outs and be free from this prison hell. But in my old age, I have come to realize one thing: taking off the handcuffs doesn't make me a free man. Freedom is about releasing all the anger and hate that got me here in the first place. It's about finding a way to escape the M&M inside me, like Jack Jones did. Writing stories like this one is my inspiration. It's how I leave my past behind. It's how I set my soul free.

Critical Thinking

Why does Sophie, the librarian, seem out of place here?

What do the inmates do to taunt Jones and why?

How is Jones's behavior transformed for the two hours a week that he was allowed to be in the library? Why do you think this was the case?

After thirty years, when Jones, angry at the world as ever, serves his time and readies to leave, what advice does Sophie give that indicates a change in Jones?

Why does Harper Lee's book *To Kill a Mockingbird* resonate with Jones?

What does Jones accomplish after his release that indicates he has changed?

What does Jones tell a columnist for a local paper was responsible for his breaking a cycle of violence once he left prison?

What ideas to help inmates "leave behind anger and . . . hate" and resentments does this story provide?

Section 5

Special Topics in Criminal Justice

Chapter 12

Juvenile Justice

Delinquency

"We Real Cool"
by Gwendolyn Brooks

NOTE: This poem is not included in this anthology but may be found on the Internet at educational sites such as poets.org and poetryfoundation.org or at your university or college library.

The short poem "We Real Cool" (1960) by Gwendolyn Brooks focuses on the issue of juvenile delinquency. Brooks reflects on young people who defiantly rebel in the form of dropping out of school and drinking underage. In addition, from the epigraph of the poem, we can assume that the dropouts are spending their time playing pool. Note that all of the verbs are capitalized; these adolescents are more concerned about their actions than to whom or what those actions are directed (the direct objects). Two of the poem's lines allude to sexuality. While not illegal necessarily, carefree sexual behavior belies an attitude of reckless decision making. The final line comes as a shock to the reader. The pool players appear to know, but are not concerned, where their decisions will lead: death. This leaves the reader to wonder how those deaths will occur—through violence, drugs, or alcohol use?

Critical Thinking

Though published over fifty years ago, does this poem address issues that are relevant today?

How does the group-think mentality of these young people compare or contrast with that of gang members today?

How is the current juvenile justice system influenced by adolescents with rebellious behaviors in regards to education and alcohol?

Though the final line of Brooks' poem indicates that the end of the road for these adolescents will be an early death, couldn't their end just as predictably be jail?

If so, should the juvenile justice system identify and address these youthful attitudes and behaviors before more significant crimes than truancy and under-age drinking occur, and by what methods would that be accomplished?

"Thank You, Ma'am"

by Langston Hughes

NOTE: This short story in not included in this anthology but may be found on the Internet or at your university or college library.

Langston Hughes (1902–1967) was a prominent African American poet and social activist (among other roles) in the United States, most famous for his leadership of the Harlem Renaissance. Much of his poetry addresses contemporary social and political issues facing black people during the first two-thirds of the twentieth century, including double-consciousness, racism, violence (physical and mental), and surveillance. In the following short story, "Thank You, Ma'am," Hughes tackles juvenile delinquency, particularly when the delinquent is a black teenager.

Published in 1958, "Thank You, Ma'am" opens with Mrs. Luella Bates Washington Jones walking home from work late at night, when a teenage boy tries to snatch her very heavy purse and run away with it. Losing his balance in the attempt, the boy falls down and Mrs. Jones gives him a swift, hard kick in the behind. What follows is her interrogation of the boy and rendering her own version of justice upon him for his attempted crime. She begins by asking him if he's ashamed of himself for his actions. Although he blurts out an affirmative answer, she catches him in a lie when he says he wasn't trying to rob her. He also admits he will run away from her if she lets him go (she's holding tight to the front of his shirt). He apologizes to her, but Mrs. Jones takes him back to her home, declaring her intention to wash his dirty face and make sure he never forgets her. Despite his attempts to get away, Mrs. Jones succeeds in dragging him into her house and getting his name: Roger. Scared, Roger asks Mrs. Jones if she intends to have him arrested and sent to jail. Mrs. Jones answers gruffly, but with compassion: she finds out that Roger is hungry, but that he wanted money to buy a pair of blue suede shoes. Rather than scold him, she is instead empathetic, telling him that she, too, was young and wanted to have things she couldn't. She also admits that, like him, she has done things she now regrets. While she makes them something to eat, Roger has a chance to escape from Mrs. Jones, but her trust in him that he will *not* run away instills a change in Roger. He sits where she can easily see him because he doesn't want her not to trust him now. They share their meal together, while she tells him about her job in a hotel beauty shop. The story ends with Mrs. Jones giving Roger ten dollars to buy the shoes he wants so badly and sending him on his way. Not knowing what to say, he merely thanks her and goes.

Critical Thinking

Why does Mrs. Jones choose not to have Roger arrested and sent to jail?

Why is her form of justice—empathy and morality—more effective than the juvenile justice system's methods?

Is Mrs. Jones' approach a viable alternative for dealing with juvenile delinquency?

How does her approach differ from current responses to juvenile delinquency, especially delinquency of black male teenagers?

Problematic Issues in Juvenile Justice

"Hard to Be Good"
by Bill Barich

Bill Barich (1943-) is an American writer born in Winona, Minnesota, and raised on Long Island. He served in the U.S. Peace Corps in Nigeria and then settled in northern California, the setting for much of his fiction, including the short story "Hard To Be Good" (1982).

This story demonstrates how easily young people who feel unconnected, purposeless, and without fair and consistent guidance can fall into the criminal justice system. Shane, the likeable protagonist in this story, is exposed to abusive family members, drugs, and peer pressure. The story begins with Shane's first encounter with the police, which involves his smoking marijuana with friends and breaking the antenna off a police car. Shane does not feel guilty about his offenses, which earn him a suspended sentence and six months' probation; his takeaway is that the police had lied, saying that he had pushed and shoved them.

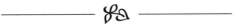

"Hard to Be Good"
by Bill Barich

Shane got arrested just before his sixteenth birthday. It was a dumb bust, out on a suburban street corner in Anaheim, California, on a warm spring night. A couple of cops were cruising through the haze and saw some kids passing around a joint, and they pulled over and did some unwarranted pushing and shoving, which resulted in a minor-league riot. Shane did not hit either of the cops, although they testified to the contrary in court, but he did break the antenna off their patrol car, so the judge was not entirely wrong to give him a suspended sentence and six months' probation. The whole affair was no big deal to Shane, since he didn't feel guilty about what he'd done—the cops had been *asking* for trouble—but it upset his grandparents, with whom he'd been living for some time.

His grandfather, Charlie Harris, drove him home after the court appearance. Harris was a retired phone-company executive, stocky and white-haired, who had great respect for the institutions of the world. "I hope you know how lucky are to get off easy," he said. "The judge could have thrown the book at you."

Shane was slumped in his seat, studying his fingernails. "It was a farce," he said.

"You take that kind of attitude and you'll wind up in the penitentiary."

"I'm not going to wind up in any penitentiary. Anyhow, the cops didn't tell the truth."

"Then they must have had a reason," Harris said.

After this, Harris made several secretive phone calls to his daughter Susan, who was Shane's mother. She lived in the redwood country north of San Francisco with her third husband, Roy Bentley. Bentley was some kind of wealthy manufacturer. Shane heard only bits of the conversations, but he was still able to guess what they were about. His grandparents were fed up with him. They'd been on his case ever since his school grades had started to drop, and it did no good anymore for him to explain that his math teacher failed everybody who wasn't a jock, or that his chemistry teacher was notoriously unfair—to the Harrises, teachers were in the same unimpeachable category as judges, cops, and ministers.

So Shane was not surprised when his grandfather broke the bad news. This happened one night when they were watching the stockcar races out in Riverside. They both loved speed and machinery. After the next-to-last race, Harris put his arm around Shane and told him that Susan wanted him to spend a couple of months with her during the summer. He used a casual tone of voice, but Shane understood that something irreversible had been set in motion.

"It's because of the bust, isn't it?" he asked. "I said it wasn't my fault."

"Nobody's blaming you. Your mother just wants to see you. Things are going well for her now."

"You really think Susan wants to see me?"

"Of course I do," said Harris, giving Shane a squeeze. "Listen, this Bentley guy's loaded. He owns a whole ranch. Your mom says you can have a separate cabin all to yourself. You'll have a wonderful visit."

"Not when all my friends are here," Shane said. "What's there to do in Mendocino?"

"Same stuff you do here. Don't be a baby, Shane. Where's your spirit of adventure?"

"It dissolved."

Harris moved his arm. "If you're going to take that attitude," he said, "we won't discuss it any further."

"It's always *my* attitude, isn't it? Never anybody else's."

"Shane," said Harris, as calmly as he could, "You just simmer down. You're not always going to get your own way in life. That's the simple truth of the matter." He paused for a moment. "The important thing for you to remember is that we love you."

"Oh sure," said Shane. "Sure you do."

Right after school let out in June, Shane got a check in the mail from his mother. She sent enough for him to buy a first-class plane ticket, but he bought a regular ticket instead and spent the difference on some Quaaludes and a bunch of new tapes for his cassette player. The drive to the airport seemed endless. At the last minute, his grandmother had decided to come along, too, so he was forced to sit in the back seat, like a little kid. The space was too small for his body; he thought he might explode through the metal and glass, the way the Incredible Hulk exploded through clothes. He watched the passing landscape with its giant neon figures, its many exaggerated hamburgers and hot dogs. It appeared to him now as a register of all the experiences he would be denied. He would have a summer without surf and beer, without friends, and possibly without sunshine.

The scene at the airport was as difficult as he feared it might be. His grandmother started sniffling, and then his grandfather went through a big hugging routine, and then Shane himself had to repress a terrible urge to cry. He was glad when the car pulled away, taking two white heads with it. In the coffee shop, he drank a Coke and swallowed a couple of 'ludes to calm his nerves. As the pills took hold, he began to be impressed by the interior of the terminal. It seemed very slick and shiny, hard-surfaced, with light bouncing around everywhere. The heels of people's shoes caused a lot of noise.

Susan had enclosed a snapshot with her check, and Shane removed it from his wallet to study it again. It showed his mother and Roy Bentley posed on the deck of their house. Bentley was skinny, sparsely bearded, with rotten teeth. He looked more like a dope dealer than a manufac-turer. Shane figured that he probably farmed marijuana in Mendocino, where sinsemilla grew with such astounding energy that it made millionaires out of extremely improbable types. He hoped that Bentley would at least be easy to get along with; in the past, he'd suffered at the hands of Susan's men. She tended to fall for losers. Shane's father had deserted her when Shane was ten months old, vanishing into Canada to avoid both his new family and the demands of his draft board. Her second husband, a frustrated drummer for a rock band, had a violent temper. He'd punched Susan, and he'd punched Shane. Their flat in the Haight-Ashbury came to resemble a combat zone. It was the drummer's random attacks that had prompted Susan to send Shane to stay with her parents. He was supposed to be there for only a few months, but the arrange-ments continued for more than three years. Shane still hated the drummer. He had fantasies about meeting him someday and smashing his fingers one by one with a ball peen hammer.

When Shane's flight was announced, he drifted down a polished corridor and gave his boarding pass to a stewardess whom he was sure he'd seen in an advertisement for shampoo. He had requested a seat over a wing, so he could watch the pilot work the flaps, and he had to slip by another young man to reach it. The young man smiled a sort of monkey smile at him. He was slightly older than Shane, maybe seventeen or eighteen, and dressed in a cheap department-store suit of Glen plaid.

Once the plane had taken off, Shane finagled a miniature bourbon from the shampoo lady and drank it in a gulp. The alcohol shot to his head. He felt exhilarated and drowsy, all at the same time. He glanced over at the young man next to him, who gave off a powerful aura of cleanliness, as though he'd been scoured with buckets and brushes, and said, without thinking much about it, "Hey, I'm really ripped."

The young man smiled his pleasant monkey smile. "It's O.K.," he said reassuringly. "Jesus loves you anyhow."

Shane thought the young man had missed the point. "I'm not talking bourbon," he whispered. "I'm talking drugs."

"I guess I must have done every drug there is," the young man said. He tugged on his right ear, which, like his left, was big. "I can understand the attraction."

The young man truned out to be Darren Grady. His parents were citrus growers. He was travelling to a seminary outside San Francisco.

"You're going to be a priest?" Shane asked.

Grady shook his head. "Its more in the nature of a brotherhood. Maybe you've seen those ads in magazines asking for new brothers?" Shane had not seen the ads. "I never noticed them, either," Grady went on, chewing a handful of peanuts, "until I got the call. You want to know how I got it? I was tripping on acid at Zuma Beach, and I saw this ball of fire over the ocean. Then I heard the ball speak. 'Judgment is near,' it said. I'm not kidding you. This really happened. At first, I thought I was hallucinating, but it wouldn't go away, even after I came down."

"So what'd you do?"

"Went and saw a doctor at the free clinic. He told me to lay off the dope. So I did. But I couldn't get rid of the ball."

"That's what made you want to be a priest?"

Grady frowned. "I can never tell it right," he said, picking through the peanut dust at the bottom of his little blue-and-silver bag.

Shane was moved by Grady's story. He'd had similar baffling trips, during which his mind had disgorged images of grievous importance, but he'd never ascribed a religious meaning to any of them. He felt foolish for bragging about taking pills. In order to set the record straight, he explained to Grady that he'd been exposed to drugs very early in life, because his mother had been a hippie; she'd named him after her favorite movie.

"It's not as bad as some names," Grady said. "I had a guy named Sunbeam in my class last year. Anyhow, you can go into court and get it changed."

Shane didn't want to see another judge, ever. "It doesn't bother me much now," he said, looking out at the sky. "When we lived in the Haight, Susan's husband, he was this drummer— he'd let me pass around joints during parties. Sometimes he'd let me have a hit. Susan knew, but I don't think she cared. I was so small, probably not much of it got into me. I don't know, though. I hate it when I see little kids smoking dope around school. You ought to be at least thirteen before you start."

"Maybe you should never start," Grady said.

"I wouldn't go that far. It helps to calm you."

"Grady tapped his breastbone. "The calm should come from inside," he said.

It seemed to Shane that Grady was truly wise for his age, so he confided all his troubles. Grady listened patiently until he was done. "I don't want to downplay it, Shane," he said, "but I'm sure it'll be over soon. that's how it is with troubles. They float from one person to the next. It's bound to come clear for you real soon."

Shane's high had worn off by the time the plane landed. He and Grady took a bus into the city, and at the Greyhound station, off Market Street, they exchanged addresses and phone numbers. The light outside the station was intense, bathing bums and commuters in gold. Shane was feeling relaxed, but he got anxious again when Grady left for the seminary. He was nervous about seeing Susan; their last visit, down in Anaheim at Christmas, had been marked by stupid quarrels. He tried talking to a soldier who was also waiting around, but it didn't work. The soldier was chewing about four sticks of gum. Shane asked him to buy a bottle of apple wine, so they could split it, and when the soldier did Shane drank most of it, washing down two more pills in the process, He was semiconscious on the bus ride up the coast. The town of Mendocino, arranged on a cliff overlooking the Pacific, struck him as a misinterpretation of New England. "It's cute," he said, to nobody in particular.

From the lobby of an inn on the main drag, he phoned his mother, and then he fell asleep in a chair. Later, he heard somebody (he thought it was Susan) say, "Aw, Roy, he's wrecked," so he said a few words in return and walked wobbly-legged to a station wagon. The next thing he knew, somebody was handing him a sandwich. He took it apart, laying the various components—cheese, tomatoes, alfalfa sprouts, two slices of bread—on the table. It occurred to him that he wasn't hungry. He said something to that effect, and somebody said something back—Bentley, the guy from the photo. He followed Bentley into a black night. Moisture from redwood branches dripped onto his head. The air seemed to be eating into his skin. Bentley unlocked the door of a cabin that smelled of pitch and camphor, and said something about extra blankets. Then Shane was alone. The whirlies hit him, and he stumbled to a small, unstable bed. After he was under the covers, the whirlies subsided, and he was able to assess his surroundings. He thought they were pretty nice. The only thing that concerned him was that there seemed to be animals in the cabin—they didn't scratch or howl, but he was aware of them anyway, lurking just beyond his line of vision.

The animals were ducks, two of them, with bulbs inside glowing like hearts. Shane saw them when he woke in the morning. Gradually, he remembered where he was, alone with the details of his arrival, and he felt disgusted and ashamed and yanked the covers over his head.

For some reason, he started thinking about Darren Grady. He was certain that Grady had never pulled such a dumb stunt. He wondered if Grady had made it to the seminary and if the other priests had shaved off his hair; he wondered, too, if Grady would recall their meeting or if all such mundane occurrences would automatically vanish from his mind, to be replaced by a steady image of God. Fifteen minutes or so passed in this fashion, helping to temper Shane's guilt and instill in him a new commitment to righteous behavior. He didn't pretend that he could ever be as wise and good as Grady, but he considered it within his power to improve. He got out of bed, examined the ducks more closely—they were lamps—and then, outside the cabin, he dumped his remaining pills on the ground and crushed them to dust. The act was like drawing breath.

Bentley's place was indeed like a ranch, fenced in and isolated from any neighbors. There were a few outbuildings, including a chicken coop and a beat-up barn missing boards from its siding. Inside the barn, Shane found birds' nests, rusty tools, and a broken-down old Chrysler with fish fins. Parts from the Chrysler's carburetor were scattered on a shelf, leaking oil.

Shane expected to be jumped on as soon as he opened the door to the main house, but nobody seemed to be around. He had no memory of its interior, except as a series of difficult-to-negotiate planes and angles. In the kitchen, he poured himself a glass of orange juice and sat down to read the sports page of a day-old paper. He heard his mother call to him from upstairs. "Is that you, Shane?" she asked. "Come up here right now. I want to talk to you."

He poured more juice and went up. "Where are you, Susan?"

"In here. I'm taking a bath."

The bathroom door was ajar; steam escaped from within. Shane-peeked and saw his mother in the tub, under a layer of froth and bubbles. Her hair was pinned up; it was thick, still mostly black, with a few gray strands. Shane thought she was immensely beautiful. He couldn't remember how old she was—maybe forty. The number was an ancient one, but he believed that it didn't really apply.

"Don't just stand there," she said. "It's drafty. Come in and shut the door." When he was inside, she said, "you look a little better today."

"Feel a little better," Shane said.

"How about a kiss for the old lady?"

He bent down, intending to kiss her on the cheek, but she lifted her arms from the water and embraced him. The sudden movement lifted her out of the soapsuds, so that her breasts were briefly visible. Shane had seen her naked before, countless times—in bathtubs and at nude beaches— but the quality of her flesh seemed different now, echoing as it did the flesh in the girlie magazines that he hid in his room in Anaheim.

"Oh, Shane," she said, pushing him away, "you were such a mess last night. What happened to you?"

Shane put his hands in his pockets. "Me and this friend of mine, Grady, we bought a bottle of apple wine and drank it at the bus station." He was quiet for a second or two. "I'm sorry I did it," he added.

"Well, you *should* be sorry. You gave us a real scare. When you behave like that, it makes me think you want me to feel guilty. I know I shouldn't have left you with Grandma and Grandpa for so long. You're my responsibility and I've done a poor job of raising you."

Shane recognized this as therapist talk; Susan was always seeing one kind of counsellor or another. Left to her own devices, she would have sputtered and thrown something at him. Once, she'd almost beaned him with a ladle; another time, an entire needlepoint kit had whistled by his ear. "You can't *raise* me, Susan," he said. "I'm not spinach."

She laughed and looked directly at him. "No, you're not spinach. But you'd better be telling me the truth about last night. It better not be pills again."

"It's not pills."

"It better not be, because if you get caught fooling with them you could go to jail, you know. It's a violation of your probation. I don't understand how you got arrested in the first place. Who were those kids you were hanging around with?"

"There's nothing wrong with the kids," Shane said heatedly. "The cops started it. Anyway, Susan since when are you so much against drugs? You used to smoke a joint every morning."

"I haven't smoked marijuana in years."

"Sure, Susan."

"Don't you dare talk to me like that, Shane," she said. "I'm your mother."

"I know."

"I'm not trying to be moralistic or anything. I just want you to keep out of trouble." She stood up in the tub; water dripped down her breasts, all down her body. "Give me that towel, will you honey?"

He grabbed a towel from the rack and threw it at her, much too hard.

She pressed the towel against her chest. "*Now* what is it?"

"What do you *think* it is? Christ, Susan, don't you have any modesty?"

"I'm sorry," she said, embarrassed. "I forgot how old you are." She wrapped herself tightly in a terry-cloth robe. "Go downstairs and I'll make us some breakfast."

The eggs she fried were brown and fertile, with brilliant orange yolks. She served them on red ceramic plates from Mexico. The colors made Shane's head swim, but he still ate with appetite. He was glad the confrontation with Susan was over. Their future together no longer seemed littered with obstacles. As she moved about the kitchen, banging pots and pans in the careless way she had, he felt a deep and abiding fondness for her, even though he knew that she had presented him with a complicated life by refusing to simplify her own. Charlie Harris called her a "nonconformist," and Shane supposed that he was right—if you ordered Susan to do one thing, she'd be certain to do the opposite. He respected her independent streak, because he had a similar streak in him; they were joined in a bond forged of trial and error.

After Susan cleared the table, she gave him some towels to put in the cabin and told him that she was going into town. He wanted to go with her, but she wouldn't let him.

"I don't mind errands," he said. He wanted to see what Mendocino looked like when it wasn't scrambled. "I could help you carry bags and stuff."

"We'll go tomorrow," Susan said firmly. "I'll have more time then. Today I've got my yoga class and a doctor's appointment." She came up behind him and hugged him. He could smell her sweet, fresh hair. Her breasts pressed against his backbone. "I love you very, very much," she said. "Now go get yourself clean."

Shane went dutifully out of the house, but he was worried a little. The word "doctor" had an awful connotation, like "teacher" or "cop." He had a terrible feeling that Susan might be sick. So a new thing began to haunt him—he ought to have been a better son. He remembered how in March his grandmother had reminded him to mail a birthday card to Susan, and how he had gone to the pharmacy and bought himself a candy bar instead. What possible use would candy be when Susan was in her grave? "You're so selfish," he said to himself, kicking at a pinecone. Every problem in the world, he saw, had its roots in some falling away from goodness.

That afternoon, around lunch time, Shane was in the old barn, sitting behind the wheel of the Chrysler and staring at the bird-peopled rafters, when Bentley wandered in and interrupted his daydream, which had to do with driving at great speeds over the surface of the moon. In person, Bentley looked even more disreputable than he had in the photograph. He could have been a bowlegged prospector who'd spent the last thirty or forty years eating nothing but desert grit. His rotten teeth were like bits of sandstone hammered into his gums. "How's the boy?" he asked in a twangy, agreeable voice, leaning his elbows on the car door.

"The boys' fine," Shane said. "He's just fine."

"Well, I'm happy about that. I'd like to have the boy step from behind the steering wheel of the car so that I can have a chat with him."

Reluctantly, Shane got out of the car. His hands were balled into fists. Down in Anaheim, he'd decided that if Bentley was a puncher, he'd punch first.

"Take it easy," Bentley said. "I'm not going to hit you."

"Wouldn't put it past you to try," Shane muttered.

Bentley lifted an expensive lizard-skin cowboy boot and ground out the cigarette he'd been smoking against the sole. "I lost my taste for violence a long time ago," he said. "Course, if I needed to, I could still fold you up and put you in my pocket with the Marlboros."

"I'm warning you," Shane said, backing off.

"The trouble is, Shane," said Bentley, following him, "your mother and I got a good thing going, and I don't want some wise-ass punk from surfer land to come around and spoil it. You pull the kind of crap you pulled last night one more time, and I'll stick you into a Jiffy bag and mail you home to the old folks."

"You can't boss me around."

At this, Bentley chuckled a bit, revealing the stumps in his mouth. "Sure I can," he said. "So long as you're on my property, and living off my kindness, I am most assuredly your boss. And here's some more news, my friend—I'm putting you to work." When Shane protested, Bentley cut him short by jabbing him in the sternum. "I'm giving you two choices. Either you can work by yourself at the ranch, and do some painting and cleaning, or your can work with me at the factory."

"What's your business?"

"I'm a manufacturer."

"Yeah, but what do you manufacture?"

"What I manufacture," said Bentley, "is ducks."

They went to visit the factory in Bentley's station wagon, which smelled of stale tobacco and leather. "See that rise?" Bentley asked Shane, as they passed a sloping hillside off to the right. "If you were to walk to the top of it and then down into the gully, you'd come to another twenty-acre parcel I own."

"Do you have another house there?"

Bentley gave him a peculiar look. "No house, no nothing," he said. "It just sits. It's appreciating in value. We'll have a picnic there someday."

"My grandfather," said Shane, "he loves to barbecue."

"We don't barbecue," Bentley said. "What we do is eat that organic food that Susan cooks. The woman has a fear of meat." He turned on the radio; a country singer was singing about beer and divorce. "Listen here, boy," Bentley continued, "I want you to have a good time this summer. I'm not naive about dope. I've done my share of it. But you have to learn yourself some moderation. Moderation is the key. You keep on abusing yourself the way you're going, you'll wind up in a pine box."

"My grandfather said I'd wind up in the penitentiary."

"That, too," Bentley said.

The factory was situated at the edge of town, in a concrete building that might once have been a machine shop. Inside, ten or twelve young longhairs, both men and women, formed an assembly line at long wooden tables. As Bentley had said, they were making ducks—or duck lamps—by gluing two pieces of heavy-duty celluloid around a metal stand that had a socket at the top for a bulb. Once the duck halves were glued together, they were secured with rubber bands and left to dry for a day or two. The excess glue was later wiped from the ducks with solvent, and they were put in cardboard boxes and cradled in excelsior. The wholesale price was twelve dollars a duck, but they were sold in trendy stores for as much as forty apiece. The materials came from Hong Kong.

Shane was shocked. His mind boggled at the notion that somebody could earn a fortune on celluloid ducks. The arithmetic didn't seem right. Forty dollars? Who'd pay forty dollars? A movie star? Were there enough duck-loving movie stars to provide Bentley with the capital to own a ranch and forty-odd acres? Apparently so. But Shane remained suspicious—the scam was too good to be true. He wished that Harris, who was always harping on the importance of hard work, could be there to watch Bentley as he lounged around the shop, smoking cigarettes and joking with his crew. Harris would go right through the roof; he'd say the whole shebang was un-American. Shane liked the atmosphere, though. Nobody treated the craft of duck-making very seriously. Besides, a tall blond girl with ironed hair kept glancing at him from across the room; he fell into an immediate fantasy about her. He told Bentley he'd prefer to work at the factory instead of at the ranch.

"I'll start you in the morning," Bentley said. "You'll be a duck packer. You'll pack so many damn ducks, you'll be quacking in your sleep."

They locked up after everybody had quit for the day. On the ride home, Shane's thoughts drifted back to Susan, and he asked Bentley if anything was wrong with her.

"No way," Bentley said. "She's a fine, fine lady. Absolutely perfect."

"I mean, is she sick or anything?"

"Sick? No, she's not sick. She's just got some female trouble. When you get older, you'll learn that every woman has it sooner or later. They can't avoid it, and you can't help 'em with it. It's just something they have to go through on their own," Bentley said with a sigh. "We'll talk about it more when we get to the ranch."

But Shane didn't bring up the subject again (he was afraid of what he might hear), and Bentley volunteered no further information. Instead, they returned to the barn and played with the Chrysler until they were both covered with oil. They cleaned the points and plugs and reinstalled the carburetor. Bentley showed Shane how the engine had been modified to make it operate at maximum efficiency. "Let's fire up the sumbitch," he said wiping his face on a polka-dotted bandanna. He let Shane sit in the driver's seat and try the ignition, but the engine wouldn't turn over. "Pump the pedal," he said. Shane pumped it and tried the ignition again. The engine roared. It sounded big in the barn, scattering robins and swallows into the dusk. Shane floored the pedal briefly and felt himself transported; energy ran through him as though he were a sieve.

After Shane had been at the factory for three weeks, he sent a postcard to his Anaheim pal Burt, the kid who'd actually hit a cop during the bust. He described his cabin, the redwoods, and the facory. "If you want to come up here," he wrote, "I can squeeze in another bed easy. And don't worry about me doing any you-know-what. I'm off that stuff for good."

Twice his grandparents called to see how he was getting along. He still felt estranged from them, and this was compounded when they told him they'd bought a camper and were going to Joshua Tree National Monument until mid-August unless Shane planned to come back before then.

"Me?" he asked, sounding wounded. "Since when do I have plans?"

For the next twenty-four hours, he was sullen and depressed, but he had to work at it, because he was having so much fun on the job. Every morning at eight, he and Bentley headed off together into a coastal fogbank that was always just beginning to disperse. They drank coffee from Styrofoam cups and told each other duck jokes while they watched the sky separate into a confetti mist under which the town of Mendocino stood exposed, back from wherever it went at night. Shane packed boxes with a ponytailed guy who was known as Eager on account of his last name, Beaver. Eager was anything but—he had a meticulous nature, and he took pains to be sure that each duck was nestled as comfortably as possible in its excelsior. He could have been packing eggs or glassware. "C'mon, Eager," Shane said to him one afternoon. "They're not alive, you know."

The tall blond girl was Emma King. She was nineteen, a college student. Shane followed her around like a dog. When the weather was hot, Emma came to the factory in white shorts and a red halter top, and Shane would monitor her every movement from his packing station, waiting for her to reach down for a tube of glue or bend low for the X-Acto knife she kept dropping on the floor. She had a boyfriend she saw on weekends, but she told Shane that she'd go to the movies with him before he returned to Anaheim. "I'm in love with this heavy girl, she's *nineteen!!!*" he wrote on another postcard to Burt. "We go drinking together after work." This was almost true, or at least at the outer fringe of validity. One Friday, Eager *had* invited him to go to a tavern in the woods where anybody could get served, but he'd decided against it to avoid trouble. Later, he heard that Emma had been there, so in his mind they were linked.

He asked her for a photo, but she didn't have any, so he borrowed Susan's camera and snapped her in different poses, while she pretended to complain. The cutest shot was one of Emma kissing a duck on its beak. Shane taped it to the dashboard of the Chrysler. He thought of it as his car now. Bentley had promised it to him in lieu of wages if he could pass his driver's test. Already, he was practicing. He did Y-turns and parallel parking. Some evenings, he and Bentley took a ride to the ocean, steaming down dirt roads that were dotted with Scotch broom and beach poppies. Once, Bentley let him go by himself, without any adult supervision, and he handled the Chrysler with such authority and skill that he developed a stitch in his side from excitement. It was a mystery to him how things kept changing.

Another mystery was his mother. He'd never seen her so happy. He could not reconcile so much happiness, in fact, with scraggly, bow-legged, rotten-toothed Bentley. Here was a man who could walk around for days with egg in his beard and never even notice. The scent of nicotine was embedded in his clothes and maybe in his skin. Could it be that love had nothing to do with beauty? If Bentley could provoke love, then so could a stone or a twig. So could a garbage can.

But there was no denying Susan's contentment. She thrived on Bentley's generosity. She seemd to float around the house, gliding barefoot an inch or two above the floor, dressed in blouses and peasant skirts that showed off her bosomy fullness. She baked bread, hummed romantic tunes, and filled all her vases with flowers. She was constantly hugging her egg-stained lover, patting him on his flat little prospector's ass. The affection spilled over to Shane. Susan's arms were always grasping for him, making up for lost time. She drew him to her for purposes of both measurement and embrace. The very size of him seemed to thrill her—he'd grown from almost nothing! "Oh, Shane," she'd say in a husky voice, holding a hunk of his cheek between her thumb and index finger. "You're such a dear boy."

If Shane hadn't known better he would have sworn that she was stoned all the time, but he'd never seen any dope in the house. As far as he could tell, the Bentleys had adopted a much more civilized vice. They drank wine—a bottle or two every evening, with Bentley leading the way. The wine burnished their faces. It made them talkative, sentimental, occasionally teary-eyed. After dinner, if the fog wasn't too thick, they'd put on sweaters and sit on the deck and speak in conspiratorial tones about the day's events, while bats sailed about overhead, like punctuation. When there was nothing on TV, Shane sat with them, shivering no matter how many layers of clothing he wore.

"Thin blood," Bentley would say, teasing him. "Goddam thin Southern California surfer's blood."

"My blood's fine."

"It's *thin,* Shane. It takes six months for blood to adapt to a new climate."

Blood was yet another mystery. Sometimes Shane thought that he understood Susan better than Bentley did, simply because they were related by blood instead of marriage. Although he and Susan had often lived apart, had quarreled and made mistakes, she was still his mother, and he was able, in a curious way, to anticipate her moods and know when something was bothering her. One night, as they sat outside, he saw that she was unusually quiet, removed from the conversation, and when Bentley went into the house he asked her if she'd got bad news at the doctor's office—she'd had another in her ongoing series of appointments that afternoon. The question made him tremble. Suppose she confessed something awful to him? Ignorance was a kind of protection. But she only smiled wistfully and patted his hand and said no, nothing very serious was wrong. It was just that the doctor had told her that she might need an operation—minor corrective surgery. She started to explain the problem to him in clinical terms, but it sounded indecent somehow to hear her describe her body as though it were an engine in need of repair, so he interrupted. "I know," he said, mimicking Bentley's sad resignation. "Female trouble." He put an arm around her, wanting to say more, but by then Bentley was back with full wineglasses and a word about the rising moon.

Shane's driving test was scheduled for a Thursday afternoon. Bentley gave him permission to come home early from work to practice. He backed the Chrysler into the barn several times without scratching it, and then he walked over to the house, hoping that Susan would make him a snack, but she'd gone to town for her yoga class. The phone rang while he was eating a boiled hot dog. Darren Grady was on the line, calling from Elk, a town south of Mendocino. Grady was upset, distressed, talking a mile a minute. He'd run away from the seminary. He was stranded, broke. Shane couldn't believe it. Where had Grady's wisdom gone? "Take it easy, Darren," he said. "Everything's going to be all right."

But Grady was blubbering. "I was trying to hitch to your place," he said, "But his highway patrol, he kicked me off the road. I cooled it in the bushes for a while and tried again, but here comes old highway patrol with his flasher on. I gave him the finger and split for town. I'm like a hunted cirminal, Shane. You got to help me."

Shane glanced at the kitchen clock. He figured that he could get to Elk and back before he and Bentley were scheduled to meet the state examiner, so he told Grady to sit tight. The drive over there took about twenty minutes and gave him a severe case of paranoia. Every car that-approached him seemed from a distance to be black and ominous and full of cops.

Grady was where he said he'd be, in front of a restaurant. He was sitting on the curb and eating a hamburger—some ketchup was on his chin—and drinking a can of beer. When he saw Shane, he waved wildly and let loose his monkey smile. Shane was surprised that Grady still had hair—there was no bald spot or anything. The only truly abused part of him was his Glen plaid suit. All its department-store slickness had been rubbed away; there were holes in the knees of his trousers, as if he'd been on a long pilgrimage over concrete. Also, he'd lost his socks. The confidence he'd had on the plane was gone; now he was nothing but fidget. "I'll never forget you for this, Shane," he said, getting to his feet. "Is this yours?" he asked in wonderment, touching the Chrysler's fins. "It's a mean machine."

Shane eyed the half-demolished burger. "I thought you were broke," he said.

"I am, but I talked up the waitress in there"—Grady jerked his streaked face in the direction of the restaurant—"and traded her my Bible."

"She gave you beer for a Bible?"

"Just the hamburger. The beer I found."

This sounded fishy to Shane. "Where'd you find it?" he asked.

"Some guy left it on the seat of his car." Grady climbed into the Chrysler. For a moment, he seemed collected, drawn virtuously into himself, but then he fell apart and started bawling. "You're the only damn friend I've got," he said, blowing his nose in the hamburger wrapper.

Grady told Shane that he'd been on the road for three days. The first night, after he'd snuck out of the seminary, he hitched to San Francisco and slept in the Greyhound station, thinking he would catch a bus to Anaheim in the morning, but when he woke he realized that he'd have to confront his parents with the sorry evidence of his failure, so, instead of phoning them, he walked over to Powell Street and ate a breakfast of crab and shrimp at a place that was shaped like the prow of a ship, and then spent twenty-two bucks playing video games at an arcade. This left him with just one dollar to his name—his emergency dollar, which he kept folded in sixteenths and hidden in the secret compartment of his wallet. When he pulled it out, the slip of paper on which Shane had written Susan's address and phone number fell to the floor.

"You get it?" Grady asked, turning towards Shane, who was paying only a little attention, since he had to watch for cops. "It was a *sign!*"

"What about the ball?" Shane asked. His forehead was wrinkled in concentration.

"Ball? What ball?"

"The ball from Zuma Beach. Did it come back while you were with the priests?"

"It never did."

"Then why'd you leave?"

Grady shrugged. His fidgety fingers picked at his knees through the holes in his pants. "It's hard to be good," he said. From the pockets of his suit coat he took two fresh cans of beer and—before Shane could protest—popped the tops. Shane accepted a can and tucked it between his thighs. He hit a bump and got doused.

On the second day, Grady said, he'd reached the town of Healdsburg. He said it was the hottest place he'd ever been to—hotter than Hell, frankly. In the evening, when it got too dark to hitch anymore, he wandered to the town square, where there were palm trees and flowers and benches, and he took off his shoes and socks and dunked his feet in a fountain. The water felt soothing as it swirled between his toes, but a bunch of Mexicans who were hanging around the square kept watching him, and he thought they might knife him or otherwise do him harm. He knew this was an irrational fear, but it was fear nonetheless, so he gathered himself together in a hurry, slipped his wet feet into his shoes, and walked briskly down a side street that led him to a vineyard, where he curled upon the warm ground and slept the night away under cover of grape leaves. A flaming sun woke him at dawn. He couldn't find his socks. Their absence seemed to hurt him more than anything else. "Everybody knows you're running away from something if you don't have socks on," he said, biting his lower lip. "Who's going to stop for a person with bare ankles?" With this, he finished his beer in a gulp and threw the empty can out the window. The can rattled over the macadam, bounced two or three times, and rolled past the nose of a highway-patrol car that was parked in the bushes, waiting for speeders.

"Aw, Grady," Shane said.

Grady swivelled around to look back. "That's the guy I gave the finger to," he said.

Shane felt as though his body had been stripped of a dimension and then spliced into a deadly, predictable horror movie. He tried to imagine that the cop hadn't seen the can—or, better, that the cop had decided to overlook it—but this didn't work, since the cop had left his hiding place and was approaching the Chrysler at a steady clip. Shane gave Grady the half-full beer he had between his thighs, and Grady dropped down in the seat and drank it off, then shoved the empty into the glove compartment. The cop came closer. Grady looked again, and, panicked, said, "He's going to bust us. Shane. I know by his face."

"You don't know for sure,"

The cops' flasher went on.

Grady sank lower in the seat. "I'm holding, Shane," he said morosely.

Shane didn't want to take his eyes from the road. "You're *what*?"

"I'm holding some speed. I bought it at that arcade." He showed Shane four pills. "Should I throw them out the window?"

The pills got swallowed—Shane couldn't think of any other way to dispose of them. He and Grady ate two apiece, which lent a hallucinatory edge to subsequent events. The cop was wearing reflector sunglasses, for instance, so that Shane was able to watch himself react to the words that bubbled from between the cop's lips when the cop pulled them over. The cop spoke of littering, of underage drinking, of operating a motor vehicle without a license and without what he called a vehicular-registration slip. Eyeless, he led Shane and Grady to his car and locked them in the back seat behind a mesh screen. The pills really took hold on the ride to the police station, and Shane was possessed by a powerful sense of urgency and a concomitant inability to stop talking. He believed that he had an important message to deliver about the nature of goodness, and he delivered it ceaselessly—to the cop, to the officer who booked him, to the ink of the fingerprint pad, and to the cold iron bars of his cell.

Roy Bentley bailed out the boys. He came to the station with his attorney, a fashionably dressed man whose hair was all gray curls. The attorney seemed to know everybody around, and after a brief back-room conversation he reported to Bentley that the charges—except for littering— had been dropped. Bentley paid a stiff fine, then put the boys in his wagon and drove them to the ranch. They were amazed to be let go so quickly. "You must be important, Mr. Bentley," Grady said.

"You two are just lucky I've got some clout," Bentley told them. "A successful businessman is not a nobody up here. I'm a Democrat and I belong to the Rotary. But don't think it's over yet. You still got Shane's mother to face."

Susan exploded. There was no therapist talk this time. When Shane came through the door, slinking like an animal, she yelled and threw a potholder at him, and then, so as not to be discriminatory, she threw one at Grady, too. She grabbed Shane by the hair and held him in place while she lectured him. She said he was an ungrateful little bastard, spoiled indifferent, snotty, rotten to the core. He refused to argue, but in the morning, when she was almost rational again, he explained to her exactly why he had done what he'd done, so that she would understand that he hadn't been frivolous or irresponsible. "It was circumstances, see?" he said, sitting forward in his chair and kneading his hands. "I couldn't just leave him in Elk, could I? How would you feel if you called some friend of yours for help and the friend said no?"

"What about Roy, Shane?" she asked. "You could have phoned him at the factory, and he would have gone for Darren."

"But it was an emergency, Susan."

"The only emergency was that you didn't think."

The next day she was more forgiving, taking into account his unblemished record, and also the fact that he had been (at least to some extent) victimized. She also agreed that Grady could stay in the cabin for a few days, provided that he let his parents know where he was. This Grady did. "Hello, Dad?" he said to his father, while Shane listened in. "It's me, Darren, your son. Remember about the seminary? Well you were right. It didn't work out."

In the cabin, Shane and Grady lay on their beds in the dark and had long philosophical discussions. Grady said that when he got home he was going to forget about religion and enroll in a junior college to study biology, so he'd have a grasp of how the universe was put together. "Science today," he said, "it has the answer to mysteries that puzzled the ancients." Shane confessed that he was dreading his senior year in high school; he would be an entirely different person when he returned to that bleak, airless building, yet nobody would acknowledge it. "The system hates what's real," he said. Grady agreed.

On more than one occasion, they talked about how strange it is that sometimes when you do everything right, everything comes out wrong. Grady had examples. "I gave my sister this kitten for her birthday," he said, "and she was allergic to it." Or "Once when I was small, I washed my mom's car to surprise her, but I used steel wool and scratched up the paint."

Shane had other questions. "If it was me stranded in Elk," he asked, "would you have come and got me?"

"You know it," Grady said, with emotion crowding his throat.

Both of them took a solemn vow never to touch dope again, ever, in any form, no matter how tempted they might be.

Grady ended up staying for better than two weeks. Several important things happened while he was around.

First, Shane passed his rescheduled driver's test and celebrated by pinstriping the Chrysler and painting flames on both its doors. Then he asked Emma King to go the drive-in with him. They went to a kung-fu double feature on a Friday night. She sat so far away from him that it seemed a deliberate attempt to deny his existence. He thought that maybe older women expected men to be bold, so after a while he walked his fingers across the seat and brushed them against Emma's thigh. She sneezed. He withdrew. Later, on the steps of her house, much to his surprise, she kissed him full on the lips and told him he was sweet. He knew it was the only kiss he'd ever get from her, so, driving home, he made a mental inventory of the moment and its various tactile sensations.

Next, on a Saturday afternoon, he and Grady took the Chrysler to the main town beach, but it was crowded with hippies throwing Frisbees to their dogs, and Shane suggested that they go instead to this great isolated spot even he had never been to before—Bentley's twenty undeveloped acres. They had to slide under a barbed-wire fence that had No Trespassing and Private Property signs plastered all over it. The trail down into the gully was steep and overgrown; the gully, in fact, was more like a canyon with a stream trickling through it, and vegetation spouting from the soil. The vegetation was so thick and matted that it was almost impossible for them to distinguish individual plants, but one of the plants they *could* distinguish was marijuana. A few stalky specimens were growing wild, like weeds. All Shane's suspicions were confirmed—Bentley was a grower.

"That's why he had the attorney," he whispered to Grady.

"Are you going to say anything?"

"Uh-uh. No way."

But Shane's conscience bothered him. In the eyes of the law, Bentley was a criminal. Did this put Susan in jeopardy, too? Would she be considered an accessory to the crime? So Shane spilled the beans to Bentley. He told him about the find and waited for Bentley to react.

Bentley tugged at the strands of his beard. "Well, you got me, all right," he said sheepishly. "I did grow me a few crops of Colombian down there a while back, before I met your mother, but the whole experience rubbed me wrong. I had a couple of brushes with John Law, and they made me real nervous. That's why I took my profits and went into ducks. Ducks are as legal as it gets."

"What about the plants we saw?"

"Must be volunteers. That happens sometimes. Stuff grows from old seeds, leftover seeds. We'll go pull 'em up."

They pulled up all the marijuana plants in the gully, arranged them in a pyre, and burned them. "It's sad," said Bentley. "But it has to be."

Next, Susan went in to the hospital for her operation. The surgery was performed in the afternoon, and Shane was allowed to visit that evening. He was scared. Susan was in a private room. She was still groggy from her anesthesia, and she had an I.V. tube in her arm. He thought she was asleep, but she called to him in a funny, childlike voice and asked him to sit in a chair by the bed. "I'm in the clouds," she said, rubbing his hand.

"But are you O.K.?"

"I'm fine," she said. "The doctor fixed everything. He says I can probably have a baby now."

"A *baby*?"

"You think I'm too old, don't you?"

"I don't know," Shane said. "How am I supposed to know about babies?"

"Lots of women have babies at my age," Susan said, rubbing and rubbing. "Roy and I want to try. Oh, Shane honey, I made things so tough on you, I want another chance. Don't I deserve another chance?"

"Sure," said Shane. "Of course you do."

But the potential baby confused him, and also depressed him a bit. In his mind, it was rotten-toothed, bearded, and smelling of tobacco. He wondered why Susan would want to introduce such a creature into the world. "I'm never going to understand anything," he complained to Grady that night. "Not anything."

"What's there to understand?" Grady asked.

"Maybe you are wise, Grady," said Shane.

Grady left at the end of the week. Shane dropped him at the Grey hound stop in Mendocino. They shook hands in a special way they'd devised, with plenty of interlocked fingers and thumbs.

"I never had a friend like you before," Grady said. "I'll never forget what you did for me."

"I'd do it again," said Shane. "Any time."

In late August, there was an unseasonal thunderstorm. It rattled window-panes and made chickens flap in their coops. When it was over, the morning sky was clear and absolutely free of fog. Shane got up early and changed the oil in the Chrysler. He filled the trunk with his belongings and put a pair of ducks for the Harrises on the back seat. Susan was not entirely recovered from her surgery, so he had to say goodbye to her in her bedroom, where she was propped up against pillows. She asked him again if he didn't want to transfer to a school in Mendocino and stay on with them, but he told her that he missed his grandparents and his friends. "I might come back next summer," he said, kissing her on the cheek. "You'll probably have the baby by then." Bentley stuck fifty dollars in the pocket of his jeans. "You ain't such a bad apple, after all," said Bentley with a smile. Shane drove off quickly, without looking back. The highway was still slick and wet from the rain, and the scent of eucalyptus was in the air.

Critical Thinking

How do you think law enforcement's unfair treatment of Shane influenced his attitude toward the justice system?

What appears unusual and unhealthy about Susan's relationship with her son?

Probation by its very nature includes supervision, which does not occur in Shane's case. Do you think supervision would have been helpful?

What rehabilitation could the courts have attempted, and do you think that would have been successful?

As the story's title states, Shane does find it hard to be good. Why?

How important are step-father Bentley's actions to Shane at this time and what might they represent to him?

At story's end, Shane has returned to his grandparents and friends. Do you think that he will be able to stay out of trouble in the future? Either way, what insights about juveniles might the criminal justice system gain from Shane's journey?

Chapter 13

Victimology and Victim's Rights

The Path from Victim Justice System to Criminal Justice System

"A Jury of Her Peers"
by Susan Glaspell

Susan Glaspell (1876–1948) was an American journalist, playwright, and novelist. Most famous for her play *Trifles*, she is recognized as an important feminist writer and modern female playwright. She adapted her 1916 one-act play *Trifles* into the well-known, heavily anthologized story "A Jury of Her Peers" (1917). The play is based on an actual murder trial that Glaspell covered for the *Des Moines Daily News*.

"A Jury of Her Peers" considers how gender figures into the determination of guilt, justice, morality, and victims' rights. The story opens on a cold March morning with Martha Hale, a farmer's wife, her husband Mr. Hale, Sheriff Peters and his wife going to the Wright farm. Mr. Wright has been murdered and his wife, Minnie Wright, has been taken into police custody. Glaspell describes the Wright farm repeatedly as a lonesome, isolated place. Upon their arrival, they meet the county attorney, Mr. Henderson, who, with Sheriff Peters' help, tries to deduce how and why Mr. Wright was murdered, beginning by asking Mr. Hale questions. (Mr. Hale and his son found the body the previous day.) Significantly, the initial questioning takes place in the kitchen, the most important room in any house, but particularly a farm wife's house, for the majority of her work—cooking, baking, canning, and cleaning—takes place there. Mr. Hale describes Mrs. Wright's seemingly odd behavior—laughing inappropriately, nervously pleating her apron, and unable to account for why she didn't wake up while her husband was being strangled in his bed. Before moving upstairs with the sheriff and Mr. Hale to examine the crime scene, Mr. Henderson asks if the kitchen might contain any evidence for a motive. The sheriff dismisses such a possibility, noting "the insignificance of kitchen things." The county attorney also ridicules Mrs. Wright's apparently inept domestic skills when he sees the dirty dish towels and burst jam jars. Resenting his criticism, both Mrs. Hale and Mrs. Peters defend Mrs. Wright, reminding the men that women's work on a farm is considerable and unending. Once again, the sheriff dismisses the women's concerns as mere "trifles."

Once the men leave the kitchen, Mrs. Hale and Mrs. Peters examine the room carefully; they know how to recognize the signs of disorder and upset in a kitchen. They begin gathering unexpected clues that point to Mrs. Wright's guilt, but that also provide justifiable motives for her crime: unfinished work in the kitchen (including an uncovered bucket of sugar and a half-empty bag beside it; a half-wiped, half-cleaned kitchen table), and a bad stove that would make cooking properly difficult. They also notice the shabbiness of Mrs. Wright's clothes when Mrs. Peters gets the items Minnie has asked for. With each clue, the two women start "seeing into things," gradually understanding what has happened in the Wright home. That understanding is solidified when they discover Mrs. Wright's quilting pieces and a broken bird cage. Some of the quilt pieces are sewn terribly, completely unlike the rest of the work. They discover a broken bird cage, but no bird. All of these discoveries lead Mrs. Hale to think about the utter loneliness of Minnie Wright's life with a husband that Mrs. Hale can only describe as "very hard" and emotionally distant and abusive. He has isolated his wife from friends and a larger community, refusing to have a telephone installed in his house.

The pivotal moment in the story occurs when Mrs. Peters discovers Mrs. Wright's bird in her sewing box, wrapped in silk and placed underneath several quilting squares. Mrs. Hale and Mrs. Peters look at each other, "in a look of dawning comprehension, of growing horror." Mr. Wright killed the bird, silencing the bit of joy that it brought to Mrs. Wright. Mrs. Peters confesses to knowing about stillness in a house, especially when there are no children. Mrs. Hale also confesses her guilt for neglecting Minnie and being complicit in her isolation. She wonders what would have happened if Mrs. Wright felt more connected to a larger community of women. These discoveries prompt both women to consider the true crime that has been committed. Although Mrs. Peters insists that "the law has got to punish crime," Mrs. Hale retorts that neglecting Mrs. Wright and not supporting her by seeing her regularly was the real crime. She continues that it's their situation as women in a rural county who "all go through the same things" that allows them to understand and know what Minnie Wright has done and why. In this way, Mrs. Hale and Mrs. Peters serve as Mrs. Wright's jury. Before the men return to the kitchen, they remove the most damning evidence that would ensure Mrs. Wright's conviction: the dead bird. Mrs. Peters rejects the notion that she is "married to the law" and sides with justice for Mrs. Wright.

———————— 🙙🙚 ————————

"A Jury of Her Peers"

by Susan Glaspell

When Martha Hale opened the storm door and got a cut of the north wind, she ran back for her big woolen scarf. As she hurriedly wound that round her head her eye made a scandalized sweep of her kitchen. It was no ordinary thing that called her away—it was probably farther from ordinary than anything that had ever happened in Dickson County. But what her eye took in was that her kitchen was in no shape for leaving: her bread all ready for mixing, half the flour sifted and half unsifted.

She hated to see things half-done; but she had been at that when the team from town stopped to get Mr. Hale, and then the sheriff came running in to say his wife wished Mrs. Hale would come too—adding, with a grin, that he guessed she was getting scary and wanted another woman along. So she had dropped everything right where it was.

"Martha!" now came her husband's impatient voice. "Don't keep folks waiting out here in the cold."

She again opened the storm door, and this time joined the three men and the one woman waiting for her in the big two-seated buggy.

After she had the robes tucked around her she took another look at the woman who sat beside her on the back seat. She had met Mrs. Peters the year before at the county fair, and the thing she remembered about her was that she didn't seem like a sheriff's wife. She was small and thin and didn't have a strong voice. Mrs. Gorman, the sheriff's wife before Gorman went out and Peters came in, had a voice that somehow seemed to be backing up the law with every word. But if Mrs. Peters didn't look like a sheriff's wife, Peters made it up in looking like a sheriff. He was to a dot the kind of man who could get himself elected sheriff—a heavy man with a big voice, who was particularly genial with the law-abiding, as if to make it plain that he knew the difference between criminals and noncriminals. And right there it came into Mrs. Hale's mind, with a stab, that this man who was so pleasant and lively with all of them was going to the Wrights' now as a sheriff.

"The country's not very pleasant this time of year," Mrs. Peters at last ventured, as if she felt they ought to be talking as well as the men.

Mrs. Hale scarcely finished her reply, for they had gone up a little hill and could see the Wright place now, and seeing it did not make her feel like talking. It looked very lonesome this cold March morning. It had always been a lonesome-looking place. It was down in a hollow, and the poplar trees around it were lonesome-looking trees. The men were looking at it and talking about what had happened. The county attorney was bending to one side of the buggy, and kept looking steadily at the place as they drew up to it.

Source: Susan Glaspell, "A Jury of Her Peers" 1917.

"I'm glad you came with me," Mrs. Peters said nervously, as the two women were about to follow the men in through the kitchen door.

Even after she had her foot on the doorstep, her hand on the knob, Martha Hale had a moment of feeling she could not cross that threshold. And the reason it seemed she couldn't cross it now was simply because she hadn't crossed it before. Time and time again it had been in her mind, "I ought to go over and see Minnie Foster"—she still thought of her as Minnie Foster, though for twenty years she had been Mrs. Wright. And then there was always something to do and Minnie Foster would go from her mind. But *now* she could come.

The men went over to the stove. The women stood close together by the door. Young Henderson, the county attorney, turned around and said:

"Come up to the fire, ladies."

Mrs. Peters took a step forward, then stopped. "I'm not—cold," she said.

The men talked for a minute about what a good thing it was the sheriff had sent his deputy out that morning to make a fire for them, and then Sheriff Peters stepped back from the stove, unbuttoned his outer coat, and leaned his hands on the kitchen table in a way that seemed to make the beginning of official business. "Now, Mr. Hale," he said in a sort of semiofficial voice, "before we move things about, you tell Mr. Henderson just what it was you saw when you came here yesterday morning."

The county attorney was looking around the kitchen.

"By the way," he said, "has anything been moved?" He turned to the sheriff. "Are things just as you left them yesterday?"

Peters looked from cupboard to sink; from that to a small worn rocker a little to one side of the kitchen table.

"It's just the same."

"Somebody should have been left here yesterday," said the county attorney.

"Oh—yesterday," returned the sheriff, with a little gesture as of yesterday having been more than he could bear to think of. "When I had to send Frank to Morris Center for that man who went crazy—let me tell you, I had my hands full *yesterday.* I knew you could get back from Omaha by today, George, and as long as I went over everything here myself. . . ."

"Well, Mr. Hale," said the county attorney, in a way of letting what was past and gone go, "tell just what happened when you came here yesterday morning."

Mrs. Hale, still leaning against the door, had that sinking feeling of the mother whose child is about to speak a piece. Lewis often wandered along and got things mixed up in a story. She hoped he would tell this straight and plain, and not say unnecessary things that would just make things harder for Minnie Foster. He didn't begin at once, and she noticed that he looked queer—as if standing in that kitchen and having to tell what he had seen there yesterday morning made him almost sick.

"Harry and I had started to town with a load of potatoes," Mrs. Hale's husband began.

Harry was Mrs. Hale's oldest boy. He wasn't with them now, for the very good reason that those potatoes never got to town yesterday and he was taking them this morning, so he hadn't been home when the sheriff stopped to say he wanted Mr. Hale to come over to the Wright place and tell the county attorney his story there, where he could point it all out.

"We came along this road," Hale was going on, with a motion of his hand to the road over which they had just come, "and as we got in sight of the house I says to Harry, 'I'm goin' to see if I can't get John Wright to take a telephone.' You see," he explained to Henderson, "unless I can get somebody to go in with me they won't come out this branch road except for a price *I* can't pay. I'd spoke to Wright about it once before; but he put me off, saying folks talked too much anyway, and all he asked was peace and quiet—guess you know about how much he talked himself. But I thought maybe if I went to the house and talked about it before his wife, and said all the womenfolks liked the telephones, and that in this lonesome stretch of road it would be a good thing—well, I said to Harry that that was what I was going to say—though I said at the same time that I didn't know as what his wife wanted made much difference to John . . ."

Now, there he was!—saying things he didn't need to say. Mrs. Hale tried to catch her husband's eye, but fortunately the county attorney interrupted with:

"Let's talk about that a little later, Mr. Hale, I do want to talk about that, but I'm anxious now to get along to just exactly what happened when you got here."

When he began this time, it was very deliberately and carefully:

"I didn't see or hear anything. I knocked at the door. And still it was all quiet inside. I knew they must be up—it was past eight o'clock. So I knocked again, louder, and I thought I heard somebody say, 'Come in.' I wasn't sure—I'm not sure yet. But I opened the door—this door," jerking a hand toward the door by which the two women stood, "and there, in that rocker"—pointing to it—"sat Mrs. Wright."

Everyone in the kitchen looked at the rocker. It came into Mrs. Hale's mind that the rocker didn't look in the least like Minnie Foster—the Minnie Foster of twenty years before. It was a dingy red, with wooden rungs up the back, and the middle rung was gone, and the chair sagged to one side.

"How did she—look?" the county attorney was inquiring.

"Well," said Hale, "she looked—queer."

"How do you mean—queer?"

As he asked it he took out a notebook and pencil. Mrs. Hale did not like the sight of that pencil. She kept her eye fixed on her husband, as if to keep him from saying unnecessary things that would go into that notebook and make trouble.

Hale did speak guardedly, as if the pencil had affected him too.

"Well, as if she didn't know what she was going to do next. And kind of—done up."

"How did she seem to feel about your coming?"

"Why, I didn't think she minded—one way or other. She didn't pay much attention. I said, 'Ho' do, Mrs. Wright? It's cold, ain't it?' And she said, 'Is it?'—and went on pleatin' at her apron.

"Well, I was surprised. She didn't ask me to come up to the stove, or to sit down, but just set there, not even lookin' at me. And so I said: 'I want to see John.' And then she laughed. I guess you would call it a laugh.

"I thought of Harry and the team outside, so I said, a little sharp, Can I see John?' 'No,' says she—kind of dull-like. 'Ain't he home?' says I. Then she looked at me. 'Yes,' says she, 'he's home.' 'Then why can't I see him?' I asked her, out of patience with her now. 'Cause he's dead,' says she, just as quiet and dull—and fell to pleatin' her apron. Dead?' says I, like you do when you can't take in what you've heard.

"She just nodded her head, not getting a bit excited, but rockin' back and forth.

"'Why—where is he?' says I, not knowing *what* to say.

"She just pointed upstairs—like this"—pointing to the room above.

"I got up, with the idea of going up there myself. By this time I—didn't know what to do. I walked from there to here; then I says: 'Why, what did he die of?'

"'He died of a rope round his neck,' says she; and just went on pleatin' at her apron."

Hale stopped speaking and stood staring at the rocker, as if he were still seeing the woman who had sat there the morning before. Nobody spoke; it was as if everyone were seeing the woman who had sat there the morning before.

"And what did you do then?" the county attorney at last broke the silence.

"I went out and called Harry. I thought I might—need help. I got Harry in, and we went upstairs." His voice fell almost to a whisper. 'There he was—lying over the . . .'

"I think I'd rather have you go into that upstairs," the attorney interrupted, "where you can point it all out. Just go on now with the rest of the story."

"Well, my first thought was to get that rope off. It looked . . .'

He stopped, his face twitching.

"But Harry, he went up to him, and he said, 'No, he's dead all right, and we'd better not touch anything.' So we went downstairs. She was still sitting that same way. 'Has anybody been notified?' I asked. 'No,' said she, unconcerned.

"'Who did this, Mrs. Wright?' said Harry. He said it business-like, and she stopped pleatin' at her apron. 'I don't know,' she says. 'You don't *know*?' says Harry. 'Weren't you sleepin' in the bed with him?' 'Yes,' says she, 'but I was on the inside.' 'Somebody slipped a rope round his neck and strangled him, and you didn't wake up?' says Harry. 'I didn't wake up,' she said after him.

"We may have looked as if we didn't see how that could be, for after a minute she said, 'I sleep sound.'

"Harry was going to ask her more questions, but I said maybe that weren't our business; maybe we ought to let her tell her story first to the coroner or the sheriff. So Harry went fast as he could over to High Road—the Rivers' place, where there's a telephone."

"And what did she do when she knew you had gone for the coroner?" The attorney got his pencil in his hand all ready for writing.

"She moved from that chair to this one over here"—Hale pointed to a small chair in the corner—"and just sat there with her hands held together and looking down. I got a feeling that I ought to make some conversation, so I said I had come in to see if John wanted to put in a telephone; and at that she started to laugh, and then she stopped and looked at me—scared."

At the sound of a moving pencil the man who was telling the story looked up.

"I dunno—maybe it wasn't scared," he hastened; "I wouldn't like to say it was. Soon Harry got back, and then Dr. Lloyd came, and you, Mr. Peters, and so I guess that's all I know that you don't."

He said that last with relief, and moved a little, as if relaxing. Everyone moved a little. The county attorney walked toward the stair door.

"I guess we'll go upstairs first—then out to the barn and around."

He paused and looked around the kitchen.

"You're convinced there was nothing important here?" he asked the sheriff. "Nothing that would—point to any motive?"

The sheriff too looked all around, as if to reconvince himself.

"Nothing here but kitchen things," he said, with a little laugh for the insignificance of kitchen things.

The county attorney was looking at the cupboard—a peculiar, ungainly structure, half closet and half cupboard, the upper part of it being built in the wall, and the lower part just the old-fashioned kitchen cupboard. As if its queerness attracted him, he got a chair and opened the upper part and looked in. After a moment he drew his hand away sticky.

"Here's a nice mess," he said resentfully.

The two women had drawn nearer, and now the sheriffs wife spoke.

"Oh—her fruit," she said, looking to Mrs. Hale for sympathetic understanding. She turned back to the county attorney and explained: "She worried about that when it turned so cold last night. She said the fire would go out and her jars burst."

Mrs. Peters' husband broke into a laugh.

"Well, can you beat the women! Held for murder, and worrying about her preserves!"

The young attorney set his lips.

"I guess before we're through she may have something more serious than preserves to worry about."

"Oh, well," said Mrs. Hale's husband, with good-natured superiority, "women are used to worrying over trifles."

The two women moved a little closer together. Neither of them spoke. The county attorney seemed suddenly to remember his manners—and think of his future.

"And yet," said he, with the gallantry of a young politician, "for all their worries, what would we do without the ladies?"

The women did not speak; did not unbend. He went to the sink and began washing his hands. He turned to wipe them on the roller towel—whirled it for a cleaner place.

"Dirty towels! Not much of a housekeeper, would you say, ladies?"

He kicked his foot against some dirty pans under the sink.

"There's a great deal of work to be done on a farm," said Mrs. Hale stiffly.

"To be sure. And yet"—with a little bow to her—"I know there are some Dickson County farmhouses that do not have such roller towels."

"Those towels get dirty awful quick. Men's hands aren't always as clean as they might be."

"Ah, loyal to your sex, I see," he laughed. He stopped and gave her a keen look. "But you and Mrs. Wright were neighbors. I suppose you were friends, too."

Martha Hale shook her head.

"I've seen little enough of her of late years. I've not been in this house—it's more than a year."

"And why was that? You didn't like her?"

"I liked her well enough," she replied with spirit. "Farmers' wives have their hands full, Mr. Henderson. And then . . ." she looked around the kitchen.

"Yes?" he encouraged.

"It never seemed a very cheerful place," said she, more to herself than to him.

"No," he agreed; "I don't think anyone would call it cheerful. I shouldn't say she had the homemaking instinct."

"Well, I don't know as Wright had, either," she muttered.

"You mean they didn't get on very well?" he was quick to ask.

"No; I don't mean anything," she answered, with decision. As she turned a little away from him, she added: "But I don't think a place would be any the cheerfuller for John Wright's bein' in it."

"I'd like to talk to you about that a little later, Mrs. Hale," he said. "I'm anxious to get the lay of things upstairs now."

He moved toward the stair door, followed by the two men.

"I suppose anything Mrs. Peters does'll be all right?" the sheriff inquired. "She was to take in some clothes for her, you know—and a few little things. We left in such a hurry yesterday."

The county attorney looked at the two women whom they were leaving alone there among the kitchen things.

"Yes—Mrs. Peters," he said, his glance resting on the woman who was not Mrs. Peters, the big farmer woman who stood behind the sheriffs wife. "Of course Mrs. Peters is one of us," he said, in a manner of entrusting responsibility. "And keep your eye out, Mrs. Peters, for anything that might be of use. No telling; you women might come upon a clue to the motive—and that's the thing we need."

Mr. Hale rubbed his face after the fashion of a showman getting ready for a pleasantry.

"But would the women know a clue if they did come upon it?" he said; and having delivered himself of this, he followed the others through the stair door.

The women stood motionless and silent, listening to the footsteps, first upon the stairs, then in the room above.

Then, as if releasing herself from something strange, Mrs. Hale began to arrange the dirty pans under the sink, which the county attorney's disdainful push of the foot had deranged.

"I'd hate to have men comin' into my kitchen," she said testily—snoopin' round and criticizin'."

"Of course it's no more than their duty," said the sheriffs wife, in her manner of timid acquiescence.

"Duty's all right," replied Mrs. Hale bluffly; "but I guess that deputy sheriff that come out to make the fire might have got a little of this on." She gave the roller towel a pull. "Wish I'd thought of that sooner! Seems mean to talk about her for not having things slicked up, when she had to come away in such a hurry."

She looked around the kitchen. Certainly it was not "slicked up." Her eye was held by a bucket of sugar on a low shelf. The cover was off the wooden bucket, and beside it was a paper bag—half full.

Mrs. Hale moved toward it.

"She was putting this in there," she said to herself—slowly.

She thought of the flour in her kitchen at home—half sifted. She had been interrupted, and had left things half done. What had interrupted Minnie Foster? Why had that work been left half done? She made a move as if to finish it—unfinished things always bothered her—and then she glanced around and saw that Mrs. Peters was watching her—and she didn't want Mrs. Peters to get that feeling she had got of work begun and then—for some reason—not finished.

"It's a shame about her fruit," she said, and walked toward the cupboard that the county attorney had opened, and got on the chair, murmuring: "I wonder if it's all gone."

It was a sorry enough looking sight, but "Here's one that's all right," she said at last. She held it toward the light. "This is cherries, too." She looked again. "I declare I believe that's the only one."

With a sigh, she got down from the chair, went to the sink, and wiped off the bottle.

"She'll feel awful bad, after all her hard work in the hot weather. I remember the afternoon I put up my cherries last summer."

She set the bottle on the table, and, with another sigh, started to sit down in the rocker. But she did not sit down. Something kept her from sitting down in that chair. She straightened— stepped back, and, half turned away, stood looking at it, seeing the woman who had sat there "pleatin' at her apron."

The thin voice of the sheriff's wife broke in upon her: "I must be getting those things from the front room closet." She opened the door into the other room, started in, stepped back. "You coming with me, Mrs. Hale?" she asked nervously. "You—you could help me get them."

They were soon back—the stark coldness of that shut-up room was not a thing to linger in.

"My!" said Mrs. Peters, dropping the things on the table and hurrying to the stove.

Mrs. Hale stood examining the clothes the woman who was being detained in town had said she wanted.

"Wright was close!" she exclaimed, holding up a shabby black skirt that bore the marks of much making over. "I think maybe that's why she kept so much to herself. I s'pose she felt she couldn't do her part; and then, you don't enjoy things when you feel shabby. She used to wear pretty clothes and be lively—when she was Minnie Foster, one of the town girls, singing in the choir. But that—oh, that was twenty years ago."

With a carefulness in which there was something tender, she folded the shabby clothes and piled them at one corner of the table. She looked up at Mrs. Peters, and there was something in the other woman's look that irritated her.

"She don't care," she said to herself. "Much difference it makes to her whether Minnie Foster had pretty clothes when she was a girl."

Then she looked again, and she wasn't so sure; in fact, she hadn't at any time been perfectly sure about Mrs. Peters. She had that shrinking manner, and yet her eyes looked as if they could see a long way into things.

"This all you was to take in?" asked Mrs. Hale.

"No," said the sheriffs wife; "she said she wanted an apron. Funny thing to want," she ventured in her nervous little way, "For there's not much to get you dirty in jail, goodness knows. But I suppose just to make her feel more natural. If you're used to wearing an apron—She said they were in the bottom drawer of this cupboard. Yes—here they are. And then her little shawl that always hung on the stair door."

She took the small gray shawl from behind the door leading upatairs.

Suddenly Mrs. Hale took a quick step toward the other woman.

"Mrs. Peters!"

"Yes, Mrs. Hale?"

"Do you think she—did it?"

A frightened look blurred the other thing in Mrs. Peters' eyes.

"Oh, I don't know," she said, in a voice that seemed to shrink away from the subject.

"Well, I don't think she did," affirmed Mrs. Hale stoutly. "Asking for an apron and her little shawl. Worryin' about her fruit."

"Mr. Peters says . . ." Footsteps were heard in the room above; she stopped, looked up, then went on in a lowered voice: "Mr. Peters says—it looks bad for her. Mr. Henderson is awful sarcastic in a speech, and he's going to make fun of her saying she didn't—wake up."

For a moment Mrs. Hale had no answer. Then, "Well, I guess John Wright didn't wake up—when they was slippin that rope under his neck," she muttered.

"No, its *strange*," breathed Mrs. Peters. "They think it was such —funny way to kill a man."

"That's just what Mr. Hale said," said Mrs. Hale, in a resolutely natural voice. "There was a gun in the house. He says that's what he can't understand."

Mr. Henderson said, coming out, that what was needed for the case was a motive. Something to show anger—or sudden feeling."

"Well, I don't see any signs of anger around here," said Mrs. Hale. "I don't . . ."

She stopped. It was as if her mind tripped on something. Her eye was caught by a dish towel in the middle of the kitchen table. Slowly she moved toward the table. One half of it was wiped clean, the other half messy. Her eyes made a slow, almost unwilling turn to the bucket of sugar and the half-empty bag beside it. Things begun—and not finished.

After a moment she stepped back, and said, in that manner of releasing herself: "Wonder how they're finding things upstairs? I hope she had it a little more red up there. You know"—she paused, and feeling gathered—"it seems kind of *sneaking*: locking her up in town and coming out here to get her own house to turn against her?"

"But, Mrs. Hale," said the sheriff's wife, "the law is the law."

"I s'pose 'tis," answered Mrs. Hale shortly.

She turned to the stove, worked with it a minute, and when she straightened up she said aggressively:

"The law is the law—and a bad stove is a bad stove. How'd you like to cook on this?"—pointing with the poker to the broken lining. She opened the oven door and started to express her opinion of the oven; but she was swept into her own thoughts, thinking of what it would mean, year after year, to have that stove to wrestle with. The thought of Minnie Foster trying to bake in that oven—and the thought of her never going over to see Minnie Foster. . ."

She was startled by hearing Mrs. Peters say:

"A person gets discouraged—and loses heart."

The sheriff's wife had looked from the stove to the pail of water which had been carried in from outside. The two women stood there, silent, above them the footsteps of the men who were looking for evidence against the woman who had worked in that kitchen. That look of seeing into things, of seeing through a thing to something else, was in the eyes of the sheriff's wife now. When Mrs. Hale next spoke to her, it was gently:

"Better loosen up your things, Mrs. Peters. We'll not feel them when we go out."

Mrs. Peters went to the back of the room to hang up the fur tippet she was wearing. A moment later she exclaimed, "Why, she was piecing a quilt," and held up a large sewing basket piled high with quilt pieces.

Mrs. Hale spread some of the blocks out on the table.

"Its' log-cabin pattern," she said, putting several of them together. "Pretty, isn't it?"

They were so engaged with the quilt that they did not hear the footsteps on the stairs. Just as the stair door opened Mrs. Hale was saying:

"Do you suppose she was going to quilt it or just knot it?"

The sheriff threw up his hands.

"They wonder whether she was going to quilt it or just knot it!" he cried.

There was a laugh for the ways of women, a warming of hands over the stove, and then the county attorney said briskly:

"Well, let's go right out to the barn and get that cleared up."

"I don't see as there's anything so strange," Mrs. Hale said resentfully, after the outside door had closed on the three men—"our taking up our time with little things while we're waiting for them to get the evidence. I don't see as it's anything to laugh about."

"Of course they've got awful important things on their minds," said the sheriff's wife apologetically.

They returned to an inspection of the block for the quilt. Mrs. Hale was looking at the fine, even sewing, and was preoccupied with thoughts of the woman who had done that sewing, when she heard the sheriff's wife say, in a queer tone:

"Why, look at this one."

She turned to take the block held out to her.

"The sewing," said Mrs. Peters, in a troubled way. "All the rest of them have been so nice and even—but—this one. Why, it looks as if she didn't know what she was about!"

Their eyes met—something flashed to life, passed between them; then, as if with an effort, they seemed to pull away from each other. A moment Mrs. Hale sat there, her hands folded over that sewing which was so unlike all the rest of the sewing. Then she had pulled a knot and drawn the threads.

"Oh, what are you doing, Mrs. Hale?" asked the sheriff's wife.

"Just pulling out a stitch or two that's not sewed very good," said Mrs. Hale mildly.

"I don't think we ought to touch things," Mrs. Peters said, a little helplessly.

"I'll just finish up this end," answered Mrs. Hale, still in that mild, matter-of-fact fashion.

She threaded a needle and started to replace bad sewing with good. For a little while she sewed in silence. Then, in that thin, timid voice, she heard:

"Mrs. Hale!"

"Yes, Mrs. Peters?"

"What do you suppose she was so—nervous about?"

"Oh, *I* don't know," said Mrs. Hale, as if dismissing a thing not important enough to spend much time on. "I don't know as she was—nervous. I sew awful queer sometimes when I'm just tired."

She cut a thread, and out of the corner of her eye looked up at Mrs. Peters. The small, lean face of the sheriff's wife seemed to have tightened up. Her eyes had that look of peering into something. But next moment she moved, and said in her indecisive way:

"Well, I must get those clothes wrapped. They may be through sooner than we think. I wonder where I could find a piece of paper—and string."

"In that cupboard, maybe," suggested Mrs. Hale, after a glance around.

One piece of the crazy sewing remained unripped. Mrs. Peters' back turned, Martha Hale now scrutinized that piece, compared it with the dainty, accurate sewing of the other blocks. The difference was startling. Holding this block made her feel queer, as if the distracted thoughts of the woman who had perhaps turned to it to try to quiet herself were communicating themselves to her.

Mrs. Peters' voice roused her.

"Here's a birdcage," she said. "Did she have a bird, Mrs. Hale?"

"Why, I don't know whether she did or not." She turned to look at the cage Mrs. Peters was holding up. "I've not been here in so long." She sighed. "There was a man last year selling canaries cheap—but I don't know as she took one. Maybe she did. She used to sing real pretty herself."

"Seems kind of funny to think of a bird here." She half laughed—an attempt to put up a barrier. "But she must have had one—or why would she have a cage? I wonder what happened to it."

"I suppose maybe the cat got it," suggested Mrs. Hale, resuming her sewing.

"No; she didn't have a cat. She's got that feeling some people have about cats—being afraid of them. When they brought her to our house yesterday, my cat got in the room, and she was real upset and asked me to take it out."

"My sister Bessie was like that." Mrs. Hale laughed.

The sheriff's wife did not reply. The silence made Mrs. Hale turn around. Mrs. Peters was examining the birdcage.

"Look at this door," she said slowly. "It's broke. One hinge has been pulled apart."

Mrs. Hale came nearer.

"Looks as if someone must have been—rough with it."

Again their eyes met—startled, questioning, apprehensive. For a moment neither spoke nor stirred. Then Mrs. Hale, turning away, said brusquely:

"If they're going to find any evidence, I wish they'd be about it. I don't like this place."

"But I'm awful glad you came with me," Mrs. Hale." Mrs. Peters put the birdcage on the table and sat down. "It would be lonesome for me—sitting here alone."

"Yes, it would, wouldn't it?" agreed Mrs. Hale, a certain very determined naturalness in her voice. She had picked up the sewing, but now it dropped in her lap, and she murmured in a different voice: "But I tell you what I *do* wish, Mrs. Peters. I wish I had come over sometimes when she was here. I wish—I had."

"But of course you were awful busy, Mrs. Hale. Your house—and your children."

"I could've come," retorted Mrs. Hale shortly. "I stayed away because it weren't cheerful—and that's why I ought to have come. I"—she looked around—"I've never liked this place. Maybe because it's down in a hollow and you don't see the road. I don't know what it is, but it's a lonesome place, and always was. I wish I had come over to see Minnie Foster sometimes. I can see now—" She did not put it into words.

"Well, you mustn't reproach yourself," counseled Mrs. Peters. "Somehow, we just don't see how it is with other folks till—something comes up."

"Not having children makes less work," mused Mrs. Hale, after a silence, "but it makes a quiet house—and Wright out to work all day—and no company when he did come in. Did you know John Wright, Mrs. Peters?"

"Not to know him. I've seen him in town. They say he was a good man."

"Yes—good," conceded John Wright's neighbor grimly. "He didn't drink, and kept his word as well as most, I guess, and paid his debts. But he was a hard man, Mrs. Peters. Just to pass the time of day with him—" She stopped, shivered a little. "Like a raw wind that gets to the bone." Her eye fell upon the cage on the table before her, and she added, almost bitterly, "I should think she would've wanted a bird!"

Suddenly she leaned forward, looking intently at the cage. "But what do you s'pose went wrong with it?"

"I don't know," returned Mrs. Peters; "unless it got sick and died."

But after she said it she reached over and swung the broken door. Both women watched it as if somehow held by it.

"You didn't know—her?" Mrs. Hale asked, a gentler note in her voice.

"Not till they brought her yesterday," said the sheriff's wife.

"She—come to think of it, she was kind of like a bird herself. Real sweet and pretty, but kind of timid and—fluttery. How—she—did—change."

That held her for a long time. Finally, as if struck with a happy thought and relieved to get back to everyday things, she exclaimed:

"Tell you what, Mrs. Peters, why don't you take the quilt in with you? It might take up her mind."

"Why, I think that's a real nice idea, Mrs. Hale," agreed the sheriff's wife, as if she too were glad to come into the atmosphere of a simple kindness. "There couldn't possibly be any objection to that, could there? Now, just what will I take? I wonder if her patches are in here—and her things."

They turned to the sewing basket.

"Here's some red," said Mrs. Hale, bringing out a roll of cloth. Underneath that was a box. "Here, maybe her scissors are in here—and her things." She held it up. "What a pretty box! I'll warrant that was something she had a long time ago—when she was a girl."

She held it in her hand a moment; then, with a little sigh, opened it.

Instantly her hand went to her nose.

"Why . . .!"

Mrs. Peters drew nearer—then turned away.

"There's something wrapped up in this piece of silk," faltered Mrs. Hale.

Her hand not steady, Mrs. Hale raised the piece of silk. "Oh, Mrs. Peters!" she cried, "It's . . ."

Mrs. Peters bent closer.

"It's the bird," she whispered.

"But, Mrs. Peters!" cried Mrs. Hale. "*Look* at it! Its *neck*—look at its neck! It's all—other side *to*."

The sheriff's wife again bent closer.

"Somebody wrung its neck," said she, in a voice that was slow and deep.

And then again the eyes of the two women met—this time clung together in a look of dawning comprehension, of growing horror. Mrs. Peters looked from the dead bird to the broken door of the cage. Again their eyes met. And just then there was a sound at the outside door.

Mrs. Hale slipped the box under the quilt pieces in the basket and sank into the chair before it. Mrs. Peters stood holding to the table. The county attorney and the sheriff came in.

"Well, ladies," said the county attorney, as one turning from serious things to little pleasantries, "have you decided whether she was going to quilt it or knot it?"

"We think," began the sheriff's wife in a flurried voice, "that she was going to—knot it."

He was too preoccupied to notice the change that came in her voice on that last.

"Well, that's very interesting, I'm sure," he said tolerantly. He caught sight of the cage. "Has the bird flown?"

"We think that the cat got it," said Mrs. Hale in a voice curiously even.

He was walking up and down, as if thinking something out.

"Is there a cat?" he asked absently.

Mrs. Hale shot a look up at the sheriff's wife.

"Well, not *now*," said Mrs. Peters. "They're superstitious, you know; they leave."

The county attorney did not heed her. "No sign at all of anyone having come in from the outside," he said to Peters, in the manner of continuing an interrupted conversation. "Their own rope. Now let's go upstairs again and go over it, piece by piece. It would have to have been someone who knew just the . . ."

The stair door closed behind them and their voices were lost.

The two women sat motionless, not looking at each other, but as if peering into something and at the same time holding back. When they spoke now it was as if they were afraid of what they were saying, but as if they could not help saying it.

"She liked the bird," said Martha Hale, low and slowly. "She was going to bury it in the pretty box."

"When I was a girl," said Mrs. Peters, under her breath, "my kitten —there was a boy took a hatchet, and before my eyes—before I could get there—" She covered her face an instant. "If they hadn't held me back I would have"—she caught herself, looked upstairs where footsteps were heard, and finished weakly—"hurt him."

Then they sat without speaking or moving.

"I wonder how it would seem," Mrs. Hale at last began, as if feeling her way over strange ground—"never to have had any children around."

Her eyes made a slow sweep of the kitchen, as if seeing what that kitchen had meant through all the years. "No, Wright wouldn't like the bird," she said after that—"a thing that sang. She used to sing. He killed that too." Her voice tightened.

Mrs. Peters moved easily.

"Of course we don't know who killed the bird."

"I knew John Wright," was Mrs. Hale's answer.

"It was an awful thing was done in this house that night, Mrs. Hale," said the sheriff's wife. "Killing a man while he slept—slipping a thing round his neck that choked the life out of him."

Mrs. Hale's hand went out to the birdcage.

"His neck, choked the life out of him."

"We don't *know* who killed him," whispered Mrs. Peters wildly. "We don't *know*."

Mrs. Hale had not moved. "If there had been years and years of—nothing, then a bird to sing to you, it would be awful—still—after the bird was still."

It was as if something within her, not herself, had spoken, and it found in Mrs. Peters something she did not know as herself.

"I know what stillness is," she said, in a queer, monotonous voice. "When we homesteaded in Dakota, and my first baby died—after he was two years old—and me with no other then . . ."

Mrs. Hale stirred.

"How soon do you suppose they'll be through looking for the evidence?"

"I know what stillness is," repeated Mrs. Peters, in just that same way. Then she too pulled back. "The law has got to punish crime, Mrs. Hale," she said in her tight little way.

"I wish you'd seen Minnie Foster," was the answer, "when she wore a white dress with blue ribbon, and stood up there in the choir and sang."

The picture of that girl, the fact that she had lived neighbor to that girl for twenty years, and had let her die for lack of life, was suddenly more than she could bear.

"Oh, I *wish* I'd come over here once in a while!" she cried. "That was a crime! That was a crime! Who's going to punish that?"

"We mustn't take on," said Mrs. Peters, with a frightened look toward the stairs.

"I might 'a' *known* she needed help! I tell you, its *queer*, Mrs. Peters. We live close together, and we live far apart. We all go through the same things—it's all just a different kind of the same thing! If it weren't—why do you and I *understand*? Why do we *know*—what we know this minute?"

She dashed her hand across her eyes. Then, seeing the jar of fruit on the table, she reached for it and choked out:

"If I was you I wouldn't *tell* her her fruit was gone! Tell her it *ain't*. Tell her it's all right—all of it. Here—take this in to prove it to her! She—she may never know whether it was broke or not."

Mrs. Peters reached out for the bottle of fruit as if she were glad to take it—as if touching a familiar thing, having something to do, could keep her from something else. She got up, looked about for something to wrap the fruit in, took a petticoat from the pile of clothes she had brought from the front room, and nervously started winding that round the bottle.

"My!" she began, in a high, false voice, "it's a good thing the men couldn't hear us! Getting all stirred up over a little thing like a—dead canary." She hurried over that. "As if that could have anything to do with—with—My, wouldn't they *laugh*?"

Footsteps were heard on the stairs.

"Maybe they would," muttered Mrs. Hale—"maybe they wouldn't."

"No, Peters," said the county attorney incisively; "it's all perfectly clear, except the reason for doing it. But you know juries when it comes to women. If there was some definite thing— something to show. Something to make a story about. A thing that would connect up with this clumsy way of doing it."

In a covert way Mrs. Hale looked at Mrs. Peters. Mrs. Peters was looking at her. Quickly they looked away from each other. The outer door opened and Mr. Hale came in.

"I've got the team round now," he said. "Pretty cold out there."

"I'm going to stay here a while by myself," the county attorney suddenly announced. "You can send Frank out for me, can't you?" he asked the sheriff. "I want to go over everything. I'm not satisfied we can't do better."

Again, for one brief moment, the two women's eyes found one another.

The sheriff came up to the table.

"Did you want to see what Mrs. Peters was going to take in?"

The county attorney picked up the apron. He laughed. "Oh, I guess they're not very dangerous things the ladies have picked out."

Mrs. Hale's hand was on the sewing basket in which the box was concealed. She felt that she ought to take her hand off the basket. She did not seem able to. He picked up one of the quilt blocks which she had piled on to cover the box. Her eyes felt like fire. She had a feeling that if he took up the basket she would snatch it from him.

But he did not take it up. With another little laugh, he turned away.

"No; Mrs. Peters doesn't need supervising. For that matter, a sheriff's wife is married to the law. Ever think of it that way, Mrs. Peters?"

Mrs. Peters was standing beside the table. Mrs. Hale shot a look up at her; but she could not see her face. Mrs. Peters had turned away. When she spoke, her voice was muffled.

"Not—just that way," she said.

"Married to the law!" chuckled Mrs. Peters' husband. He moved toward the door into the front room and said to the county attorney:

"I just want you to come in here a minute, George. We ought to take a look at these windows."

"Oh—windows," said the county attorney scoffingly.

"We'll be right out, Mr. Hale," said the sheriff to the farmer.

Hale went to look after the horses. The sheriff followed the county attorney into the other room. Again—for one final moment—the two women were alone in that kitchen.

Martha Hale sprang up, her hands tight together, looking at that other woman, with whom it rested. At first she could not see her eyes, for the sheriff's wife had not turned back since she turned away at that suggestion of being married to the law. But now Mrs. Hale made her turn back. Her eyes made her turn back. Slowly, unwillingly, Mrs. Peters turned her head until her eyes met the eyes of the other woman. There was a moment when they held each other in a steady, burning look in which there was no evasion nor flinching.

Then Martha Hale's eyes pointed the way to the basket in which was hidden the thing that would make certain the conviction of the other woman—that woman who was not there and yet who had been there with them all through that hour.

For a moment Mrs. Peters did not move. And then she did it. With a rush forward, she threw back the quilt pieces, got the box, tried to put it in her handbag. It was too big. Desperately she opened it, started to take the bird out. But there she broke—she could not touch the bird. She stood there helpless, foolish.

There was the sound of a knob turning in the inner door. Martha Hale snatched the box from the sheriff's wife, and got it in the pocket of her big coat just as the sheriff and the county attorney came back.

"Well, Henry," said the county attorney facetiously, "at least we found out that she was not going to quilt it. She was going to—what is it you call it, ladies?"

Mrs. Hale's hand was against the pocket of her coat.

"We call it—knot it, Mr. Henderson."

Critical Thinking

Why does Glaspell title the story "A Jury of Her Peers"?

What is the significance of the repeated phrase, "quilt it or knot it?

How likely is it that Mrs. Wright will have a jury of her peers during her actual trial? What does it even mean when we refer to someone's peers?

Why are the men in the story, especially the sheriff and the district attorney, unable to see the clues that the women discover?

How does the justice system now treat domestic abuse, both emotional and physical?

How does such abuse and women's response to it, including killing their abusive spouses, affect how they are charged and prosecuted?

Do you believe Mrs. Wright will be convicted? Why or why not?

Should she be convicted for murder or a lesser charge? Or should she be exonerated?

What social services are now available to domestic abuse victims?

"Closure"

by Stephen D. Rogers

When considering the concepts of victimization and victimology, people generally think of the interactions of an offender and their victim. That victimization extends beyond simply the pain of a battery or the loss of one's property. Being the victim of a crime also has a psychological and emotional cost that can far exceed the tangible financial expenses that may include medical costs, property loss, and work missed.

Those emotional costs may be exacerbated by the very justice system meant to address the victimization. Having to miss work as one constantly returns to court for a variety of judicial proceedings to then dealing with a hostile examination by a defense attorney trying to discredit one's testimony or character during the actual trial contribute to the emotional expense of a crime.

What may be one of the more egregious examples of being traumatized by a representative of the criminal justice system was the arrest of a homeless rape victim, devastated by having to appear on the witness stand against the accused serial rapist. When the witness was later found wandering in traffic in front of the courthouse, she was admitted to a psychiatric ward of a hospital, only to be detained by the prosecutor, under court order, to guarantee her later appearance at the trial, which had been postponed over the Christmas holiday. But instead of being detained in a mental health facility or a local hotel, she was secured in the county jail for the next month.

Jail paperwork accidently identified her as a criminal suspect instead of as a victim and reluctant witness being detained to guarantee her court appearance. While in the jail she was reportedly attacked by another inmate. She eventually had another breakdown leading to a confrontation with a jailer, who later filed charges for assault, a felony. Only after she testified in the original trial were charges dropped and she was released from custody.

The prosecutor assumed he had found a balance between addressing the victim's needs while fulfilling his responsibility to prosecute a serial rapist, but the difficulty was that he wasn't seeing the world from a mentally ill individual's perspective, one suffering from both bipolar order and symptoms of schizophrenia. His was the perspective of a prosecutor and even of a cop—that jail isn't such a big deal as they put people in it all the time, as shown by the thousands who were already in that very jail. He lost sight of the fact that jail exists as a tool to punish, even if not convicted.

For the investigator that detained her, it was just another court order addressed to keep the prosecutor happy; for the prosecutor handling it, it was just a tool to get the testimony he needed for a conviction. For the judge, the one ultimately responsible to protect the innocent from the excesses of the government, it was simply another file on her bench to be addressed, another piece of paperwork needing her signature. Few in the justice system acted as if they recognized the psychological damage done by deciding that jail was appropriate for anyone in such a situation, let alone a mentally ill victim of a sexual assault.

The justice system can be demeaning, degrading, and dehumanizing and it can corrupt the perspective of all the players within it. For a crime victim, the justice system itself may simply re-victimize them, placing the supposed greater good ahead of the needs of the victim it serves and, in some cases, possibly taking a greater psychological toll than the original crime itself.

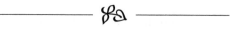

"Closure"

by Stephen D. Rogers

The police informed me they caught the suspects
Recovered all my belongings
Suggested I change my locks
As if
There was some kind of closure there
My residence no longer violated
My space once again my own

Critical Thinking

How does the justice system currently attempt to address the needs of victims?

Is there an alternative to prosecuting a suspect while also addressing the needs of a victim?

How does the criminal justice system make one insensitive, and can anything be done to address it?

Chapter 14

Future of Criminal Justice

Case Study

"Harrison Bergeron"

by Kurt Vonnegut, Jr.

Kurt Vonnegut (1922–2007) was a prolific American writer of novels, short stories, and nonfiction. A native of Indianapolis, Indiana, he grew up during the Depression in poverty and difficult family circumstances. *Slaughterhouse Five* (1969), his sixth novel, was immediately successful (largely due to its anti-war point of view) and garnered his subsequent fame after years of struggling as a writer. Social critique—including unequal distribution of wealth and social Darwinism—is a hallmark of his writing. Existential questions about the purpose of life also figure into Vonnegut's work. An avowed atheist, Vonnegut considered himself a free thinker and was a member of the American Humanist Association. He eschewed affiliation with American political parties, favoring socialism instead.

Published in 1961 in *The Magazine of Fantasy and Science Fiction*, "Harrison Bergeron" is a dystopian story set in 2081 America and a savage attack against the dangers of authoritarian, government-sponsored thought policing that recalls George Orwell's *1984* (1949). At the story's start, the narrator tells us that all Americans are now completely equal: no one is smarter, prettier, more handsome, or more talented than anyone else. This equality has been achieved following the passage of the 211th, 212th, and 213th Amendments to the U.S. Constitution, and enforced by the United States Handicapper General. Most people are of average intelligence, but those who are above average must wear a radio at all times to which the government sends noise of various frequencies to quell any critical thinking. Moreover, citizens that display any kind of beauty, strength, or talent wear extra weights, masks, and other encumbrances to remain equal. The government's efforts mean that no one has an attention span of more than a few minutes or any long-term memory. Thus, George and Hazel Bergeron are unable to comprehend the horror of their fourteen-year-old son Harrison being removed from their home by the Handicapper General for being too smart and too strong. George, who must wear a radio transmitter, is regularly assaulted by noise to prevent him from thinking about his son's fate, while Hazel is just average enough to think about it at all. As they watch a television program featuring ballerinas (most of whom wear ugly masks to cover their beauty and weights to prevent them from dancing at more than an average level), George and Hazel watch an announcement interrupting the program: Harrison has escaped from jail and is considered extremely dangerous because of his intellectual and athletic abilities. A police photograph shows Harrison wearing huge earphones rather than the usual radio transmitter, glasses designed to prevent him from seeing properly, and scrap metal all over his body to keep him from moving too quickly. Shortly thereafter, the news announcement is interrupted by Harrison, who stands defiant in the broadcast studio as he removes all of his handicaps and declares his intention to become Emperor and select an Empress to rule with him. When a ballerina joins him, Harrison removes her mask, ear radio, and physical handicaps, and then orders the musicians to play above average. Harrison and the ballerina begin dancing, displaying amazing feats and joy. Just as they kiss each other, Diana Moon Glampers, the Handicapper General, kills them both with a double-barreled ten-gauge shotgun. Hazel and George see their son murdered but are unable to process what has happened. Hazel only recalls that she saw something sad on television, while George receives a debilitating zap in his head.

"Harrison Bergeron"

by Kurt Vonnegut, Jr.

The year was 2081, and everybody was finally equal. They weren't only equal before God and the law. They were equal every which way. Nobody was smarter than anybody else. Nobody was better looking than anybody else. Nobody was stronger or quicker than anybody else. All this equality was due to the 211th, 212th, and 213th Amendments to the Constitution, and to the unceasing vigilance of agents of the United States Handicapper General.

Some things about living still weren't quite right, though. April, for instance, still drove people crazy by not being springtime. And it was in that clammy month that the H-G men took George and Hazel Bergeron's fourteen-year-old son, Harrison, away.

It was tragic, all right, but George and Hazel couldn't think about it very hard. Hazel had a perfectly average intelligence, which meant she couldn't think about anything except in short bursts. And George, while his intelligence was way above normal, had a little mental handicap radio in his ear. He was required by law to wear it at all times. It was tuned to a government transmitter. Every twenty seconds or so, the transmitter would send out some sharp noise to keep people like George from taking unfair advantage of their brains.

George and Hazel were watching television. There were tears on Hazel's cheeks, but she'd forgotten for the moment what they were about.

On the television screen were ballerinas.

A buzzer sounded in George's head. His thoughts fled in panic, like bandits from a burglar alarm.

"That was a real pretty dance, that dance they just did," said Hazel.

"Hugh?" said George.

"That dance—it was nice," said Hazel.

"Yup," said George. He tried to think a little about the ballerinas. They weren't really very good—no better than anybody else would have been anyway. They were burdened with sashweights and bags of birdshot, and their faces were masked, so that no one, seeing a free and graceful gesture or a pretty face, would feel like something the cat drug in. George was toying with the vague notion that maybe dancers shouldn't be handicapped. But he didn't get very far with it before another noise in his ear radio scattered his thoughts.

George winced. So did two of the eight ballerinas.

Hazel saw him wince. Having no mental handicap herself, she had to ask George what the latest sound had been.

"Sounded like somebody hitting a milk bottle with a ball peen hammer," said George.

"I'd think it would be real interesting, hearing all the different sounds," said Hazel, a little envious. "All the things they think up."

"Um," said George.

"Only, if I was Handicapper General, you know what I would do?" said Hazel. Hazel, as a matter of fact, bore a strong resemblance to the Handicapper General, a woman named Diana Moon Glampers. "If I was Diana Moon Glampers," said Hazel. "I'd have chimes on Sunday—just chimes. Kind of in honor of religion."

"I could think, if it was just chimes," said George.

"Well—maybe make 'em real loud," said Hazel. "I think I'd make a good Handicapper General."

"Good as anybody else," said George.

"Who knows better'n I do what normal is?" said Hazel.

"Right," said George. He began to think glimmeringly about his abnormal son who was now in jail, about Harrison, but a twenty-one-gun salute in his head stopped that.

"Boy!" said Hazel, "that was a doozy, wasn't it?"

It was such a doozy that George was white and trembling, and tears stood on the rims of his red eyes. Two of the eight ballerinas had collapsed to the studio floor, were holding their temples.

"All of a sudden you look so tired," said Hazel. "Why don't you stretch out on the sofa, so's you can rest your handicap bag on the pillows, honeybunch." She was referring to the forty-seven pounds of birdshot in a canvas bag, which was padlocked around George's neck. "Go on and rest the bag for a little while," she said. "I don't care if you're not equal to me for a while."

George weighted the bag with his hands. "I don't mind it," he said. "I don't notice it any more. It's just a part of me."

"You been so tired lately—kind of wore out," said Hazel. "If there was just some way we could make a little hole in the bottom of the bag, and just take out a few of them lead balls. Just a few."

"Two years in prison and two thousand dollars fine for every ball I took out," said George. "I don't call that a bargain."

"If you could just take a few out when you came home from work," said Hazel. "I mean—you don't compete with anybody around here. You just set around."

"If I tried to get away with it," said George, "then other people'd get away with it—and pretty soon we'd be right back to the dark ages again, with everybody competing against everybody else. You wouldn't like that, would you?"

"I'd hate it," said Hazel.

"There you are," said George. "The minute people start cheating on laws, what do you think happens to society?"

If Hazel hadn't been able to come up with an answer to this question, George couldn't have supplied one. A siren was going off in his head.

"Reckon it'd fall all apart," said Hazel.

"What would?" said George blankly.

"Society," said Hazel uncertainly. "Wasn't that what you just said?"

"Who knows?" said George.

The television program was suddenly interrupted for a news bulleting. It wasn't clear at first as to what the bulletin was about, since the announcer, like all announcers, had a serious speech impediment. For about half a minute, and in a state of high excitement, the announcer tried to say, "Ladies and gentlemen—"

He finally gave up, handed the bulletin to a ballerina to read.

"That's all right—" Hazel said of the announcer, "he tried. That's the big thing. He tried to do the best he could with what God gave him. He should get a nice raise for trying so hard."

"Ladies and gentlemen—" said the ballerina, reading the bulletin. She must have been extraordinarily beautiful, because the mask she wore was hideous. And it was easy to see that she was the strongest and most graceful of all the dancers, for her handicap bags were as big as those worn by two-hundred-pound men.

And she had to apologize at once for her voice, which was a very unfair voice for a woman to use. Her voice was a warm, luminous, timeless melody. "Excuse me—" she said, and she began again, making her voice absolutely uncompetitive.

"Harrison Bergeron, age fourteen," she said in a grackle squawk, "Has just escaped from jail, where he was held on suspicion of plotting to overthrow the government. He is a genius and an athlete, is underhandicapped, and should be regarded as extremely dangerous."

A police photograph of Harrison Bergeron was flashed on the screen upside down, then sideways, upside down again, then right side up. The picture showed the full length of Harrison against a background calibrated in feet and inches. He was exactly seven feet tall.

The rest of Harrison's appearance was Halloween and hardware. Nobody had ever borne heavier handicaps. He had outgrown hindrances faster than the H-G men could think them up. Instead of a little ear radio for a mental handicap, he wore a tremendous pair of earphones, and spectacles with thick wavy lenses. The spectacles were intended to make him not only half blind, but to give him whanging headaches besides.

Scrap metal was hung all over him. Ordinarily, there was a certain symmetry, a military neatness to the handicaps issued to strong people, but Harrison looked like a walking junkyard. In the race of life, Harrison carried three hundred pounds.

And to offset his good looks, the H-G men required that he wear at all times a red rubber ball for a nose, keep his eyebrows shaved off, and cover his even white teeth with black caps at snaggle-tooth random.

"If you see this boy," said the ballerina, "do not—I repeat, do not—try to reason with him."

There was the shriek of a door being torn from its hinges.

Screams and barking cries of consternation came from the television set. The photograph of Harrison Bergeron on the screen jumped again and again, as though dancing to the tune of an earthquake.

George Bergeron correctly identified the earthquake, and well he might have—for many was the time his own home had danced to the same crashing tune. "My god—" said George, "that must be Harrison!"

The realization was blasted from his mind instantly by the sound of an automobile collision in his head.

When George could open his eyes again, the photograph of Harrison was gone. A living, breathing Harrison filled the screen.

Clanking, clownish, and huge, Harrison stood in the center of the studio. The knob of the uprooted studio door was still in his hand. Ballerinas, technicians, musicians, and announcers cowered on their knees before him, expecting to die.

"I am the Emperor!" cried Harrison. "Do you hear? I am the Emperor! Everybody must do what I say at once!" He stamped his foot and the studio shook.

"Even as I stand here—" he bellowed, "crippled, hobbled, sickened—I am a greater ruler than any man who ever lived! Now watch me become what I can become!"

Harrison tore the straps of his handicap harness like wet tissue paper, tore straps guaranteed to support five thousand pounds.

Harrison's scrap-iron handicaps crashed to the floor.

Harrison thrust his thumbs under the bar of the padlock that secured his head harness. The bar snapped like celery. Harrison smashed his headphones and spectacles against the wall.

He flung away his rubber-ball nose, revealed a man that would have awed Thor, the god of thunder.

"I shall now select my Empress!" he said, looking down on the cowering people. "Let the first woman who dares rise to her feet claim her mate and her throne!"

A moment passed, and then a ballerina arose, swaying like a willow.

Harrison plucked the mental handicap from her ear, snapped off her physical handicaps with marvelous delicacy. Last of all, he removed her mask.

She was blindingly beautiful.

"Now—" said Harrison, taking her hand, "shall we show the people the meaning of the word dance? Music!" he commanded.

The musicians scrambled back into their chairs, and Harrison stripped them of their handicaps, too. "Play your best," he told them, "and I'll make you barons and dukes and earls."

The music began. It was normal at first—cheap, silly, false. But Harrison snatched two musicians from their chairs, waved them like batons as he sang the music as he wanted it played. He slammed them back into their chairs.

The music began again and was much improved.

Harrison and his Empress merely listened to the music for a while—listened gravely, as though synchronizing their heartbeats with it.

They shifted their weights to their toes.

Harrison placed his big hands on the girl's tiny waist, letting her sense the weightlessness that would soon be hers.

And then, in an explosion of joy and grace, into the air they sprang!

Not only were the laws of the land abandoned, but the law of gravity and the laws of motion as well.

They reeled, whirled, swiveled, flounced, capered, gamboled, and spun.

They leaped like deer on the moon.

The studio ceiling was thirty feet high, but each leap brought the dancers nearer to it.

It became their obvious intention to kiss the ceiling.

They kissed it.

And then, neutralizing gravity with love and pure will, they remained suspended in air inches below the ceiling, and they kissed each other for a long, long time.

It was then that Diana Moon Glampers, the Handicapper General, came into the studio with a double-barreled ten-gauge shotgun. She fired twice, and the Emperor and the Empress were dead before they hit the floor.

Diana Moon Glampers loaded the gun again. She aimed it at the musicians and told them they had ten seconds to get their handicaps back on.

It was then that the Bergerons' television tube burned out.

Hazel turned to comment about the blackout to George. But George had gone out into the kitchen for a can of beer.

George came back in with the beer, paused while a handicap signal shook him up. And then he sat down again. "You been crying?" he said to Hazel.

"Yup," she said.

"What about?" he said

"I forget," she said. "Something real sad on television."

"What was it?" he said.

"It's all kind of mixed up in my mind," said Hazel.

"Forget sad things," said George.

"I always do," said Hazel.

"That's my girl," said George. He winced. There was the sound of a rivetting gun in his head.

"Gee—I could tell that one was a doozy," said Hazel.

"You can say that again," said George.

"Gee—" said Hazel, "I could tell that one was a doozy."

Critical Thinking

What are the dangers of total equality in society, especially with regard to the criminal justice system?

Is Vonnegut suggesting that equality is not a worthy ideal? Why or why not?

What role does television play in deterring crime, and imposing and maintaining justice?

What does Harrison Bergeron symbolize in the story?

What is Vonnegut suggesting about the relationship between individuality, defiance of authority, and criminal justice?

What is the significance of Vonnegut choosing "Harrison Bergeron" as the title for his story?

CPSIA information can be obtained
at www.ICGtesting.com
Printed in the USA
LVHW02s2320100118
562505LV00003B/14/P